GEORGE ELIOT AND EUROPE

Warwick Studies in the European Humanities

Warwick Studies in the European Humanities, edited from the Humanities Research Centre, University of Warwick, will publish monographs and collections of essays across the whole range of humanities subjects including classics, history, philosophy, modern languages, literary and cultural studies, theatre, film and the visual arts. There will be a special emphasis on interdisciplinary topics and the series will include books which discuss the relationship between Europe and the rest of the world.

George Eliot and Europe

edited by

JOHN RIGNALL

Routledge
Taylor & Francis Group

LONDON AND NEW YORK

First published 1997 by Ashgate Publishing

2 Park Square, Milton Park, Abingdon, Oxfordshire OX14 4RN
52 Vanderbilt Avenue, New York, NY 10017

Routledge is an imprint of the Taylor & Francis Group, an informa business

First issued in paperback 2019

British Library Cataloguing in Publication Data
George Eliot and Europe – (Warwick studies in
    the European humanities)
    1. Eliot, George, 1819–1880 – Criticism and interpretation
    2. English fiction – 19th century – History and criticism
    3. Europe – In literature
    I. Rignall, John, 1942–
    823.8

Library of Congress Catalog Card Number :96-71122

ISBN 978-1-85928-334-9 (hbk)
ISBN 978-0-367-88823-7 (pbk)

Contents

List of Illustrations

Thanks are due to the Henry E. Huntington Library, San Marino, California, for permission to publish Illustrations 1, 2, and 4, and to The Mauritshuis in The Hague and to Joel Snyder for Illustration 3.

Preface

The majority of these essays began life as papers delivered at the conference on 'George Eliot and Europe' held at the University of Warwick from 14 to 16 July 1995 (Tom Winnifrith's 'Renaissance and Risorgimento in *Romola*' was on the original programme but could not in the end be delivered). 'George Eliot and Europe' was organized under the auspices of the Humanities Research Centre at the University of Warwick and in collaboration with the George Eliot Fellowship, and the editor would like to thank Dr Peter Mack and Marian Franklin, the Director and the Secretary of the Centre, and Kathleen Adams, the Secretary of the Fellowship, for their support and invaluable practical assistance in arranging the conference and making it run smoothly.

Peter Mack and the Centre have also been generous with guidance and support in preparing this volume for publication, while the editor owes a particular debt of gratitude to Rachel Parkins and Athena Economides for their skill and patience in helping produce the final version of the text.

Notes on the Contributors

Margaret Harris is Professor of English Literature at the University of Sydney. With Judith Johnston she has edited *The Journals of George Eliot* (Cambridge University Press, forthcoming), and *Middlemarch* (Everyman Paperbacks).

Hans Ulrich Seeber is Professor of English at Stuttgart University and has written widely on Victorian literature. He is editor of a new standard history of English literature in German, *Englische Literaturgeschichte* (Metzler, 1993), and the author of the sections on the nineteenth and early twentieth centuries.

Elizabeth Deeds Ermarth is Saintsbury Professor of English Literature at the University of Edinburgh and her many publications include *Realism and Consensus in the English Novel* (1983), the Twayne monograph on George Eliot, and *Sequel to History* (1992).

Nancy Henry is Assistant Professor of English at the State University of New York at Binghamton and the editor of the first annotated edition of George Eliot's *Impressions of Theophrastus Such* (Pickering & Chatto, 1994).

Barbara Hardy is Emeritus Professor of English at Birkbeck College, University of London, and her extensive work on George Eliot, starting with *The Novels of George Eliot* (1959) and including *Critical Essays on George Eliot* (1970) and *Particularities* (1982), has been instrumental in establishing the modern reputation of the novelist.

Nancy Cervetti is Assistant Professor of English and Director of the Women's Studies Programme at Avila College in Kansas City, Missouri. Her publications include articles on George Eliot in the *Victorian Newsletter* (1991) and *Women's Studies* (1992).

Delia da Sousa Correa teaches nineteenth and twentieth-century literature and culture at Oriel and Manchester Colleges, Oxford, and lectures part-time at the Worcester College of Higher Education. She is completing a book on *Music in Victorian Literary Culture: George Eliot and her Contemporaries* (Cambridge University Press, forthcoming).

Derek Miller received his PhD from the Graduate Centre of the City University of New York for a dissertation on 'Imperial Anxieties in English Fiction, 1870s to 1930s'.

Bonnie McMullen holds degrees from Bryn Mawr College, the University of Pittsburgh, and the University of Toronto, where she wrote a PhD dissertation on George Eliot. She lives in Oxford, where she teaches English and American Literature.

Beryl Gray lectures at Birkbeck College, University of London, and is the author of *George Eliot and Music* (1989). She has edited 'The Lifted Veil' and 'Brother Jacob' (Virago Press), and *Adam Bede* and *The Mill on the Floss* (Everyman Paperbacks).

Linda K. Robertson is Professor of English at the University of Arkansas, Monticello. She has published a number of articles on George Eliot and on Victorian fiction, and her book *The Power of Knowledge: George Eliot and Education* is in press.

Tom Winnifrith is Senior Lecturer in English at the University of Warwick and the author of many books on the Brontës and of *Fallen Women in the Nineteenth-Century Novel* (1994).

Lesley Gordon is a librarian in the Robinson Library at the University of Newcastle and wrote her PhD thesis on 'Concepts from Classical Greek Literature in the Novels of George Eliot'.

Shoshana Milgram Knapp is Associate Professor of English at Virginia Tech and her publications include articles on George Eliot in *Nineteenth-Century Fiction* and on George Eliot and Tolstoy in the *Slavic and East European Journal*, as well as articles on, among others, Victor Hugo, George Sand, Dostoyevsky, and Chekhov.

John Rignall is Senior Lecturer in English at the University of Warwick and the author of *Realist Fiction and the Strolling Spectator* (1992). He has recently edited *Daniel Deronda* (Everyman Paperbacks, forthcoming).

Gill Frith is Lecturer in English at the University of Warwick and the author of *Dreams of Difference: Women and Fantasy* (1991). She is currently working on a book about female friendship and national identity in novels by nineteenth and twentieth-century British women writers.

Introduction

The essays in this collection aim to illuminate different aspects of George Eliot's relation to the literature and culture of Continental Europe. The European dimension of her work was central and enduring. Her first book was a translation from the German of David Strauß and her last, *Impressions of Theophrastus Such*, alludes in its title to a Greek philosopher of the fourth century BC and owes an obvious debt to the work of a seventeenth-century French satirist, La Bruyère's *Caractères*. In between, although her novels deal mainly with English provincial life, that circumscribed world is conceived and scrutinized by a mind not bounded by those narrow horizons, but deeply versed in the literature, philosophy and culture of Europe and the wider world. A glance at the chapter epigraphs to *Middlemarch* gives some indication of how widely her net is cast: from Chaucer, Shakespeare and Milton, to Dante, Pascal, Cervantes, Goethe, de Musset, Hugo, and Italian and Spanish proverbs. With her early work as a translator of Feuerbach and Spinoza as well as Strauß; with her knowledge of Latin and Greek, and French, German, Italian, Spanish, and Hebrew; with her frequent and often lengthy visits to the Continent from the age of twenty-nine until the last year of her life; and with her lifetime of extraordinarily wide and intensive reading, she is the most knowledgeably European of English novelists in an age when, as Hans Ulrich Seeber points out in his essay, Europe was generally understood to include the British Isles rather than to begin at Calais.

For George Eliot Europe was no monolithic 'other' but a naturally accepted part of her heritage as an educated Englishwoman, and one whose diversity she appreciated. As she puts it in 'A Word for the Germans', '[...] it is precisely that partition of mankind into races and nations, resulting in various national points of view or varieties of national genius, which has been the means of enriching and rendering more and more complete man's knowledge of the inner and outer world'.[1] How her own knowledge of the world was enriched by her contact with other races and nations should become clear in the following pages; and the variety which she acclaims in that article is reflected in the range and diversity of the topics addressed in this collection. The essays focus on different countries and cultures, including not only France, Germany and Italy, but also the relatively neglected subject of Spain. Some examine the complex general issues of language and culture raised by her work, while others concentrate on her response to specific European

---

[1] *Essays of George Eliot*, ed. by Thomas Pinney (London: Routledge and Kegan Paul, 1963), p. 388.

writers and texts. There are investigations of intertextualities and possibilities
of influence, as well as comparative discussions of the novels, like Barbara
Hardy's, which reads George Eliot alongside two other great European
novelists, Tolstoy and Fontane. Those novels whose action is set entirely or
significantly in Europe, *Romola* and *Daniel Deronda*, feature prominently, as
is to be expected, but the European connections of *Middlemarch* and *The Mill
on the Floss* also receive attention, as do her journals and *Impressions of
Theophrastus Such*. In many of these essays the role of that other
cosmopolitan intellectual, G. H. Lewes, figures significantly, for it is with him
that George Eliot shared so much of her experience of foreign literatures and
foreign parts. When Lewes died he was probably best known for his *Life of
Goethe*. When George Eliot died, Lord Acton, reaching for superlatives, had
recourse to other great names from European literature: 'If Sophocles or
Cervantes had lived in the light of our culture, if Dante had prospered like
Manzoni, George Eliot might have had a rival'.[2] It is in such company that
she properly belongs, and it is in that wider European context that these
essays seek to place her.

---

[2] *George Eliot: The Critical Heritage*, ed. by David Carroll (London: Routledge & Kegan
Paul, 1971), p. 461.

Chapter One

What George Eliot Saw in Europe: The Evidence of her Journals

Margaret Harris

The title of this paper works both with the literal sense of 'what George Eliot saw' (at its most literal, detailed itineraries of her travels in Continental Europe), and with the more colloquial and analytic sense of 'what she saw in Europe': what she made of it, what it meant to her. Readers of her journals, from Henry James on, have taken the view that these journals are bland, offering not much more than lists of where she went and what, in the literal sense, she saw. Thus James reviewing *George Eliot's Life as related in her letters and journals*, compiled by her widower John Cross:

> The various journals and notes of her visits to the Continent are [...] singularly vague in expression on the subject of the general and particular spectacle — the life and manners, the works of art. She enumerates diligently all the pictures and statues she sees, and the way she does so is proof of her active, earnest intellectual habits; but it is rarely apparent that they have, as the phrase is, said much to her, or that what they have said is one of their deeper secrets.[1]

James, always a creative reader of George Eliot, tacitly requires more conspicuous writerliness than he finds in the selections from her journals available to him. He apparently regrets that the journals are not the polished kind of travel-writing represented by his own *Transatlantic Sketches* (1875), which dwell on the alterity of the experience of travel, contrasting 'abroad' where imaginative and emotional energies are stimulated, with the

[1] *George Eliot: The Critical Heritage*, ed. by David Carroll (London: Routledge & Kegan Paul, 1971), p. 499. This paper draws on the edition of *The Journals of George Eliot*, edited by Margaret Harris and Judith Johnston (Cambridge University Press, forthcoming). The editors thank Jennifer Moore for her invaluable research assistance, and acknowledge the support provided by an Australian Research Council Large Grant, 1991-2. The permission of Mr Jonathan Ouvry to quote unpublished material is gratefully acknowledged; as is the permission of the Beinecke Rare Book and Manuscript Library, Yale University Library, to publish material held there.

authenticity of 'home', typified by the mundane and routine, at once stable and constraining.[2] Read complete, George Eliot's travel journals, for all that they are 'private' writing, not prepared for publication, turn out to be texts as self-conscious as James's own. Their piecemeal publication has distracted attention from the craft of their construction.

Extracts from the journals have been available in Cross's version, and in selections included by George Eliot's twentieth-century champion Gordon Haight in his magisterial edition of her letters. While Haight identified many of Cross's editorial interventions (in addition to leaving out a good deal, Cross conflated letters, and also sections of letter with sections of journal),[3] naturally enough he treated the text of the journals as illustrative of or ancillary to the text of the letter. Thus while he includes in full in *The George Eliot Letters* some of the essay-type, set-piece journals such as 'Recollections of Ilfracombe' and 'How I came to write fiction',[4] for the most part, snippets from the journals appear as footnotes.

My argument about what George Eliot saw in Europe depends on a set of convictions about her journals, developed during the preparation of an edition of them. On the whole, the journals do not generate instant new insight into George Eliot's life and work. Reading the journals, like reading any George Eliot text, is a matter of longterm rewards, not only of immediate gratifications. They can be read with and against other George Eliot texts: they complement such records as letters, as well as her fiction.[5] In this essay, I am principally concerned to demonstrate her engagement with discourses of travel in the earliest extant journal material, dealing with her sojourn in Weimar in 1854, and in 'Recollections of Italy. 1860', her account of 'one of those journies that seem to divide one's life in two' (*Letters*, III, 311).

---

[2] See James Buzard, *The Beaten Track: European Tourism, Literature, and the Ways to 'Culture' 1800-1918* (Oxford: Oxford University Press, 1993), especially pp. 176 ff. Buzard's discussion, in particular Chapter 3, 'A Scripted Continent: British and American Travel-Writers in Europe, *c.* 1825-1875', provides context for my account of George Eliot in Europe.

[3] Gordon S. Haight, *The George Eliot Letters*, 9 vols (New Haven: Yale University Press, 1954-78), I, pp. xiii-xv.

[4] *The George Eliot Letters*, II, 238-52, and II, 406-10. Cross had published extracts from each.

[5] An analogous reading of George Eliot's personal writings is developed by Rosemarie Bodenheimer in *The Real Life of Mary Ann Evans: George Eliot, Her Letters and Fiction* (Ithaca and London: Cornell University Press, 1994), which makes a case for the letters as a more fully biographical text (of Marian Evans) than has been recognized, and demonstrates how subtly and deviously George Eliot wrote herself out in letters and fiction.

The journals are a discontinuous text, and while together they are as close as George Eliot comes to autobiography, they are not straightforward self-writing (though the full text does restore George Eliot as the speaking subject, rather than the subject of Cross's or Haight's narration). There is a major instance of self-construction to be discerned as a consequence of seeing the journals entire: at one point the physical arrangement of the material within a manuscript volume enacts a version of the 'split self' of autobiography, as the journals provide a covert account both of the adoption of the pseudonym 'George Eliot', and of the surrender of the secret of the identity of Marian Evans Lewes with George Eliot.[6] This is a particularly striking example of George Eliot's exercise of authority and control in all her writing.

The journals include two kinds of writing: daily diary entries ranging from a phrase to a page or so, and longer essays, which in some cases re-write the diary and in others complement it.[7] The journals and diaries run from the time of her union with George Henry Lewes in 1854 to her death in 1880: we know of a lost journal of the Spanish expedition of 1866-7, and the diary for 1878 is missing. However she used other notebooks concurrently: that edited by Joseph Wiesenfarth as *George Eliot: A Writer's Notebook 1854-1879* covers pretty well the same timespan, and at any one time she was likely to have several volumes on the go (as she did while working on *Middlemarch*, for example).[8] These various files reveal George Eliot's deliberate division and disposition of her notes and memoranda, part of the justification of my claim for her particular kind of control even of her most private and informal writing.

The journals began in Europe, in the winter of 1849 which Marian Evans (not yet George Eliot) spent in Geneva after the Brays took her on tour

[6] This claim is presented in detail in the introduction to *The Journals of George Eliot*.

[7] The extant material is contained in six volumes (all in the Beinecke Rare Book and Manuscript Library, Yale University, except for the 1879 diary, which is in the Berg Collection, New York Public Library): Her diary for 1854-61, which includes also 'Recollections of Weimar', 'Recollections of Berlin', 'Ilfracombe', 'Scilly' and 'Jersey', 'How I came to write fiction' and 'History of Adam Bede'; the diary for 1861-77; separate diaries for each of 1879 and 1880; a notebook containing 'Germany. 1858', with 'Recollections of Italy. 1860'; and another containing 'Italy. 1864', with 'Normandy and Brittany. 1865'.

[8] *George Eliot: A Writer's Notebook 1854-1879* (Charlottesville: University Press of Virginia, 1981); *George Eliot's Middlemarch Notebooks: A Transcription*, ed. by John Clark Pratt and Victor A. Neufeldt (Los Angeles and London: University of California Press, 1979) and *George Eliot's Quarry for 'Middlemarch'*, ed. by A. T. Kitchel (Los Angeles: University of California Press, 1950).

following the death of her father. We have her word for the origin of the
journal, at the end of the first diary:

> This is the last entry I mean to make in my old book in which I wrote for the first time
> at Geneva, in 1849. What moments of despair I passed through after that – despair that
> life would ever be made precious to me by the consciousness that I lived to some good
> purpose! It was that sort of despair that sucked away the sap of half the hours which
> might have been filled by energetic youthful activity: and the same demon tries to get
> hold of me again whenever an old work is dismissed and a new one is being meditated.
>
> June 19th 1861.

The extant text, however, dates from July 1854. It is assumed that Cross
destroyed the earlier section *(Letters,* I, xv), so that the text now opens with
Marian Evans (still not George Eliot) crossing again to Europe for the first
time since her return from Geneva in 1850. On that occasion she was
travelling after a major life crisis, and now there is another rite of passage: the
journal begins with an elopement.

> July 20th 1854
> I said a last farewell to Cambridge street this morning and found myself on board the
> Ravensbourne, bound for Antwerp about 1/2 an hour earlier than a sensible person
> would have been aboard, and in consequence I had 20 minutes of terrible fear lest
> something should have delayed G. But before long I saw his welcome face looking for
> me over the porter's shoulder, and all was well. The day was glorious and our passage
> perfect. Mr R. Noel happened to be a fellow-passenger. The sunset was lovely but still
> lovelier the dawn as we were passing up the Scheldt between 2 and 3 in the morning.
> The crescent moon, the stars, the first faint blush of the dawn reflected in the glassy
> river, the dark mass of clouds on the horizon, which sent forth flashes of lightning, and
> the graceful forms of the boats and sailing vessels painted in jet black on the reddish
> gold of the sky and water, made up an unforgettable picture. Then the sun rose and
> lighted up the sleepy shores of Belgium with their fringe of long grass, their rows of
> poplars, their church spires and farm buildings.

Haight quotes most of this passage, though not consecutively;   Cross's
version runs: 'I said a last farewell to Cambridge Street on 20th July 1854,
and found myself on board the Ravensbourne, bound for Antwerp. The day
was glorious and our passage perfect. The sunset was lovely', and so on.[9]
This is characteristic of Cross's editorial procedure. He retains the 'fine
writing' of the description of dawn: though George Eliot the novelist does not
yet exist, the descriptive powers of Marian Evans, journalist, can be
demonstrated, but not her amused self-deprecation as she waits for Lewes
(who is generally edited out where possible).

---

[9] Gordon S. Haight, *George Eliot* (Oxford: Oxford University Press, 1968), p. 148; J. W.
Cross, *George Eliot's Life,* 3 vols (Edinburgh and London: Blackwood, 1885), I, 332.

The journals, then, open as George Eliot embarks not only on the 'Ravensbourne', but on her life with Lewes — a union ended by his death in 1878. George Eliot's diary during these months in Germany is full, and interesting; generally, its preoccupations persist in varying proportions in later journals. Her impressions of the places they go are sharp, suffused with happiness: she presents vignettes of fellow travellers, or of people glimpsed in passing, or of buildings or landscapes. Her descriptions of the Rubens paintings they see in Antwerp are the beginning of the commentary on art which later occupies a good deal of the journals. There is little political comment beyond a passing reference to the Crimean War. Similarly, there are some generalisations about national stereotypes, but no significant social comment. Neither is there significant economic comment, except on a domestic level, since concern about money is acute. There is a record of their ailments (a familiar refrain). Above all, their work — reading and writing — is recorded. The professional purpose of this journey was Lewes's research in Weimar and Berlin for his study of Goethe (published in 1855), and George Eliot — Dorothea-like? — assisted him in translation and other ways, as well as doing her own journalistic work and a translation of Spinoza's *Ethics*.

However, it is not only a case of what the writer tells us, since the journals also show the writer at work. There is evidence of her reworking the same material in different contexts: the diary at times has parallel texts in letters (the letter to Charles Bray from Weimar dated 16 August 1854, parallels and summarises the diary, by contrast with the self-justificatory one of 20 October to the same correspondent which exposes the anxiety about her reputation that finds no expression in the euphoric diary pages [*Letters*, II, 170-2 and 178-9]). Also, once in Berlin, she rewrote her Weimar diary as an essay called 'Recollections of Weimar'. 'Recollections' provides more of a summary and an overview than the diary; impressions are assimilated and organised, modifying the narrator's initial unfavourable impression of Weimar (this narrator is never identified, nor even gendered). The essay emphasizes the travellers' reactions to the place and the people they met, and obscures the working aspect of their visit which is so strongly marked in the diary. Though the focus is on the cultured environment in Weimar — hearing Liszt play is a high point — and on the customs and characteristics of the people, the pleasures of the flesh are not disregarded. There is a good deal of comment on food (uncommon elsewhere in George Eliot's journals, and indeed in her fiction), and on their walks — of which this picnic with wine and Keats is a notable example:

A beautiful walk through a beech-wood took us to the Mooshütte where we rested on the rustic bench near the door and took our luncheon. Before this Mooshütte stands the beech on which Goethe and his friends cut their names and from which Goethe denounced Woldemar. We could recognize some of the initials. The tree has been shattered by lightning and is protected by a piece of sheet-lead. We were very jolly over our luncheon and right glad of the small bottle of wine which we had felt it rather a corvée to carry. We rested an hour on the grass under the shade of the beeches and then set off again, while the sun was still burning, on our way home. But we rested again and slept when we got among the trees, then took another stage, and sat down on the grass to read Keats. I read aloud St Agnes' Eve, and at another resting place, part of Hyperion. The solemn pine forest looked still grander than in the morning, and we richly enjoyed it in spite of our weariness. About half past five, hot, aching and adust, we entered Weimar and found a glass of cold water from a pump by the roadside delicious as nectar.

(Cross published only a few lines relating to the Goethe pilgrimage; Haight nowhere printed any of this idyll.)

There are further versions of 'Recollections of Weimar', which George Eliot recast into two articles in a recognisable strain of travel writing published in *Fraser's Magazine* in 1855.[10] In their presentation of the exotic culture to an indigenous readership are discernible already the characteristic emphases of George Eliot's prose, which suggest that on any matter there can be different points of view, perhaps equally valid. These essays include elements of both entertainment and instruction, and with her translations and some major reviews form her contribution to the propagation of German culture in Britain.[11] There are inevitably intertextualities with Goethe; perhaps also with Thackeray, whose Pumpernickel is very different from George Eliot's Weimar. These are unique instances of journal material going fairly direct to print (there is another smaller but engaging instance when Lewes apparently borrowed some descriptions of Ilfracombe for *Sea-Side Studies*).[12]

---

[10] 'Three Months in Weimar', *Fraser's Magazine*, 51 (June 1855), 699-706, and 'Liszt, Wagner and Weimar', 52 (July 1855), 48-62, reprinted in *Essays of George Eliot*, ed. by Thomas Pinney (London: Routledge and Kegan Paul, 1963): Pinney indicates the further cuts George Eliot made to these essays when she revised them for inclusion in *Essays and Leaves from a Notebook*, ed. by Charles Lee Lewes (1884). Also, Pinney points out (p. 96) that the second essay defends Wagner, who had been criticised during his visit with the London Philarmonia Orchestra in March-June 1855: a specific instance of George Eliot's championing German culture.

[11] The fullest discussion of this aspect of Europe in George Eliot is Rosemary Ashton, *The German Idea: Four English Writers and the Reception of German Thought* (Cambridge: Cambridge University Press, 1980).

[12] Haight, *George Eliot*, p. 198.

What, then, did George Eliot see in Weimar? (Facetiously, one might say that whatever she saw was through rose-coloured spectacles.) In the first place, she saw scenery, people, buildings and artefacts: Goethe was a determinant of what she saw, and in some measure of how she saw it. Certainly the Weimar where she spent three months was liberated and liberating: there is an important sense of the validity of different cultures and lifestyles, as well as the freer social code that countenanced irregular unions.

She saw also opportunities for writing: indeed at this time the journals are in an important sense where George Eliot-to-be is writing (and hence one interest of the various versions of the Weimar material). Of these 1854-5 journals, there is not much trace in the novels, though clearly this work, along with the major reviews like 'The Natural History of German Life', forms an important body of writing preparatory to the novels. Meanwhile Marian Evans, journalist, plied her trade, mindful of her mission on behalf of German culture, and the need to earn a living.

Before moving to 'Recollections of Italy. 1860', I must return George Eliot and Lewes from Europe to England to their post-honeymoon life together. Early in 'Recollections of Berlin', we find the following:

> We were amused to hear that Carlyle said he should think no one could die at Berlin, for in beds *without curtains* what Christian could give up the ghost? To us, the lack of curtains was the smallest fault of German beds.

(Cross omits the second of these sentences.) Comment on German beds recurs in the closing section of 'Berlin' (bold type restores Cross's omissions):

> **We soon became ill, and so were even thankful to see the cliffs of Dover.**
>
> English mutton, an English fire **and an English bed** were likely to be appreciated by creatures who had had eight months of Germany with its questionable meat, its stove-heated rooms **and beds warranted not to tuck up.** The taste and quietude of a first-rate English hotel were also in striking contrast with the heavy finery, the noise, and the indiscriminate smoking of German inns. But after all, Germany is no bad place to live in, and the Germans, to counterbalance their want of taste and politeness, are at least free from the bigotry and exclusiveness of their more refined cousins. I even long to be amongst them again – to see Dresden, and Munich and Nürnberg and the Rhine country. May the day soon come!
>
> Dover. March 27 1855.

The excision of the German beds is a nice instance of Cross's censorship — and the extent of the bedtalk in the journals. And in the peroration George Eliot provides her own summary of what she saw in Europe.

The antipathy to German beds was far from idiosyncratic. I invoke the authority of Murray's *Handbook for Travellers on the Continent:*

One of the first complaints of an Englishman on arriving in Germany will be directed against the beds. It is therefore as well to make him aware beforehand of the full extent of misery to which he will be subjected on this score. A German bed is made only for one; it may be compared to an open wooden box, often hardly wide enough to turn in, and rarely long enough for any man of moderate stature to lie down in [...]. Curtains are almost always wanting. The place of blankets is sometimes supplied by a light puffy feather-bed, which is likely to be kicked off, and forsake in his utmost need the sleeper [...]. Mr Coleridge has recorded his abhorrence of a German bed, declaring 'he would rather carry his blanket about him, like a wild Indian, than submit to this abominable custom'.[13]

The phenomenon represented by the handbooks put out from the late 1820s by the London publishing house of John Murray is germane to an estimation of George Eliot's independence as traveller and tourist.   Murray was also Byron's publisher, and Byron pervades the handbooks: *Childe Harold's Pilgrimage* is frequently cited. Murray's guides are a product of the boom in English tourism on the Continent in the years after the Napoleonic wars.[14] John Murray offered his personal experience as guidance to a clientele among the affluent middle class, for whom the railway provided new horizons. Murray had clear assumptions about the English traveller, who is admonished to 'divest himself, as soon as possible, of his prejudices, and especially of the idea of the amazing superiority of England above all other countries, in all respects';[15] who is warned that the Continent must be assumed to be dirty and populated by rogues; and to whom useful tips (such as the utility of separate passports for servants) are imparted. George Eliot clearly was not in need of such exhortation (though she does comment approvingly on the cleanliness of Belgium).   None the less, what George Eliot saw, especially in Italy, substantially conforms to the orthodoxy represented by Murray.

This said, there are times when George Eliot sees more sharply than 'Murray'. In 'Normandy and Brittany. 1865', her account of what she saw was in places directly dependent on Murray, which she quotes liberally (in inverted commas, unsourced). At one stage, Murray reports that the south portal of the church of St Ouen in Rouen is called *des Marmouzets*. Instead of Murray's 'from the figures of the animals carved on it',[16] George Eliot writes

---

[13] *A Handbook for Travellers on the Continent: Being a Guide to Holland, Belgium, Prussia, Northern Germany, and the Rhine from Holland to Switzerland,* 10th edn, corrected (London: John Murray, 1854), para. 30, p. 200.

[14] Buzard provides a fuller account in Chapter 1, 'Tourist and Traveller in the Network of Nineteenth-Century Travel', esp. pp. 65-79.

[15] *A Handbook for Travellers on the Continent,* pp. xv-xvi.

[16] *Handbook for Travellers in France,* 9th edn, (London: John Murray, 1864), p. 39.

'from the little baboon-like demons who are oozing out below the arch of the doorway': a nice instance of 'what she saw' improving on what others saw.

To turn now to the first Italian tour in 1860, a much-anticipated journey. In a letter of 5 June 1857, George Eliot wrote to Cara Bray: 'We mean to settle down (after we have once been to Italy) and buy pots and kettles and keep a dog' *(Letters, II, 339)*. She was not disappointed in the experience: writing to Sara Hennell on 2 July 1860 she declared, 'We have had an unspeakably delightful journey — one of those journies that seem to divide one's life in two by the new ideas they suggest and the new veins of interest they open' *(Letters, III, 311)*. I think this is accurate comment in respect of her writing life, perhaps self-fulfilling prophecy. A reading of 'Recollections of Italy' casts light on the well-recognized division between the early novels, drawn in such large measure from her own family recollections, and the later works. In her relationship with Lewes, this journey also marks a shift in what I can only call the balance of power between them. George Eliot's reputation and finances are now secure, and from this point hers is to be the dominant career. There is also an imminent change in their domestic arrangements, since Charles Lewes comes home from Hofwyl with them, and they set up house in central London.

This journey marks the first occasion when Eliot and Lewes travelled abroad avowedly for pleasure. It also establishes a pattern of their taking off for foreign parts immediately a book is finished (in this case, they had both completed major works, respectively *The Mill on the Floss* and *The Physiology of Common Life)*. Their relative affluence makes this possible. It is notable that money matters, which had bulked so large in the 1854-5 journals, are in the background now.

The remark about travelling for pleasure needs to be qualified, however: it is the pleasure of improvement rather than hedonism on the one hand, or on the other a more specific motive like research on Goethe or physiology (which took them to Germany in 1858). They set themselves a steady curriculum, which owes a great deal to Ruskin though he is not mentioned: the Ruskin who proclaims the power of art to translate, not just to transcribe, the natural world. The journal is concerned both with natural beauty and with works of art (George Eliot copied passages of *The Stones of Venice* in her commonplace book).[17] They acquired a small library en route, including Liddell's *History of Rome*, 'to repair the breaches in our historical

---

[17] *George Eliot: A Writer's Notebook,* pp. 39-42 and 169. Wiesenfarth conjectures that these notes were made in preparation for the 1860 expedition.

knowledge', Stendhal's *Histoire de la Peinture,* Kugler's *Handbook of Italian Painters,* and Murray on Naples.[18]

This journal was written up from now-vanished memoranda, and there is no parallel diary as for the German visit of 1854-5. Writing in retrospect, George Eliot constructs her Italian journey as a version of the Grand Tour inflected by English Romanticism. Her account acknowledges the class (aristocratic) and gender (male) implications of the Grand Tour, and is frequently cast in Romantic tropes of dream and transport. Throughout, there is appraisal of the experiences of the travellers against a set of romantic expectations of the classical world, for the most part tacit, which George Eliot finds fulfilled without either reaching heights of romantic epiphany, or confronting Italy as a mystic Other, symbol of the sensuous South. There is no declared self-scrutiny such as Goethe avowed in his *Italian Journey* (one of the texts against which George Eliot's essay resonates): 'My purpose in making this wonderful journey is not to delude myself but to discover myself in the objects I see.'[19]   Goethe of course relished his incognito on his Italian journey: George Eliot sometimes seems to have had a sense of another self when abroad. Cross rather wistfully describes her stamina on their honeymoon:

> I had never seen my wife out of England, previous to our marriage, except the first time at Rome, when she was suffering. My general impression, therefore, had been that her health was always very low, and that she was almost constantly ailing. I was the more surprised, after our marriage, to find that from the day she set her foot on Continental soil, till the day she returned to Witley, she was never ill – never even unwell. She began at once to look many years younger.[20]

As well as physical invigoration, like most travellers George Eliot at times experienced some dissolution of self in travel. In 'Recollections of Italy' there is a textual embodiment of a narrator much more strongly characterised than in 'Weimar' as she adopts something of the male-gendered traveller's persona, in part by deployment of her classical learning.

'Recollections of Italy' has a set-piece opening. First, sententious moralising of a characteristic kind, which in its use of the phrase 'double consciousness' makes clear that what a traveller sees at any given moment

---

[18] G. H. Lewes, Journal, 7, 21 and 27 April 1860 (Beinecke). The Murray in question is presumably *A Handbook for Travellers in Southern Italy; being a guide for the continental portion of the Kingdom of the Two Sicilies,* 3rd edn., 1858.

[19] J. W. Goethe, *Italian Journey [1786-1788],* trans. by W. H. Auden and Elizabeth Mayer, (Harmondsworth: Penguin Books, 1970), p. 57.

[20] *George Eliot's Life,* III, 417.

may not be fully grasped in that moment; and then interpretation of the Alpine crossing as a transcendent experience:

> We have finished our journey to Italy — the journey I had looked forward to for years, rather with the hope of the new elements it would bring to my culture, than with the hope of immediate pleasure. Travelling can hardly be without a continual current of disappointment if the main object is not the enlargement of one's general life, so as to make even weariness and annoyances enter into the sum of benefit. One great deduction to me from the delight of seeing world-famous objects is the frequent double consciousness which tells me that I am not enjoying the actual vision enough, and that when higher enjoyment comes with the reproduction of the scene in my imagination I shall have lost some of the details, which impress me too feebly in the present because the faculties are not wrought up into energetic action.
>
> I have no other journal than the briefest record of what we did each day; so I shall put down my recollections whenever I happen to have leisure and inclination — just for the sake of making clear to myself the impressions I have brought away from our three months' travel.
>
> The first striking moment in our journey was when we arrived, I think about eleven o'clock at night, at the point in the ascent of the Mont Cenis where we were to quit the diligences and take to the sledges. After a hasty drink of hot coffee in the roadside inn, our large party — the inmates of three diligences — turned out into the starlight to await the signal for getting into the sledges. That signal seemed to be considerably on in the future, to be arrived at through much confusion of luggage-lifting, voices, and leading about of mules. The human bustle and confusion made a poetic contrast with the sublime stillness of the starlit heavens spread over the snowy tableland and surrounding heights. The keenness of the air contributed strongly to the sense of novelty: we had left our everyday conventional world quite behind us and were on a visit to Nature in her private home.

They had spent some time in Paris and other places en route; in a letter to John Blackwood she described 'the passage over the Mont Cenis, in the cramping diligence and traineau [...] with no food except a small loaf' (*Letters*, III, 285). The decision to open narration with the dramatic nocturnal scene in the Alps is strategic, launching an explicit account of crossing a boundary from the dulness of the mundane into experience of heightened sensibility and romantic dream (she sleeps and wakes several times before dawn). There is an assumption of a male gaze in the conventional gendering of Nature as female, which is tacitly reinforced as the journal proceeds — although the romantic discourse of the opening is not uniformly sustained throughout the essay.

Over the Alps, they proceed to Turin, where they 'had a sight of the man whose name will always be connected with the story of that widening life — Count Cavour': Again, as in Weimar, politics are remote — the more surprising given the turbulence of Italy at this time. As in the Weimar journal, there are telling vignettes, like the meeting en route to Pisa with 'an

Irish family who had been settled in Australia for 20 years, and were come to Europe on account of their son's education and purposed entrance at the bar'; or her account of the protracted business of getting luggage ashore at Civita Vecchia, about which Murray warns and Lewes expostulates, with its amused observation of a dog and a bone.

They make their way to Rome:

> At last we came in sight of Rome, but there was nothing imposing to be seen. The chief object was what I afterwards knew to be one of the aqueducts, but which I then in the vagueness of my conceptions guessed to be the ruins of baths. The railway station where we alighted looked remote and countrified: only three omnibuses and one family carriage were waiting, so that we were obliged to take our chance in one of the omnibuses – that is, the chance of finding no place left for us in the hotels. And so it was. Every one wanted to go to the Hotel d'Angleterre, and every one was disappointed. We, at last, by help of some fellow-travellers, got a small room *au troisième* at the Hotel d'Amérique, and as soon as that business was settled we walked out to look at Rome — not without a rather heavy load of disappointment on our minds from the vision we had had of it from the omnibus windows. A weary length of dirty uninteresting streets had brought us within sight of the dome of St Peter's which was not impressive, seen in a peeping makeshift manner, just rising above the houses; and the Castle of St Angelo seemed but a shabby likeness of the engravings. Not one iota had I seen that corresponded with my preconceptions.

Rome is the test case for the traveller in Italy, as Goethe emphasized (like Eliot and Lewes, he hurried to be there for a particular religious festival — All Saints in his case — and experienced some initial disappointment).[21] George Eliot's spirits improved on the morning after their arrival, and she soon experienced at the sight of two weatherbeaten statues of colossi 'a thrill of awe, half like what might have been felt by the men of old who saw the divine twins watering their steeds when they brought the news of victory'. This retrieval of the past is continued: in the Campo Vaccino she describes carts and animals 'mingling a simple form of actual life with those signs of the highly artificial life that had been crowded here in ages gone by': pillars, temple, the arch of Titus and so on. The Forum near the Coliseum became 'our favourite haunt', where vestiges of pedestals are 'utterly confused to all but erudite eyes'. Rome is a text she learns to read, through her knowledge of other texts about it.

'Let me see what I most delighted in, in Rome', she asks, and gives a lengthy list of 'the traces of Ancient Rome that have left the strongest image of themselves in my mind' — including some picturesque features and a number of views. Lewes writes of buying cameos (GHL Journal, 18 April

---

[21] *Italian Journey*, p. 129.

1860), as Dorothea does for Celia — but George Eliot is silent about this activity. Her journal concentrates on the challenge of travel to the exclusion of 'home thoughts'. She makes no mention even of the good news of the sales of *The Mill on the Floss* that reached them in Rome, with better news to come in Florence (including word of the highly favourable review in *The Times*: *Letters*, III, 289 and 296). Yet her writing has made their travel possible: by the end of the year, she has made over £3,000 from *The Mill*.

The essayist declares, 'How much more I have to write about Rome!' — which, effectively, she reserves for a decade until she writes *Middlemarch*. There are some direct transpositions into *Middlemarch*: Dorothea's disorientation, obviously; the painter Overbeck, whose maroon velvet cap and grey scarf are given to Naumann; Eliot and Lewes's disappointment in the frescoes of Cupid and Psyche in the Farnesina palace, transmuted in Casaubon's obtuse scholarly comments in Chapter 20; her pleasure in the Campagna. But there are, too, more profound reflections which may have germinated over time: questions about scholarship, art, history, and the relativity of knowledge. These issues are inscribed in the novel in such details as the misattribution of Raphael's 'Coronation of the Virgin' referred to in Chapter 19. What George Eliot is pointing to in the works of art in the Vatican — the statue of Cleopatra, or Ariadne, for example — is not the fixed 'meaning' of a recoverable past, but the continual process of making new meanings.[22] From now on, her fiction was to be explicitly concerned with the presence of the past in the present, with the resonance of Savonarola's Florence in nineteenth century England, or the interaction in *Middlemarch* of the 1830s and 1870s. The major 'division' for George Eliot before and after the Italian journey of 1860 is evident in her writing life: in the shift from the working out of childhood memories to more studied work on the past in relation to the present, both reading the past in relation to the present, and writing it. The journal gives her account at the time of these issues taking hold: not a new concern for her, but one which now emerges with a new focus and emphasis, to be painfully worked through in the writing of *Romola* and the shorter fictions that intervened between its conception and completion, *Silas Marner* and 'Brother Jacob'.

---

[22] These claims depend on such detailed exegeses as Joseph Wiesenfarth, '*Middlemarch*: The Language of Art', *PMLA*, 97 (1982), 363-77 and Kathleen McCormack, '*Middlemarch*: Dorothea's Husbands in the Vatican Museums', *VIJ*, 20 (1992), 75-91, which show how the whole discourse of art is working in the novel – particularly the capacity of art to interpret and be reinterpreted.

On they go to Naples, their base for expeditions to a number of places including Pompeii, which moved them deeply, and Amalfi, where they had a variation in their regime: 'We stupidly neglected seeing the Cathedral; but we saw a macaroni mill and a paper mill'. The next place where they spend any length of time is Florence, where Lewes's journal for 21 May records his inspiration that Savonarola 'afforded fine material for an historical romance. Polly at once caught at the idea with enthusiasm' — though George Eliot's journal makes no reference to the matter. Then to Siena, Bologna, Padua — and Venice, of which she gives a conventionally rhapsodic account: 'What stillness! What beauty! Looking out from the high window of our hotel on the Grand Canal, I felt that it was a pity to go to bed: Venice was more beautiful than romances had feigned'. There can be no doubt that she was enthralled, but as in Rome her response, conditioned by her textual expectations, lacks the more individual abandon of her account (say) of Weimar. At a later point, she describes a sunset ride in a gondola — 'it is the sort of scene in which I could most readily forget my own existence and feel melted into the general life'. The section on Venice is the clearest evidence of the extent to which 'Recollections of Italy' is an account of George Eliot 'melted into the general life' of the tourist registering prescribed sights and reactions to them.

The special, set apart quality of the Italian experience is sustained to the end of the narrative. They proceed out of Italy via Milan and the lakes: 'The next day we reached lovely Chiavenna at the foot of the Splugen pass, and spent the evening in company with a glorious mountain torrent, mountain peaks, huge boulders, with rippling miniature torrents and lovely wild flowers among them, and grassy heights with rich Spanish chesnuts [sic] shadowing them'.[23] The following day they travel in heavy rain to Splügen, which they find 'thoroughly German'. The significant crossing of the Alps at the beginning of the journal is recalled as from 'the climax of grand, nay terrible scenery' they enter 'open green valleys with dotted white churches and

---

[23] This is a convenient point to comment on the treatment of 'Recollections of Italy' by Cross and Haight. Cross prints it almost complete (with a nice small mistranscription in this quotation, where he reads *young* for *wild* flowers). Haight, curiously, quotes it hardly at all. Indeed, in *Letters,* he prints excerpts from Lewes's journals in preference to George Eliot's: the passage about the inspiration for *Romola*, and another about Pompeii which among other things deplores the impropriety of some frescoes ('It was curious to see the schoolboy like tendency in these Pompeians, to ornament their bedrooms with pictures of hideous obscenity': III, 291).

homesteads. We were in Switzerland, and the mighty wall of the Valteline Alps shut us out from Italy, on the 21st of June'.

The account of the whole experience is concluded and contained, though they are not home yet.

This journal reads as the fulfilment of expectations which are the outcome of quite conventional (male) assumptions. But George Eliot is rarely accommodated within a genre, and she treats with the assumptions of travel writing in this journal only to repudiate them in later writing. Even in this journal, which so comprehensively shows her stimulation by the exotic aspects of Italy (climatic, topographical, cultural, and antiquarian), she is not seduced by the genre into representing a quest for buried truth or a purer state of being as the goal of her travels. There is a consciousness in the journal of history being constantly re-made: in her fiction especially from *Romola* on there is an engagement with the layers of previous civilisations and with competing histories (individual and collective). This is a concept of history and historical process which is far from being simply archaeological on the one hand or progressivist on the other.

George Eliot of course made subsequent visits to Italy, whose agendas provide some gloss on 'what she saw'. She and Lewes made a trip in 1861 to research *Romola*, which was marred by sickness, and for which there is no separate journal; in 1864, they made a dedicated study tour with the painter Frederick Burton, recorded in the brief journal 'Italy. 1864'; in 1869 there was the trip on which she first met Cross, an encounter not mentioned in the few lines given to this expedition in her diary. And, of course, she went to Italy on her honeymoon in 1880. Her diary gives no explicit preparation for the entry of 6 May, 'Married this day at 10.15 to John Walter Cross, at St. George's, Hanover Square'. Subsequent entries are generally brief and factual as the wedding journey of the Crosses in part retraces routes George Eliot had taken with Lewes. The experience of Venice this time proves very different from the saturation in picturesqueness described in 1860, for Cross (later to claim that he was overcome by heat) allegedly threw himself into the Grand Canal from their hotel. This drama, the occasion of concupiscent consternation ever since, is barely discernible in George Eliot's diary, which records only visits from doctors and the arrival of Cross's brother, who accompanies them when after a week they resume their journey and take a leisurely route home via Switzerland, Germany, and Belgium. It was George Eliot's last time in Europe.

The evidence of the journals concerning what George Eliot saw in Europe, I have tried to suggest, is various. Europe was important to her in a number of ways: she went there at critical times in her life (after the death of her father, when she eloped with Lewes, when she had completed a novel, on her honeymoon). In general, the journals provide evidence of her ways of seeing, in the moment and over time. In particular, in the examples I have considered, the journals constitute a text aside from her fictional explorations of some of the same intellectual — and geographical — territory, and revealingly document turning points in her creation of her writing self.

Chapter Two

Cultural Synthesis in George Eliot's *Middlemarch*

Hans Ulrich Seeber

> ... all meanings, we know, depend on the key of interpretation.
> (George Eliot, *Daniel Deronda*, Ch. 5)

Middlemarch — a European Novel

In matter and manner, George Eliot's *Middlemarch* reflects and enacts that modernizing process which changed Europe from the end of the eighteenth century almost out of recognition. The obvious matter of the novel is social change. Its major characters are actively involved in that change as doctors, scientists, political reformers, manufacturers and bankers. The aim of the protagonists — Lydgate, Dorothea and Ladislaw in particular — is not merely a functional and quantitative one, namely increased efficiency of production and organization, but a combination of scientific and social improvement. It is this endeavour which links them, as I have tried to show elsewhere, with the utopian projects of the nineteenth century and their complete or partial failures. The characteristic occidental conjunction of rational research, economic and technological application explodes holistic, static, circular concepts of order, thereby unleashing a feverish dynamism totally unknown in the nineteenth century outside Europe — with the exception of the United States. The secularization of Christianity and the increasingly rapid division of labour produces the endlessly complex 'web' of modern society which looks towards the future and uses its newly awakened sense of history for purposes of self-definition. For where everything seems to flow and to float, where time rules triumphant, memory is called upon to describe the river of change and to account for the emergence of the disturbing here and now.

It is precisely the recording of change which the historian or narrator of the tale *Middlemarch* sets herself as her task. Compared with what Fielding had to do, the modern historian's task is complicated by the acceleration of time and change implying the emergence of an increasingly complex social world. To tackle such a task the historian, as George Eliot calls her role as narrator, needs to confine herself or himself to the thorough study of a limited area. In a review of the state of German philosophy in 1855, discussed by George Eliot with approval,[1] Otto Friedrich Gruppe insists that the sober investigation of a limited field is more appropriate for a truly modern philosophic mind than the building of grand systems after the fashion of Hegel. Accordingly, *Middlemarch* presents itself as a case-study of social and historical research. The observed facts of social behaviour, which the dialogues in a sense document (hence the importance of the presentation of gossip and party-talk), are analysed, interpreted and evaluated by a sophisticated philosophic mind which is in full possession of the contemporary theories, concepts and discourses for her/his analytical and hermeneutic work. The narrator's epistemological situation in fact reflects that of historians, sociologists and scientists in general, who are all engaged in the Kantian project of bridging the gap between the subject and the object, the observer and the observed, abstract discourse and concrete experience.

If my woefully brief and reductive description of the matter and the manner of *Middlemarch* is not totally wrong, the conclusion seems inevitable that the novel is both modern and European in a most emphatic sense. This emphasis is strengthened by the author's seemingly European vision and European frame of reference. Just like Matthew Arnold, Thomas Carlyle and Samuel Taylor Coleridge, to name only a few obvious cases, George Eliot knew that Europe, owing to its classical, Christian, philosophical and economic traditions, is something unique in the context of nineteenth-century world cultures and that England, partaking of these traditions and ceaselessly exchanging knowledge and ideas with the European Continent, plays a vital part in that European project. Despite references to imperialism in *Daniel Deronda*, this project was for George Eliot not yet as darkened by the shadow of European colonialism and European nationalism as it was for Conrad and for E. M. Forster. Instead, Eliot stresses the possibility of redemption by transcending the self, whereby she means both the individual self and the collective national self. The self, educating itself and increasing its

---

[1] George Eliot, 'The Future of German Philosophy', review of Otto Friedrich Gruppe's *Gegenwart und Zukunft der Philosophie in Deutschland* (1855), in *Essays of George Eliot*, ed. by Thomas Pinney (New York: Columbia University Press, 1963), pp. 148-153.

knowledge, thereby gaining the required 'breadth of horizon'[2] as Herr Klesmer puts it in *Daniel Deronda*, needs to absorb the other in acts of sympathetic understanding, in order to become a true self. A true self is never closed, it preserves its propensity for growth. Unknown alien cultures and experiences are accessible by acts of hermeneutic understanding. Theorizing about the possibilities of understanding them ('verstehen') was the major preoccupation of nineteenth-century hermeneutics and historiography. To appropriate other cultures results in personal growth and the formation of an identity which is complex and alive. This is what is meant by the Goethean idea of *Bildung*, well-known to George Eliot. It can, however, also be related to the more scientific notion of evolutionary emergence, first posited by George Henry Lewes.

Indeed, there is no such thing as a pure collective or personal identity. A host of different genetic, ethnic, cultural and systemic strands contribute to the making of a personal or collective identity even within comparatively close-knit communities. To a greater or lesser extent we are all hybrids. And only synthetic judgements, as Kant emphasized in his *Critique of Pure Reason* and which Eliot noted with approval, are capable of adding something to our knowledge. In this paper I work on the assumption that one of the methods employed in *Middlemarch* stresses the necessity of growth and change by showing examples of more or less successful cultural syntheses. The attempt at synthesis always implies the danger or the chance of unresolved conflicts and frictions. In the case of Dorothea Brooke, Tertius Lydgate and Will Ladislaw it seems clear that cultural inspiration and cultural interaction lead to the formation of specifically Anglo-European identities which, not surprisingly, provoke mixed reactions from the representatives of provincial English society. Taking the concept of cultural synthesis as my key to the text, I hope to shed some light on European aspects of the novel which perhaps have not received the attention they deserve. I shall first look at the demands its many voices make on the reader. I shall then proceed to comment upon some European aspects of the characters of Dorothea and Will Ladislaw.

---

[2] George Eliot, *Daniel Deronda* (Harmondsworth: Penguin Books, 1983), p. 79. References in the text are to this edition. It is significant that 'horizon' has been and still is one of the key concepts of the German hermeneutic tradition (cf. Gadamer, Jauss).

Eliot's European Voices

It has often been observed that Eliot's texts, *Middlemarch* and *Daniel Deronda* in particular, make extraordinary demands on the intellectual capacity of the reader. To begin with, her implied reader must be a polyglot. Since Eliot usually does not translate the epigraphs introducing the chapters, the reader who does not have a good command of French, Italian, Spanish and German is reduced to an impoverished appreciation of the text and its voices. Rather like the arguments preceding the text in old novels, the epigraphs usually sum up an important theme of the respective chapter. As such, they might be considered superfluous as the diligent reader can be expected to find out for himself. Their contribution to the overall effect and flavour of the novel, however, is not merely to help the reader's understanding or, even more superficially, to show off the author's impressive reading. Rather, they embed the text and its configurations in a European context of shared aesthetic, moral and intellectual values. We are constantly reminded of a common cultural heritage feeding into the text, illuminating it and being illumined by it in a process of mutual recognition. The chorus of voices from Dante to Goethe, from Shakespeare to Wordsworth and Victor Hugo, from proverb to lyric song and essay, enriches the polyphony of a composition modelled on the example of a symphony. Unlike T. S. Eliot's *The Waste Land*, this symphony of European voices is not marred by discordant notes. Instead of emphasizing the discord between traditional harmony and modern disharmony, George Eliot's text displays and enacts a tonality which in a sense disavows the element of discontinuity contained in the Theresa-Dorothea analogy. For Eliot Theresas are no longer possible in the modern world, but her artistic handling of European voices past and present emphasizes synthesis and harmony rather than dissonance. However, this does not mean that the novel's diversity of viewpoints and its openness are displaced by the possibly suffocating unity of an organic whole.

Although Eliot makes use of national stereotypes for purposes of characterization and classification — Germany is equated with, for instance, art, Spain with heroism, France with sexual temptation and science, etc. — nationalism does not rank high on her list of priorities. Both in her novels and in her essays she looks at Continental Europe with remarkable sympathy. Being perfectly confident of her English identity she is bent upon widening her horizon, appreciating the achievements of continental cultures and depreciating their defects. Her criticism is good-humoured, her appreciation notably warm. Standing in Goethe's study at Weimar, she is moved to tears by its very simplicity. Praising French lady novelists, she objects to national arguments with gentle irony: 'Patriotic gallantry may perhaps contend that English women could, if they had liked, have written as well as their neighbours; but we will leave the consideration of that question to the reviewers of the literature that might have been. In the literature that actually is, we must turn to France for the highest examples of womanly achievement in almost every department'.[3]

Eliot had the good fortune to live at a time when Anglo-German relations were not darkened by bad memories. This allows her to look at German life with a completely unprejudiced eye. There may be another reason for her astonishing and admirable objectivity. Eliot continues an eighteenth-century transnational discourse of humanitarian values and cultural endeavour. Right up to the First World War the *Respublica literaria* of Europe never completely succumbed to nationalism. In the preface to *De L'Allemagne*, published in London in 1813, Madame de Staël bitterly complains of the new nationalism which made it impossible to publish her book in France. Similarly Stendhal, in the preface to his *De L'Amour* (1823), appeals to the reader to value the truth higher than specifically French prejudices. For Stendhal a blind, fanatical sort of patriotism is incompatible with the notion of a truly civilized man or a truly civilized nation. It is well-known that Goethe, Germany's national writer *par excellence*, did not think much of German nationalism. Again, the utopian and idealistic movements of the nineteenth century appeal to a European audience. They deplore the negative effects of national egoisms which were largely absent during the Middle Ages, mainly because the Christian faith provided a common bond strong enough to make joint actions possible. It seems obvious that the Theresa-Dorothea analogy, with its reference to the crusades, reflects this European dimension of nineteenth-century thinking. Sympathizing with the Saint-Simonians in Paris, Lydgate does not merely express his momentary admiration for early socialist ideas, he also subscribes to their idea of a common European project. Saint-Simon admires the cultural and spiritual unity of mediaeval Europe, and both the French Saint-Simonians and the German Romantics look back to the Middle Ages as a source of redemption from the ills of modern society, its materialism and egotism. Hugh Whitemeyer characterizes George Eliot's view of Romanticism as follows:

> By Romanticism in this context [...] George Eliot meant a German, Catholic, neo-medieval movement whose 'main feature [...] was the exaltation of the Medieval above the Classic, of art animated by Greek humanism'. Naumann is explicitly associated with

---

[3] *Essays of George Eliot*, ed. by Thomas Pinney (London: Routledge and Kegan Paul, 1963), p. 54.

this movement when he is described as 'one of the chief renovators of Christian art .[...]'.[4]

One of the chief inspirations of such a view of Romanticism and the Middle Ages was Novalis's essay *Die Christenheit oder Europa*. However, Eliot's attitude towards Romanticism and the Middle Ages is ambivalent. While approving of the contribution the Romantics made to the understanding of the complex symbolism of mediaeval art and of their vision of European culture, she is not at all in favour of reactionary politics or aesthetics.

Classic English dictionaries do not define the word Europe. They request the reader to check the entry 'European'. The scarce information given there does not include the opposition of Europe and England which is perfectly common in present-day English usage. I surmise that a narrowing down and a connotative charging of the meaning of the word must have happened within the last hundred years. Dr Johnson, in his dictionary, plainly states that 'European' means 'belonging to Europe', using examples from poems by Waller, Dryden and Phillips. Thomas de Quincey uses the term 'European literature' which for him includes the English branch. He deplores the 'imperfect literary organization of Europe'[5] of the eighteenth century which explains the fact that Samuel Johnson and Gotthold Ephraim Lessing, the two great critics, had not heard of each other. The well-informed and extensive surveys of nineteenth-century European thought and literature written by British authors of the time show how much the situation has changed. I need mention only three works: William Lecky, *History of European Morals*, published in 1869; George Saintsbury, *A History of Criticism and Literary Taste in Europe* (3 vols, 1900, 1902, 1904), and John Theodore Merz, *A History of European Scientific Thought in the Nineteenth Century* (1904-1912). Merz states: 'The subject before us, then, is European Thought — i.e. the thought of France, Germany, and England — during the greater part of the Nineteenth Century.'[6] Merz assumes the existence of a European cultural elite engaged in the pursuit of widening our horizon and increasing our

---

[4] Hugh Whitemeyer, 'George Eliot, Naumann and the Nazarenes', *Victorian Studies*, 18, 2 (1974), 150.

On George Eliot's literary appropriation of abroad cf. Deirdre David, '"Getting Out of the Eel Jar": George Eliot's literary appropriation of abroad', in *1830-1876 Creditable Warriors: English Literature and the Wider World*, No. 3, ed. by Michael Cotsell (London, Atlantic Highlands: The Ashfield Press, 1990), pp. 257-72.

[5] *The Collected Writings of Thomas de Quincey*, ed. by David Masson (London: Black, 1896-1897), XI, 160.

[6] John Theodore Merz, *A History of European Scientific Thought in the Nineteenth Century*, 4 vols (1904-1912; repr. Gloucester, Mass: Peter Smith, 1976), I, 15.

knowledge. Lydgate, just like George Eliot herself and George Henry Lewes, is obviously a member of that elite. Discussing Lydgate's scientific project, the narrator explicitly classifies it as one of the remarkable efforts made by the 'European mind': 'Of this sequence to Bichat's work, already vibrating along many currents of the European mind, Lydgate was enamoured.'[7] Middlemarch opinion notes with uneasiness and even disapproval his 'odd name' — ' "I thought it was an odd name was Tertius," said the bright-faced matron [...]', (128) — and his 'foreign ideas' (186). To emphasize shared values and aims, this European elite quite consciously uses a polyglot Eurocentric discourse to signal its awareness of what has been done elsewhere. I must confine myself to quoting only one characteristic example from Saintsbury: 'I may at least hope that I shall not be charged with "la fretta/Che l'onestade ad ogni atto dismaga", in regard to a book which has been the actual work and companion of seven years in its composition [...]'.[8] Defending his work against criticism levelled at it he declares: 'I am very sorry to appear stiff-necked in reference to criticism made with many obliging expressions, but *Ich kann nicht anders*, [...]' (III, vii). Saintsbury repeats Martin Luther's famous statement made before the Reichstag held at Worms in 1525.

Saintsbury moves effortlessly from one language to the other. He displays the characteristic traffic of ideas and of idioms which one can also observe in *Middlemarch*. To study and to evaluate provincial life properly apparently requires a frame of reference and a vantage point transcending national boundaries. In the examples given so far the voices were distinct. A fictional text can present them simultaneously whenever a non-English person's foreign idiom is rendered in English. This is the case with Naumann and Klesmer. Both, from the point of view of a German reader, are strikingly convincing, because their uncompromising professionalism and their linguistic behaviour are rendered superbly well. Both represent the German artist who was a stereotype at the time, but a stereotype based on fact. Eliot distinguishes between caricature based on truth and, by implication, caricature produced by fantasy and used for purposes of defamation. In the following example taken from *Daniel Deronda*, the reader is invited to listen to two voices at the same time, the English spoken by the character and the German subtext it is supposed to represent. Joseph Kalonymos addresses Daniel

---

[7] George Eliot, *Middlemarch* (Harmondsworth: Penguin Books, 1976), p. 178. References in the text are to this edition.

[8] George Saintsbury, *A History of Criticism and Literary Taste in Europe* (Edinburgh and London: William Blackwood & Sons, 1949), III, pp. v-vi.

Deronda in German: 'So — you are no longer angry at being something more than an Englishman?' (787). The particle 'so' introducing the sentence reflects idiomatic German. However, Eliot changes the German model to create an acceptable stylistic synthesis. In German I would expect a 'so, so', suggesting an attitude of wondering appreciation toward Deronda's change of mind. The blending of the two voices in fact enacts the blending of two identities which creates something richer and more exciting than the old 'pure' self. Deronda remains an Englishman, but an Englishman who is also something else. Klesmer's identity is also presented in terms of ethnic and cultural synthesis: 'Herr Klesmer being a felicitous combination of the German, the Sclave [i.e. Slav], and the Semite' (77). Again, in *Scenes of Clerical Life* Amos Barton is characterized thus: 'He was like an onion that has been rubbed with spices; the strong original odour was blended with something new and foreign.'[9] Contrasting life at St Ogg's with mediaeval reminiscences evoked by the Rhineland, the narrator of *The Mill on the Floss* declares:

> You could not live among such people; you are stifled for want of an outlet towards something beautiful, great, or noble: you are irritated with these dull men and women, as a kind of population out of keeping with the earth on which they live — with this rich plain where the great river flows for ever onward and links the small pulse of the old English town with the beatings of the world's mighty heart.[10]

In order to avoid a stifling provincialism England apparently needs to develop vital links with Europe and the rest of the world.

In other cases a successful blend or synthesis is carefully avoided, either to show the speaker's insufficient command of English or to demonstrate a momentary breakdown of such a command because of a sudden inner turmoil. After listening to Gwendolen's less than perfect musical performance Klesmer's English suddenly falters. He responds to Mr Arrowsmith's conciliatory sentence, 'You cannot like to hear poor amateur singing' in the following manner: '"No, truly, but that makes nothing," said Herr Klesmer, suddenly speaking in an odious German fashion with staccato endings, quite unobservable in him before, and apparently depending on a change of mood, as Irishmen resume their strongest brogue when they are fervid or quarrelsome' (78). Herr Klesmer does not merely get his pronunciation wrong; by translating the German idiom 'das macht nichts' literally, he also produces a wrong combination of words. An uncontrolled cultural interference puts him at a distinct social disadvantage. Another instance of a

---

[9] George Eliot, *Scenes of Clerical Life* (Harmondsworth: Penguin Books, 1982), p. 67.
[10] George Eliot, *The Mill on the Floss* (Harmondsworth: Penguin Books, 1988), pp. 362-3.

not quite successful synthesis is Brooke, who does not seem to have digested completely the new ideas and images he met with on his European travels.

In Eliot's works the narrator's comments are often interspersed and studded with ironic quotations of European key-words and discourses. To examine the uses of this strategy, let us consider the following example from *Scenes of Clerical Life*:

> 'Ah!' said Mr Hackit, 'and my wife makes Mr Barton a good stiff glass o' brandy-and-water, when he comes into supper after his cottage preaching. The parson likes it; it puts a bit o' colour into his face, and makes him look a deal handsomer.'
>
> This allusion to brandy-and-water suggested to Miss Gibbs the introduction of the liquor decanters, now that the tea was cleared away; for in bucolic society five-and-twenty years ago, the human animal of the male sex was understood to be perpetually athirst, and 'something to drink' was as necessary a 'condition of thought' as Time and Space. (49)

The passage juxtaposes provincial speech and an ironic quasi-historical explanation by the narrator couched partly in philosophical terms. A slightly humorous and satiric touch is thus introduced which distances the reader from the provincial speakers and reveals their limitations and defects. The stance adopted by the narrator is that of an educated, metropolitan observer looking at the scene with philosophical reflectiveness. The *experience* of provincial gossip gives way to an act of *thinking* and evaluating. The excessive drinking habits of the male section of provincial society are exposed to the ironic gaze of the narrator, who ridicules them by claiming for them an importance as high as the categories of transcendental philosophy. Such an incongruous combination of male thirst and quasi-philosophical speech, however, damages transcendental philosophy itself. And indeed, in her review of Gruppe's book, Eliot disapproves of Kant's transcendental categories from the point of view of English empiricism and of Gruppe's antimetaphysical philosophy based on linguistic analyses. Gruppe denounces German philosophical idealism as a 'speculative error' ('spekulative[r] Irrtum').[11] Kant, according to Gruppe, failed to see the 'nature of abstract notions' ('Verkennen des Wesens abstracter Begriffe').[12] If one does not realize that abstract notions originated in concrete, sensuous experience, they tend to trick their users into the belief that there is something real corresponding to them. The phrase 'condition of thought' and the words 'Time' and 'Space', beginning with a capital letter, refer to Kant's *Critique of Pure Reason*.

---

[11] O. F. Gruppe, *Gegenwart und Zukunft der Philosophie in Deutschland* (Berlin: Georg Reimer, 1855), p. 239.

[12] Gruppe, p. 246.

Eliot's commentary thus contains discursive elements culled from Kant's philosophy, from the pastoral poetry of the ancients ('bucolic') and from eighteenth-century definitions of the nature of man ('human animal'). The collocation 'bucolic society' implies an attitude of humorous condescension towards provincial life, a mixture of love and ironic distance. Although no doubt used interchangeably with 'rural', it also conjures up memories of bucolic poetry reaching back to Vergil and Theocritus. The phrase 'human animal' varies, with satiric intent, the classic definition of man as an *animal rationale*.

The defining feature of Eliot's mode of narrative, in other words, is a disjunction and a correlation between quasi-theoretical discourse and scenic presentation of English life. Such a structure is reminiscent of the Kantian disjunction and correlation between 'Begriff' and 'Anschauung', i.e. between abstract notion and concrete experience. The one cannot do without the other. Knowledge is indeed produced by the interaction and synthesis of the two. However, in fictional composition this synthesis is left to the activity of the reader. The modern fissure between thought and emotion, abstract notion and image, so much deplored by T. S. Eliot as a defining characteristic of modern as opposed to Elizabethan literature, is the result of the European intellectual movement initiated by Bacon and Descartes. Having this movement in mind, Kant states pointedly in his *Kritik der reinen Vernunft*:

> Gedanken ohne Inhalt sind leer, Anschauungen ohne Begriffe sind blind. (A 51) Der Verstand mag nichts anzuschauen, und die Sinne nichts zu denken. Nur daraus, daß Sie sich vereinigen, kann Erkenntnis entspringen. (A 51) [13]

> Thoughts without content are empty, intuitions without concepts are blind. (A 51) The understanding can intuit nothing, and the senses can think nothing. Only through their union can knowledge arise. (A 51) [14]

Identity and Synthesis

The strongest, most persistent and largely victorious voice to be heard in *Middlemarch* expresses conservative wisdom and conservative prejudices. The narrative voice, however, commenting upon the opinions prevalent in *Middlemarch*, regularly indicates the narrowness and limitations of the persons venting such opinions. Thus the attitude adopted by the characters towards the cultures of the Continent can be used as a yardstick to gauge their

---

[13] Immanuel Kant, *Kritik der reinen Vernunft* (Hamburg: Meiner, 1956), p. 95.

[14] *Immanuel Kant's Critique of Pure Reason*, trans. by Norman Kemp Smith, 2nd imp. (London: Macmillan, 1933), p. 93.

potential for growth and *Bildung*. Those minor characters who express their dislike of foreign ideas and of foreign blood are usually not presented in a favourable light. Eliot quite evidently supports the party of knowledge, education and growth, in fact, of meliorism. For her such a position is incompatible with anti-European attitudes. The critics of Lydgate's European training are ironically disposed of:

> It was clear that Lydgate, by not dispensing drugs, intended to cast imputations on his equals, and also to obscure the limit between his own rank as a general practitioner and that of the physicians, who, in the interest of the profession, felt bound to maintain its various grades. Especially against a man who had not been to either of the English universities and enjoyed the absence of anatomical and bedside study there, but came with a libellous pretension to experience in Edinburgh and Paris, where observation might be abundant indeed, but hardly sound. (213)

Significantly, even characters who strike one as quintessentially English such as the Garths, Farebrother or Bulstrode are linked to a European background. Bulstrode is convinced that medical reform in Middlemarch needs an infusion of Parisian knowledge via Lydgate. Farebrother exchanges letters with the utopian socialist Trawley and is likeable and somewhat exceptional for being remarkably fair, open-minded and unconstrained: 'As the Vicar walked to Lowick, anyone watching him closely might have seen him twice shrug his shoulders. I think that the rare Englishmen who have this gesture are never of the heavy type' (444). The endearing virtues of the Garth family are given a typological dimension by a reference to the Roman hero Cincinnatus. The qualities of Mary Garth's mother are summed up as follows: 'In her snowy-frilled cap she reminded one of that delightful Frenchwoman whom we have all seen marketing, basket on arm' (276). The implied reader is expected to have had the same positive French experiences as the narrator, no matter whether those experiences were gained from life or from art.

The extraordinary strength of Eliot's novel is due to her ability to represent so many different voices of a changing community. To present voices and change is precisely what the medium of the novel can do, unlike the medium of the fine arts. This is an insight which was first developed systematically by Gotthold Ephraim Lessing in his *Laokoon: oder über die Grenzen der Mahlerey und Poesie*. Painting is restricted to representing bodies only in space and at a given moment. Laokoon's voice and his actions as they change and modulate are beyond the scope of painting. The function of narrative and of dramatic poetry, on the other hand, is to present 'articulated tones in time'.[15] Will Ladislaw uses the same arguments in his memorable dispute with Naumann about the respective virtues of painting and of poetry. And for once, I believe, Will gets the better of Naumann, speaking as he does with the tacit approval of the novelist George Eliot:

> Language gives a fuller image, which is all the better for being vague. After all, the true seeing is within; and painting stares at you with an insistent imperfection. I feel that especially about representations of women. As if a woman were a mere coloured superficies! You must wait for a movement and tone. There is a difference in their very breathing: they change from moment to moment. — This woman whom you have just seen, for example: how would you paint her voice, pray? But her voice is much diviner than anything you have seen of her. (222)

Dorothea's heavenly voice synthesizes nature and art. As such it can express the uncommon qualities of Dorothea's soul. The strings of the Romantic Aeolian harp, to which Will frequently compares Dorothea's voice, are not vibrated by human fingers but by the wind, by nature itself. Dorothea's uncontaminated nature is at odds with the common voices of Middlemarch. Though using the same English sounds, she seems to be using a remote, foreign code, thus combining in fact two different voices. This clash of voices and codes comes out particularly well in her following encounter with Mrs Cadwallader:

> 'I never called everything by the same name that all the people about me did,' said Dorothea, stoutly.
> 'But I suppose you have found out your mistake, my dear,' said Mrs Cadwallader, 'and that is a proof of sanity.'
> Dorothea was aware of the sting, but it did not hurt her. 'No,' she said, 'I still think that the greater part of the world is mistaken about many things.' (581)

Cadwallader implicitly accuses Dorothea of insanity. What we would nowadays call Dorothea's utopian mentality and utopian code confront the 'petty medium' of Middlemarch opinion. It will not do to discuss Dorothea's attitude simply as the immature romantic idealism of an exalted young woman. In fact, her idealism synthesizes a variety of models and influences, some of which seem to have escaped the attention of the critics. Dorothea's constant preoccupation with schemes and plans remind one of nineteenth-century utopianism, which was not necessarily incompatible with religious fervour of a Methodist kind. Her attempt to combine religious faith with rationalism reflects a characteristic theological obsession of the nineteenth century. Again, European influences contribute decisively to the making of

---

[15] Lessing, in *Laokoon*, speaks of 'artikulierte Töne in der Zeit'. Quoted in Volker Meid, *Metzler Literaturchronik: Werke deutschsprachiger Autoren* (Stuttgart, Weimar: Metzler, 1993), p. 228.

her identity. It is she, not Celia, who responds passionately to Monsieur Liret's teaching and to the organ music at Freiburg cathedral (not Freiberg, as the Penguin edition has it). It is she who deplores the fact that she did not learn German as well as French during her stay at Lausanne.

Being exposed to the pagan sensuous relicts of Rome, Will's remarks on German scholarship, and Naumann's aesthetic professionalism, Dorothea is forced to subject her own marriage and her own Puritan identity to a thorough re-assessment. The very name 'Dorothea' chosen by Eliot for Miss Brooke bestows a typological identity on the young woman which links her with both English and continental saints of Christianity and women's emancipation. It establishes an interfigural relationship which illuminates her identity rather more than the extremely scant information we are given about her childhood and youth. The narrator does not fail to mention 'that mysterious influence of Naming which determines so much of mortal choice' (268). The paradigms determining both the character of Dorothea and of Ladislaw are saints. The parallels and the differences are unmistakeable. Dorothea, the martyr, who lived at the time of Diocletian, converted her accuser by sending him apples and roses from beyond the grave. The name Ladislaw is a compound combining the meanings 'to govern' ('vladati') and 'fame' ('slava'). Ladislaw I (1077-95) of Poland was declared a saint and won recognition by successful reform work.

In a sense the text explores the fate of heroism and saintliness under the 'prosaic' conditions of the modern world. Why then does Eliot produce a semantic gap to be filled by the reader, why does she not acknowledge the more obvious contemporary members of the family of Dorotheas? After all the narrator considers Dorothea to be a modern type, i.e. an abstraction of 'the lives of many Dorotheas' (86). Presumably Eliot avoided disclosing Dorothea's contemporary sisters in the text in order to play down the erotic and political potential of her heroine which is less obtrusively implied in the references to Ariadne and Theresa. First of all, there is an obvious kinship with Dorothea Beale of Cheltenham, the pioneer of women's education. In German Classicism and Romanticism the name Dorothea became a synonym for a curious combination, also characteristic of Eliot's heroine, of women's emancipation and wifely devotion to a husband. Dorothea Tieck made contributions to that famous translation of Shakespeare into German known under the name of Schlegel and Tieck. Dorothea Schlegel, famous and notorious for her passionate relationship with the Romantic critic and philologist Friedrich Schlegel, left her former husband, a Jewish banker from Frankfurt, to join Friedrich. She gave up her Jewish beliefs for her husband,

and even joined the Catholic church when Friedrich found his spiritual home in Catholicism. Dorothea, under the influence of her husband, developed strong literary interests and wrote a novel herself. One of the most erotic novels in the German language, *Lucinde*, written by Friedrich, reflects the free love between the two Romantics in their early, revolutionary period. Again, Goethe in *Hermann und Dorothea* portrays a woman who, in the aftermath of the French revolutionary wars spilling over to Germany, leaves her fellow refugees to join Hermann in an act of utter devotion and trust. Despite the sequence of names of the title, the real hero of Goethe's idyll is Dorothea, who is not merely remarkable for her altruism, but also for her role as a political interpreter of the rapid changes defining the modern world. Marriage and family life are understood to give stability to modern life threatened by rapid change and disruption. Furthermore, just like Eliot's Dorothea, Dorothea Schlegel and Goethe's Dorothea move from one husband or fiancé to another one, the second relationship being the happier one and having political implications. George Henry Lewes, in his *Life of Goethe*,[16] calls *Hermann und Dorothea* 'one of the most faultless of modern poems' (II, 195) and a 'Hymn to the Family' (II, 207). In varying degrees the German models emphasize altruism, love, even eroticism, politics, wifely devotion and education, but, unlike Eliot, they do not yet probe realistically into the limitations and sacrifices which are in store for women under given social conditions. Still, Dorothea's breathtaking innocence and idealism, particularly in her relationship with Will while still a married woman, remind one of the exalted German Dorotheas rather than of Madame Bovary.

Unlike Dorothea's, Will Ladislaw's Anglo-European identity is so obvious that it hardly needs elaborating. Brought up in England as the grandson of a Polish refugee and educated at Heidelberg, in almost every detail he conforms both to the stereotype of the Romantic intellectual influenced by German romanticism and the Polish rebel. For the narrator his redeeming feature is his ability to transform himself, under the impact of his love for Dorothea, from a rootless would-be poet and artist to a political journalist and reformer. It is no surprise at all that Middlemarch society emphasizes his foreignness and treats him with suspicion and contempt. However, Will's alleged foreignness, conveniently attributed to his foreign blood, is really a cultural perception produced by the synthesis of English, Polish and German elements which he represents. While provincial opinion in *Middlemarch* deplores Will's 'dangerously mixed blood' (503), the narrator emphatically

---

[16] *The Life of Goethe*, ed. by George Henry Lewes, 3rd edn, 2 vols (Leipzig: Brockhaus, 1882).

recommends new ethnic and cultural syntheses. Will may not be an ideal choice for Dorothea. For anyone knowing English and German romanticism he certainly is a believable character. What is more, from the point of view of Dorothea's obvious sexual needs, of which she becomes aware during her stay in Rome, Will is not the wrong choice. The stereotype of the Pole in nineteenth-century culture emphasizes both his love of freedom and his erotic attractions.

Let me add a final observation. It was precisely the failure of this progressive European discourse and synthesis, epitomized by the figure of Kurtz in Conrad's *Heart of Darkness*, which marked the beginning of modernism as an intellectual and artistic project. Modernism registers both the crisis and possible modes of reconstruction. Marlow has this to say about Kurtz's mixed identity:

> The original Kurtz had been educated partly in England, and — as he was good enough to say himself — his sympathies were in the right place. His mother was half-English, his father was half-French. All Europe contributed to the making of Kurtz; and by-and-by I learned that, most appropriately, the International Society for the Suppression of Savage Customs had entrusted him with the making of a report, for its future guidance. And he had written it, too. I've seen it. I have read it. It was eloquent, vibrating with eloquence, but too high-strung. Seventeen pages of close writing he had found time for! But this must have been before his — let us say — nerves, went wrong, and caused him to preside at certain midnight dances ending with unspeakable rites, [...].[17]

Why did the failure mentioned above happen?[18] This is a question which takes us right to the heart of the contemporary debate about Eurocentric culture and its problematic relationship with other cultures. The obvious way out is to say that Kurtz and his twentieth-century disciples betrayed the humanist heritage of Europe. One could also say that Conrad reaffirms the static, pessimistic anthropology of the Christian tradition: man's instincts are

---

[17] Joseph Conrad, *Heart of Darkness* (Harmondsworth: Penguin Books, 1985), p. 86.

[18] I thank Elizabeth Deeds Ermarth for raising this question during the discussion of my paper at the Warwick conference.

After completing my essay I notice that K. M. Newton pointed out revealing parallels between Dorothea Schlegel and Dorothea Brooke, Friedrich Schlegel and Will Ladislaw in 'Historical prototypes in *Middlemarch', English Studies*, 56 (1975), 403-8. According to him, Will's transformation from a capricious romantic to an active political man was modelled on Friedrich's similar development. In both cases the change is due to the influence of one of the two Dorotheas. I find Ken Newton's argument completely convincing and wish to thank him for sending me an offprint of his article.

Another article which I wish I had read before embarking upon my own study is Barbara Hardy's illuminating essay 'Rome in Middlemarch: A Need for Foreignness', *George Eliot — George Henry Lewes Studies*, 24-25 (September 1993), 1-16.

stronger than his reason. However, cultural critics like D. H. Lawrence and Heidegger ('Seinsvergessenheit') probe deeper and raise more disturbing questions. Is Western civilization with its exploitative attitude towards nature, its capacity for abstractions and reifications, its economic individualism and expansionism, inherently aggressive? If we do need a radical re-examination and reorientation of European (and American) culture, Eliot's notion of 'sympathy' — towards nature, towards our fellow human beings — will have to play a major role.

Chapter Three

George Eliot and the World as Language

Elizabeth Deeds Ermarth

The particular topical issue that my title suggests is the role of language in our lives, and the extent to which language constructs rather than passively reflects reality, if we can still use such a word as 'reality'.

This issue is not a particularly new one; it goes back well through the nineteenth century. George Eliot certainly knew as well as anyone that, like languages, cultural values deeply differ. She emphasizes the fact that cultural values are just that, cultural, *not* natural, and that much unhappiness is caused by the naturalization of those constructs. 'Construct' is a word that would not have surprised her or sent her scurrying for cover. Her novels prepare us to understand how languages, and the systems of belief and value that act like languages, provide differing habitations in the world. To inhabit a language, as Cortázar says, is to inhabit a world: a world of systemic differences that shape and limit and enable all kinds of function.

But there *is* a point of emphasis at which the problem of language becomes controversial: the point of distinguishing between relativism on the one hand and relativity on the other. What is at stake in this distinction is whether the constructed world is one or many: whether the grammatical differences between systems can be mediated according to some common denominator, perhaps even a common grammar of some kind, or whether their differences are absolute and unmediateable. I shall come back to this problem later.

But first, I would like to begin considering how the world is language by reflecting on my experience of writing about George Eliot — an experience that I know is not limited to me. For me, then, writing on George Eliot usually is a particularly mixed experience consisting of both pleasure and frustration. On the one hand, she says complex things with such wit and generosity, that I feel delighted, and compelled to assent. There is always an extra margin for amusement in the narrative language, a kind of chronic

33

risibility in the text. Taking *Middlemarch* as perhaps the most familiar example, there are those continuous small turns of vocabulary that open new vistas, like the description of Lydgate's situation in terms of 'the hampering threadlike pressure of small social conditions' — a quiet, literary joke linking Middlemarchers with Lilliputians. There are the little dramas of indirection, like that immortal breakfast conversation between Rosamond and Fred Vincy on various matters of accompaniment: her piano to his flute, in return for his accompaniment on her expedition to encounter Lydgate; and with the implicit extension of their musical duo playing in the background.[1] The little dramas and new vistas sometimes even include me, the reader, as for example when her narrator speaks of 'the grins of suppressed bitterness or other conversational flavours which make half of us an affliction to our friends' (Ch. 18, 132-3).

To take a final example, here is a little commentary from *Middlemarch* on the subject of French influence and English tradition:

> 'Lydgate has lots of ideas, quite new, about ventilation and diet, that sort of thing,' resumed Mr Brooke, after he had handed out Lady Chettam, and had returned to be civil to a group of Middlemarchers.
>
> 'Hang it, do you think that is quite sound? — upsetting the old treatment, which has made Englishmen what they are?' said Mr Standish. (Ch. 10, 68)

There is some continuing topicality in this conversation on the subject of French influence; similar ones still do take place, here and there, in British Universities. But the best fun here is in the way perspectives multiply and balance. Lydgate's ideas receive a certain transfiguration in Mr Brooke's way of putting things; thus transfigured these ideas receive decided opposition from Mr Standish, whose own interest itself requires such deconstruction. Throughout such passages I especially enjoy the extra edge that belongs to the narrative voice, that margin of wider perspective that implicates much that is not explicit in these speeches.

The pleasure I find in such narrative moments has to do with the complexity of the viewpoint and the clarity concerning differences between one and another. Taken in series moments such as this constitute George Eliot's narrative sequence. Around one centre of interest and attention, and then the next, and the next, shifting constellations of viewpoint gather, and dissolve. This complex treatment of perspective is a mystery of realist narration that we have only begun to recognize. In these constellations are

---

[1] George Eliot, *Middlemarch, A Study of Provincial Life* (1871-72), ed. by Gordon S. Haight (Boston: Houghton Mifflin Riverside, 1956), Ch. 11. All references will be to this edition.

embodied the collective awareness of a culture, perhaps even the self-consciousness of the species, but in any case an invisible community of awareness in each novel, that transcends the particular moment at the same time as it finds expression there. George Eliot has few equals — perhaps no equals — when it comes to presenting this complex of awareness. Elsewhere I have called this representation the 'Nobody' narrator in order to distinguish it from anything so limited as a particular individual viewpoint.[2] This blend of consciousness, time, and language does not belong exclusively to any character or even to the historical George Eliot; the entire range of narrative awareness constitutes it; its narrative expression is precisely Nobody. George Eliot's management of this complex perspectival system constitutes one of her great achievements and accounts for much of the fun of reading her. That narrative slide from one view to another engages readers in a kind of suspense that has little to do with plot, and it reminds us continually that nothing is final.

Such are the pleasures of writing on George Eliot. They are also the basis of the frustration I mentioned. The frustration lies in the fact that all but the most carefully formulated conclusions about George Eliot are reversible. No sooner do you say something definitive about her novels than you confront a counterbalancing consideration, a qualifying remark, that inevitable 'on the other hand'. Perhaps the archetype of such moments is that one in Chapter 29 of *Middlemarch* , when the narrator says: 'One morning, some weeks after her arrival at Lowick, Dorothea — but why always Dorothea? Was her point of view the only possible one with regard to this marriage?'. The narrative then gives us the counterbalancing viewpoint. There is never a single way of looking at things in George Eliot. There is always that 'on the other hand' that makes conclusions difficult.

Just to confirm this for any remaining skeptics, consider those commonplaces of George Eliot criticism, the subject of egoism and her particular treatment of it in the pier-glass description. There are many examples in George Eliot's novels of egoism working its destructiveness. Arthur Donnithorne, Tito Melema, Edward Casaubon, Henleigh Grandcourt — the destructiveness of such egoists might seem rather unproblematically to recommend altruism. If thinking of oneself is worst, then thinking of others must be best. It seems an obvious conclusion, and has often been stated in George Eliot criticism. The pier-glass often been taken as a comment at the

---

[2] Elizabeth Deeds Ermarth, *Realism and Consensus in the English Novel* (Princeton: Princeton University Press, 1983).

expense of egoism.   But no sooner does one think of this, than something whispers, 'on the other hand'.   Let me refresh memory briefly with this familiar passage:

> Your pier-glass or extensive surface of polished steel made to be rubbed by a housemaid, will be minutely and multitudinously scratched in all directions; but place now against it a lighted candle as a centre of illumination, and lo! the scratches will seem to arrange themselves in a fine series of concentric circles round that little sun. It is demonstrable that the scratches are going everywhere impartially, and it is only your candle which produces the flattering illusion of concentric arrangement, its light falling with an exclusive optical selection. These things are a parable. The scratches are events, and the candle is the egoism of any person now absent — of Miss Vincy, for example. (Ch. 27, 195)

That little reduction at the end — the remark about someone who is absent — might sound the warning that all is not quite as it seems here. The curious thing about this pier-glass metaphor is its double message about egoism. On the one hand I can think of several examples of egoism in *Middlemarch* to which this passage might apply — Casaubon, Raffles, Bulstrode, and of course poor Miss Vincy. Clearly egoism cannot be a good thing. But no sooner do these applications appear than, 'on the other hand', I recognize in Dorothea Brooke an important exception. She is always thinking of others; she considers Sir James from Celia's point of view. She *likes* giving up things as her carnally minded sister complains. In fact Dorothea is far too good at the selflessness business and it gets her into trouble. She is so badly inexperienced at acting on, or even knowing her own personal feelings that she very nearly leaves her chance for happiness pointlessly in the dust. She is the altruist whose example recommends egoism. George Eliot explicitly comments in an essay, 'We should distrust a man who sets up shop purely for the good of the community'.[3] Altruism in George Eliot has little to do with selflessness or lack of ego; instead, it has to do with balancing the conflicting claims of ego and of community. Pure egoism may be destructive on the one hand; but (and here it is again) 'on the other hand', a developed ego is necessary to independent and adult life. Dorothea's example simply stands in the way of what might otherwise have been an easy generalization about the pier-glass and about egoism. The metaphor asserts the powerfully narcissistic potential of ego, but it also asserts the *importance* of ego as a condition of light and order.

George Eliot often causes such havoc with interpretive generalizations. At least one reason for this is that she undermines the dualisms that such

---

[3] *Essays of George Eliot*, ed. by Thomas Pinney (New York: Columbia University Press, 1963), p. 156.

generalizations depend upon.   She pushes readers beyond the dualism between egoism and altruism, and beyond the implicit hierarchies that always underlie such a dualism.   Her narratives engage us in a different kind of problematic, where the important questions are matters of scope and emphasis, and not at all of deciding which side wins in a dualistic competition.   When we come across that inevitable 'on the other hand', hang it (as Mr Standish would say), we are probably being required to deconstruct a dual opposition.   This commitment in George Eliot's work is, I think, one reason why she favours metaphors of webs or networks: because they are headless and footless systems of relationship without a common centre. There are many centres in George Eliot, not one.   In any case, the dual experience of interpretive enjoyment and frustration amounts to a reader's version of that 'antagonism of valid claims' that is a familiar moral problem to most of the characters in George Eliot's novels.

This 'on the other hand' brings me around again to language because, with each such shift of viewpoint, George Eliot invokes a difference, and a difference that depends upon deep structures, not superficial accidents alone. In her novels a 'valid claim' is never *solely* an individual matter; it is always cultural and systemic as well.   Rosamond Vincy is, after all, the flower of Mrs Lemon's school, and Lydgate chooses her for that reason; it is no good then complaining of narcissistic performances that are put on in the first place at the request of the community and with their entire approval.   Where was Rosamond to learn otherwise?   She meets *her* first 'on the other hand' from Will Ladislaw, a man who is not interested in female flowers.   And her husband Lydgate also depends on systems much larger than he is, both for his strengths and his weaknesses; his intellectual independence has been fostered by science; his carelessness is gender-specific.   Just as Antigone's claims rest on a religion and Creon's on a political system, so the conflicting claims of Rosamond and Lydgate, and every other George Eliot character, rest on something larger and more grammatical in the sense already hinted at.

It is precisely because of what we can call their grammatical properties that actions and events are intelligible or perhaps even possible at all.   George Eliot's genius appears in the way she makes visible the difficult, complex fact that each individual act specifies anew some traditional arrangement, some systemic order, modifying in some minuscule way a broadly interconnected balance of things.   It is precisely thus that unheroic acts become powerful: in their specification and possible modification of a grammar of belief and value.

Such grammars become evident at crucial moments in her novels.   The effort to understand a strange book, the refusal to burn a will, the silence about injustice that breeds guilt and violence. These moments have to do with more than an individual or a single event; they carry the traces of systemic organization. The religious tradition that brings Thomas à Kempis to Maggie Tulliver combines fatally with the tribal narrowness that prompts her to heed him. Mary Garth's family life gives her a set of principles, a grammar of independence, that prepares her to refuse Featherstone's request to burn his will. Gwendolen Harleth grows up in a culture and a family riddled with prejudice against women and obsequiousness before money and rank; these are powerful preparations for her fatal choices.

So the conflict of valid claims is never an individual matter only but always a discursive one having to do with a cultural grammar. Because this is true, the conflict can *not* be settled easily, or perhaps at all. The conflicts between systems, between languages, between discursive formations in George Eliot admit of no absolute distinction between right and wrong. What solution is easy or 'right' to the conflict in *Adam Bede* between feudalism and modernity; to the conflict in *The Mill on the Floss* between clan law and more modern rules; to the conflict in *Daniel Deronda* between national and ethnic cultures? What is right for one is wrong for another, what invigorates a strong mind may derange a weak one. There is always that 'on the other hand'. Even Rosamond Vincy has her excellent reasons. Even Rosamond Vincy has her chance to differ from herself.

This uniquely sophisticated emphasis on the balance between systemic claims has much to do with George Eliot's knowledge of language: knowledge that she deliberately cultivated early in her career. She was close to forty when she published her first stories. She was in her thirties when she published those brilliant essays and reviews. She was still in her formative twenties when she worked on her translations, and when, on top of the French she had learned at school, she added not one, not two, not even three or four, but *five* new languages: Italian, German, Latin, Greek, and Hebrew. Very few English novelists, for that matter very few novelists have had anything like this grasp of the fundamental differences between languages. More than anything else, I think, George Eliot's knowledge of language accounts for her happy grasp of systemic limitation. Her chronic 'on the other hand' belongs to this deep knowledge.

To reflect a minute on this claim, it seems obvious that knowledge of languages teaches the limits of all systems as nothing else can do. To learn a second language is to discover a second system for formulating everything. The gain in perspective is powerful. A second or third language, even if one rarely uses it, always presents a limit to any way of formulating or perceiving.

One's native language is no longer *the* language, but instead only *a* language among others: one way, and only one way, of mapping the world and managing practical affairs. As a thoroughly modern philologist, George Eliot knew that language determines possible perception.

Even more to the point, linguistic differences demonstrate that language is not a matter of vocabulary. It is not a collection of little stickers to put on things, as Garcia-Marquez's characters do in *One Hundred Years of Solitude* when the great forgetfulness plague falls on them and they run around putting little signs on things so that they will remember what they are called. Language is more than a collection of tags; it is a system of relationship and value that must make sense internally, grammatically. But while the speech act, the *parole*, even the unspoken gesture all are tangible, a linguistic system *itself* never appears explicitly, except in grammar books or other secondary derivations from usage. We do not go about actually saying 'subject, verb, object'. We speak, using the implicit structure, the common *langue* that supports the *parole* invisibly. Various overlapping systems of value and expression at once hamper Rosamond Vincy and support her: systems that are not unique to her but that nevertheless do not at all foreclose on the unique and unrepeatable poetry of an individual life.

If I were to carry this line of inquiry only one step further — over the hedge, in fact — I might ask, Where does the grammar of English exist? Not in textbooks, certainly, which are merely partial records of speech acts; not in some permanent world of Platonic Forms above and beyond speech acts; no, English, as a living and changing language, exists distributed, and very broadly distributed, in all, and only, the particular expressions of native speakers. Its grammar — that is, its *langue* — though never itself spoken, nevertheless remains a powerful condition of intelligibility for what *is* spoken, for the *parole*. The difference between English and another language, say Chinese, lies not merely in different words for things but in entirely different systemic *preparations* for expression. For example, English separates agent and action; Chinese does not. How much of cultural practice, I wonder, must follow from such deep linguistic preparations of discourse? George Eliot's writing has done much to prepare us for our current interest in language as a model for all systems, for all economies of belief and value. As she so brilliantly shows, to know a language, to know a discourse, is to inhabit a world.

Moments when such grammatically separate worlds intersect constitute the cruxes of all George Eliot's novels. The fistfight between Adam Bede and Arthur Donnithorne brings two systems into conflict: one where men are

equals and one where they are not. When Arthur Donnithorne gallops in with
the last minute pardon, he reenacts an gesture of ancient privilege, but he does
so under constraint of a new world where law, not privilege, prevails. In
Renaissance Florence various worlds collide that inform individual lives. In
the confrontation between Romola and Tito we find writ small certain cultural
differences that are also writ large in the reactionary religious teaching of
Savonarola and in the garden of humanist scholars. Dorothea's world and that
of the Vincys' revolve side by side, encountering each other occasionally but
remaining pointedly separate. When Lydgate leaves Miss Vincy in the lane to
go and attend Casaubon, or when Dorothea goes to Rosamond about
Lydgate's disgrace, two individuals meet but so do two different ways of
constructing the world; the meeting is informed not only by the sympathy that
Dorothea attempts, more successfully in their second meeting than in their
first, but also by the powerful disparity between these two women's
conditions of intelligibility, the difference in their grammars of experience.
And those differences are nothing to the differences between the planetary
systems of her next novel, *Daniel Deronda*, that brilliant, massive, and
completely unified epic. Gwendolen's tight little, right little world comes into
contact with inescapable, intractable cultural difference; and she, at least,
begins to encompass it.

The growing points of the novels — the moments of opportunity for
individuals and plot — are almost always such moments of encounter
between one system of intelligibility and another. Throughout the Nobody
narrator hovers, always maintaining its promise of relatedness between
systems.

Such an encounter dramatically redirects many a character. Gwendolen
Harleth has such an encounter most strikingly when she realizes that the man
she has mentally wrapped and delivered as a husband is not only an English
aristocrat but also ('on the other hand') a Jew, and a Zionist to boot.
Suddenly an entire order of things, a grammar of belief and value that 'had
lain aloof in newspapers and other neglected reading' enters her life 'like an
earthquake' and dislodges her for the first time 'from her supremacy in her
own world' so that she is reduced in her own mind 'to a mere speck' (Ch. 69,
875-6).[4] When Deronda tries to reassure her that, though they are parted, their
'minds may get nearer', it could seem a bit lame, except for the fact that it has
the authority of George Eliot's whole narrative style behind it: the authority of

---

[4] George Eliot, *Daniel Deronda* (1876), ed. by Barbara Hardy (Harmondsworth: Penguin
Books, 1967). All references are to this edition.

that invisible community maintained by the Nobody narrator, that formality which includes all individuals and is congruent with none. The invisible bridge Deronda mentions is the thing that really counts in realism because it is the potential of the future — the more-than-this that makes not for righteousness but for experiment, adventure, generosity, even play.

George Eliot does not leave Gwendolen a mere speck in her encounter with the wide ranging 'purposes of others'. That encounter is precisely a beginning, as well as an end. Not for nothing does George Eliot dramatize this young woman's determination as well as her disadvantages, her wit and intelligence as well as her thoroughly-cultivated mercenary selfishness. Just as Deronda is more than an English gentleman, Gwendolen is more than an individual girl; she is one of those girls with 'their blind visions' who are the 'delicate vessels' bearing onward the treasure of human affections (Ch. 11, 160). Whatever we make of this claim, it is clear enough that Gwendolen manages to accomplish something that few others do: she begins actually to change her vision, her grammar, her expectations, her acts of attention. By the end of the novel she is back where she must be in order to survive: re-negotiating her relationship with her mother and, notably, through that act re-negotiating her relationship with the plurality of worlds. *Daniel Deronda*, even more than her other novels, asserts the radical relativism of cultural value. From one side of London to the other, as from West to East, grammars differ.

In this discussion you will have heard echoes of contemporary theoretical debate about language as a model of systemic order. Since Saussure, it has become increasingly useful — we may even say profitable — for those interested in language to consider the extent to which *everything* operates like language. Politics. Music. Fashion. These operate as English and Hebrew do, according to invisible grammars or discursive rules that govern what it is possible to do, and not do: that govern what it is possible to say and what it is possible to hear; that govern who may speak. Awareness of this power of discourse to form perception and to limit it comes directly from the nineteenth century, and is not at all the recent brainchild of what Lionel Robbins once called 'the stunt anti-rationalism' of certain French intellectuals.[5] With post-structuralist theory we are still working on this problem of plural systems, and the difficult problem of negotiating between them where there seem to be *no* common denominators, and no possibility of a common world. Even though

---

[5] Lionel Robbins, *The Economic Basis of Class Conflict and Other Essays in Political Economy* (London: Macmillan, 1939), p. viii.

temporal and spatial horizons may seem to be continuous, language and discourse may not be. This is precisely the problem that post-structuralist theory presents to us. It is precisely the intractable, perhaps absolute differences between one language, one discourse, and another, that Jean-Francois Lyotard has christened 'the differend': 'a case of conflict, between (at least) two parties, that cannot be equitably resolved for lack of a rule of judgement applicable to both arguments. One side's legitimacy does not imply the other's lack of legitimacy' and 'applying a single rule of judgement to both in order to settle their differend as though it were merely a litigation would wrong (at least) one of them (and both of them if neither side admits this rule)'.[6]

This description may claim only what George Eliot claims, that what is right for one is wrong for another; that what stimulates a strong mind only deranges a weak one; that what applies in the one system simply does not apply in the other. What then? Lyotard asks, what do we do when there seems to be no way to establish privilege between systems, even between moral systems: no common denominator, but only 'phrases in dispute'? Whatever the outcome of the complex debate on this point, Lyotard's discussion provides an example of that situation beyond relativism — of that condition of relativity — where the conflict of claims must be negotiated *without* the possibility of resolution or even of mediation. In various forms, most fundamentally in our scientific description of nature since 1900, relativity has already challenged the common denominators with which nineteenth-century writers unified the world, especially the common denominators of time and space.

The cultural implications of this step beyond relativism are profound — none more so for a democratic society. Truthfully, and even while our tastes in narrative may run to the objectivity of realists like George Eliot, we know that our political world is fractured by tribal warfare in ways that make a joke of mediation. What resolution, what translation, what mediation is possible between the grammar of awareness in Palé, Bosnia, on the one hand and in Paris or Geneva on the other?

Still, intractable as these discursive differences seem, they are fundamentally the same differences the nineteenth century faced. The difference between Lyotard and George Eliot is that he pushes relativism to relativity, and here I return to my opening remark about the point at which

---

[6] Jean-Francois Lyotard, *The Differend: Phrases in Dispute*, trans. by George Van den Abbeele (Minneapolis: University of Minnesota Press, 1983), p. xi.

language becomes controversial. To Lyotard all systems are finite and self-contained so that negotiations between them *can* find no common denominator. The problem of relationship must be deeply reconceived. The relativism we find in George Eliot, on the other hand, insists on the possibility of common denominators. In contradistinction with Mr Dagley's darkness, or Rosamond's or Casaubon's or even Dorothea's, the novel presents us with the ripple and amplification of language and of the narrative perspective system that contains so much, much more than these limited cases. George Eliot acknowledges that every language has its limit, but in her work crucially all limited languages coexist in a common world. Communication between them may be difficult; it may be hampered by traditional usage and prejudice; but communication remains possible. Communication may require separateness, but as Deronda tells Gwendolen, across that gap minds may get nearer.

George Eliot's novels characteristically cruise the boundaries between different systems of intelligibility, but her narrative style always maintains a common horizon. It is the same world for everyone, even Henleigh Grandcourt; he practically mutates into a sub-human species, but he, too, was once young and impressionable.

The real beneficiaries of George Eliot's narrative style are of course not her characters but her readers. We are the ones, unlike Maggie or Tito, who are continually forced to move from one private centre of interest to another, one place to another, one discourse or system of values to another. Some readers report feeling positively harried by the shifting in perspective at all levels: from the microscopic level of sentences and brief dialogue to the macroscopic level of the whole narration, itself implicated by continuous extension in a yet wider world. This highly achieved narrative medium provides an outside to every inside, a margin to every system. It is a trial for those who, like old Mrs Farebrother, have determined never to change; but it is a welcome opportunity for those interested in a plurality of worlds, for those interested in languages.

Chapter Four

George Eliot, George Henry Lewes, and Comparative Anatomy

Nancy Henry

'A difference of taste in jokes is a great strain on the affections'.
(George Eliot, *Daniel Deronda*)

I

In 1852, George Henry Lewes resumed work on his biography of Goethe by inquiring into the poet's influence on the study of comparative anatomy.[1] His research produced an article for the *Westminster Review*, 'Goethe as a Man of Science'. In *The Life and Works of Goethe*, published in 1855, the *Westminster* article was rewritten as a chapter entitled, 'The Poet as Man of Science'. In the early version, Lewes defended Goethe's contributions to science against sceptics, complaining that 'professional men, with professional contempt, shrugged their shoulders at the "amateur". They did so then, they do so now' (October 1852, p. 258). In defending Goethe, Lewes defended himself. He would soon, and for the rest of his career, experience 'professional contempt' for the work of the non-professional, and his exclusion from the scientific establishment was a point of identification with Goethe. Whereas Lewes initially presented his cause as one of establishing Goethe's reputation as a scientist, in his rewritten chapter he argued that elitist snobbery on the part of 'professional men' threatened the very vitality of scientific inquiry: 'When the amateur brings forward crudities, which he announces to be discoveries, their scorn may be legitimate enough; but when he happens to bring forward a discovery, and they treat it as a crudity, their

---

[1] Rosemary Ashton, *G. H. Lewes, A Life* (Oxford: Oxford Universiy Press, 1991), p. 122.

scorn becomes self-stultification'.[2] As an amateur and a popularizer with no university education, no institutional support, and no laboratory, Lewes suffered an uncomfortable consciousness of his outsider status.[3]

Goethe, of course, was not merely an amateur scientist; he was a great poet, and Lewes's analysis of Goethe's life succeeds in breaking down an accepted opposition between Science and Art. Lewes aimed to show, by quoting scientists, that Goethe was accepted among them. At the same time, he seems to construct a genealogy of men who contributed to both scientific and artistic discourses and in which he might take a place. In 'The Poet as a Man of Science', Lewes elaborated his praise for Goethe's 1790 treatise on the 'Metamorphoses of Plants' (*Life*, 331). In making his case for the importance of the 'Metamorphoses', Lewes cites various authorities, among them Nees von Esenbeck, one of the 'greatest names' in the science of botany. Lewes quotes a passage from Esenbeck that invokes the ancient philosopher Theophrastus: ' "Theophrastus is the creator of modern botany. Goethe is its tender father, to whom it will raise looks full of love and gratitude, as soon as it grows out of its infancy, and acquires the sentiment which it owes to him who has raised it to so high a position" ' (*Life*, 332). Theophrastus, like Goethe and Lewes, was both philosopher and scientist, the creator of the literary genre of character writing as well as the creator of modern botany. In George Eliot's last work of fiction, the figure of Theophrastus would unite literary and scientific cultures and would represent as well the modern type of the author/outsider.

Impressions of Theophrastus Such (1879), George Eliot's last book, is decipherable in full only when seen as a dialogue with Lewes, which, reflecting both of their careers, consistently yokes art and science. One clue to the puzzling question of why George Eliot chose to give Aristotle's pupil, Theophrastus, a modern incarnation may be found in Lewes's implied connection between himself, Goethe, and Theophrastus. Because *Impressions* was written during the summer of 1878 in the last months of Lewes's life, the presence and play of science in it represents a layering of personal associations. Various aspects of nineteenth-century science pervade Eliot's fiction. The professionals include medical doctors such as Meunier, who

---

[2] George Henry Lewes, *The Life of Goethe*, 2nd edition (London: George Routledge & Sons Ltd, n.d.), p. 337.

[3] Ashton writes that Lewes always felt anxiety about his 'credentials': 'It was the one sore spot in a man otherwise remarkable for his lack of sensitivity about his reputation' (147). See also Alain Barrat, 'G. H. Lewes, Goethe and Science: From Romanticism to Positivism', *George Eliot — George Henry Lewes Studies*, 28-9 (September 1995), 42-49.

performs a chilling experiment on the body of Mrs Archer at the end of 'The Lifted Veil' (1859), and Lydgate, whose attempts at medical reform are frustrated by the provincial conservatism of Middlemarch and whose misguided quest for an 'originary tissue' insures his failure as a researcher. Among the amateur dabblers in natural history are *Middlemarch*'s Mr Farebrother and *Felix Holt*'s old Mr Transome.   Eliot's intellectual and literary engagement with scientific issues has been treated in a number of important critical works, yet all neglect the web of scientific allusions in *Impressions*.[4]   Of Eliot's works, *Impressions* is the most permeated with concerns about the Victorian culture of science, about technology and new kinds of knowledge which were raising intellectual and ethical problems for future generations.   Eliot's attitude toward scientific change was always broadly social; that is, she cared about the implications of discoveries and their applications for every aspect of human (and particularly English) society.   Toward the end of her career, Eliot chose to make scientific inquiry her particular, personal means of coded signaling with Lewes, acknowledging in her allusions the intersection of her private life and public writing. *Impressions* reflects a shared feeling of outsiderness generated by Eliot's and Lewes's sense that their work could not be understood by the majority of their respective readers.   In the pages of *Impressions*, the Eliot-Lewes relationship is simultaneously exposed and protected because their private communication is public but invisible.

Particularly because Lewes's biography of Goethe occupied his time during the early years of their relationship, its association of Theophrastus, Goethe and Lewes is a useful starting point for looking at the secret but public communication between Eliot and Lewes as it existed in the 1850s and again in the 1870s.[5]   Like the ancient philosopher Theophrastus and the Romantic poet Goethe, Lewes saw his studies of plant and animal life as continuous

---

[4] See especially Gillian Beer, *Darwin's Plots: Evolutionary Narrative in Darwin, George Eliot, and Nineteenth-Century Fiction* (London: Routledge and Kegan Paul, 1983) and Sally Shuttleworth, *George Eliot and Nineteenth-Century Science* (Cambridge: Cambridge University Press, 1984).

[5] Mark Wormald has recently traced connections between *Middlemarch* and Lewes's essays on natural history of the 1850s.   He notes that certain metaphors involving the microscope and microscopic views in that novel were 'surely written with Lewes's "Only a Pond!" in mind, if not actually at hand'.   What *Impressions* shows is that she not only had Lewes in mind, she was writing to and joking with him in a way that necessarily could be recognized by him alone.   It was in this way that important aspects of her work became increasingly inaccessible to her general readership.   See 'Microscopy and Semiotic in *Middlemarch*', *Nineteenth-Century Literature*, 50 (March 1996), 517.

with his observations of human behaviour and psychology. He believed particularly that what he called 'the Philosophy of the infinitely little' was a noble and ultimately humanistic pursuit. He wrote in *Studies in Animal Life*: 'But I cannot think any serious study is without its serious value to the human race; and I know that the great problem of Life can never be solved while we are in ignorance of its simpler forms'.[6] From his research on Goethe, and under the influence of scientific-minded friends such as Herbert Spencer and Richard Owen, Lewes became a committed amateur comparative anatomist. The experiments he performed, the texts he read, and the status of his reputation became a part of George Eliot's experience. The 1852 article, 'Goethe as a Man of Science', was published under her editorship at the *Westminster*, and in 1854 she attempted to block the publication of a review by T. H. Huxley, which was critical of Lewes's scientific qualifications and therefore detrimental to his reputation.[7]

Eliot's participation in Lewes's experiments began with the trip to Ilfracombe, recorded in her 'Ilfracombe Journal' of 1856.[8] *Sea-Side Studies at Ilfracombe, Tenby, The Scilly Isles, and Jersey*, which is dedicated to 'our great anatomist', Richard Owen, contains the following description of what Lewes calls 'the most piquant of all paradoxes', the parasitic Crustacean, *Lernaea*:

> The female, ensconced in the eye, or gills, of a fish, lives a lazy life at the fish's expense, and the male lives upon her as she lives on the fish (not unlike some disreputable males of the human species), and this male is himself infested with parasitic Vorticellae, so that we find parasites of parasites of parasites! (56).[9]

Lewes's tone is casual and humorous, one of the ways he found to make dry scientific observations palatable to his audience. His joke, however, is not directed merely to his reading public. This passage about parasitic Vorticellae did not appear in the original 'Sea-side Studies', serialized in *Blackwood's Magazine* in 1856. It was added (to accompany an illustration, see p. 48) in the revisions for his book, *Sea-Side Studies* (1858). The significant change in the lives of Lewes and George Eliot between the two versions of 'Sea-Side

---

[6] *Studies in Animal Life* (London: Smith, Elder, and Co., 1862), p. 41.

[7] See Ashton, pp. 146-7.

[8] Reprinted in *George Eliot, Selected Essays, Poems and Other Writings*, ed. by A. S. Byatt and Nicholas Warren (London: Penguin, 1990).

[9] *Sea-Side Studies at Ilfracombe, Tenby, The Scilly Isles, and Jersey* (Edinburgh and London: Blackwood and Sons, 1858) originally ran in *Blackwood's Magazine* from August-October 1856 and June-October 1857. *Studies in Animal Life* (London: Smith, Elder, and Co., 1862) originally ran in the *Cornhill Magazine* between January and June 1860.

their office in your own organism. The lining
membrane of your air-passages is covered with

Fig. 2.

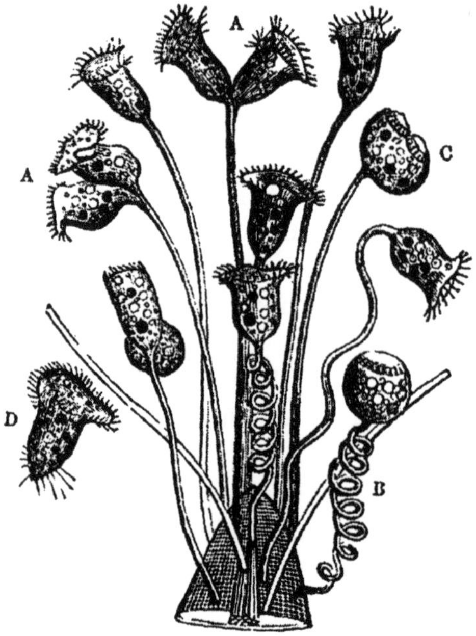

GROUP OF VORTICELLA NEBULIFERA, on a Stem of Weed,
Magnified.

A　One undergoing spontaneous division.
B　Another spirally retracted on its stalk.
C　One with cilia retracted.
D　A bud detached and swimming free.

cilia; which may be observed by following the
directions of Professor Sharpey, to whom science

1. *Vorticella* from G. H. Lewes, *Studies in Animal Life*, p. 12

Studies' was the publication of her first work of fiction, 'Scenes of Clerical Life', also in *Blackwood's Magazine* (1857). The success of that work, published as a book in 1858, gave Lewes every reason to anticipate what would eventually be the case — that her earnings would far exceed his in the years ahead. With typically good-humoured self-deprecation, Lewes refers to himself as the 'disreputable male' living parasitically on the female. He would later extend his analysis of the Vorticella's parasitism in his essay 'Only a Pond!'. Speaking of the 'elegant Vorticella — the bell-shaped animalcule', he writes: 'We have all laughed at Thackeray's poor Irishman having always some poorer Irishman living on him, as he lives on society; and here we see the very system carried on by the tiny denizens of that tiny ocean'.[10] In an article intended to help popularise the study of natural science, Lewes finds common ground with his readers in examples from literature to illustrate his microscopic observations.

Twenty years later in 1878, looking back on their life together, George Eliot appropriated the names and characteristics of the very animalcules Lewes had once studied and through which he signaled to her. In Chapter XV of *Impressions*, entitled 'Diseases of Small Authorship', the primary character is a literary 'authoress' named Vorticella. Just as Eliot was returning to associations of her time in Ilfracombe, Tenby, and the Scilly Isles with Lewes, her narrator Theophrastus is returning to the small provincial town where Vorticella 'flourished' in his youth. Eliot seems to be literalising Lewes's metaphor in 'Only a Pond!': 'The drop of water is a microcosm — the world in miniature' (595). Eliot's Vorticella is such a 'small' author that she, as well as her fellow authors in 'Pumpiter', are metaphorically speaking, microscopic. When Theophrastus visits the author Vorticella, she bores him with details about the reception of her book, *The Channel Isles with Notes and an Appendix*. Vorticella is a parasite on her husband's wealth and status, which allow her to write irrelevant books and to magnify her self-importance. She boasts:

> The fact is that no critic in this town is fit to meddle with such subjects, unless it be Volvox, and he, with all his command of language, is very superficial [...] I hope you noticed how he contradicts himself.[11]

Eliot's critique of 'small authorship' is enriched by its intertextual associations with Lewes's writing, and the game, which characterizes all of *Impressions*, consists of more than word-play: it refers specifically to

---

[10] *Blackwood's Edinburgh Magazine*, 85 (May 1859), 597.

[11] George Eliot, *Impressions of Theophrastus Such* [1879], edited with an introduction by Nancy Henry (London: Pickering and Chatto, 1994), p. 124.

male Rotifers, the usual organs of sense and locomotion are wanting; and in a parasitic Lernæa, the degradation is moral as well as physical: the female lives in the gills of a fish, sucking its juices, and the ignoble husband lives as a parasite upon her!

But this digression is becoming humiliating, and meanwhile our hands are getting benumbed with cold. In spite of that, I hold the jar up to the light, and make a background of my forefingers, to throw into relief some of the trans-

Fig. 11.

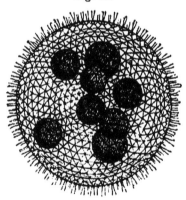

VOLVOX GLOBATOR, with eight volvoces enclosed (Magnified).

parent animals. Look at those light green crystal spheres sailing along with slow revolv-

Lewes's texts. The fact that Volvox, an organism which figured in Lewes's *Studies in Animal Life* (see Illustration 2, p. 50), contradicts himself, puts a twist on one of Lewes's favourite categories of microscopic organisms — the 'paradox'. [12]

In 1856, Lewes published his own 'Metamorphoses: A Tale'. The title of this fictional work recalls Goethe's 'Metamorphoses of Plants'. Goethe's 'Metamorphoses' was published in 1790; Lewes's story opens in 1789. Lewes's writing on Goethe as man of science emphasizes the latter's theory of metamorphoses as 'development'. The history of scientific discovery is invoked in Lewes's 'Metamorphoses' as part of his analysis of social change following the French Revolution. His narrator pays homage to Jan Swammerdam, whose microscopic dissections contributed to human knowledge of the infinitely little, and most importantly for Lewes, demystified the process of metamorphoses by detecting the stages of development. The reference to Swammerdam emphasizes the act of dissection — of disengaging the body parts one by one for examination — as a central metaphor in 'Metamorphoses', which is explicitly concerned with providing an anatomy, in fiction, of French society:

> Swammerdam, the great naturalist, astonished the world by showing that even in the chrysalis the butterfly was discernible; he disengaged the antennae, wings, and legs which had been folded up in the chrysalis, hidden from sight, and proved that the transformation which astounded men was no transformation at all, but a development.[13]

Swammerdam (1637-1680) lived during a remarkable period in the history of anatomical studies. His father kept a 'cabinet' in Amsterdam and he devoted his own life to the study of anatomy. In seventeenth-century Amsterdam, the most distinguished medical men performed anatomies, their students as well as community members in attendance. Lewes read Swammerdam's *Bibel der Natur* in the original Dutch, and, in *Studies in Animal Life*, praised him as 'that incarnation of patience and exactness' (27).[14] In 'Metamorphoses', Lewes's narrator introduces the figure of Swammerdam to establish

---

[12] In his discussion of paradoxes, Lewes quotes: 'Great fleas have little fleas, and lesser fleas to bite 'em, | And these again have other fleas, and so ad infinitum' (56). Appropriately, the lines are by Augustus De Morgan from his book, *A Budget of Paradoxes*. See *OED* on 'Paradox'.

[13] Lewes, G. H., 'Metamorphoses: A Tale', *Blackwood's Edinburgh Magazine*, 79 (May and June 1856) and 80 (July 1856), Pt III, Ch. 2.

[14] Lewes's copy of Swammerdam's *Bibel der Natur* (1644-75) in an 1752 edition is in the Dr Williams Library. It was signed 'G. H. Lewes' in 1856. His notes in the text point especially to discussions of spontaneous generation and metamorphoses.

anatomical observation as a metaphor for the development of human character. He then continues:

> The grown man amazes us by his seeming difference from the growing youth [...] we marvel at the change, because we had not the power of moral anatomy to detect in the chrysalis state all the indications of the perfect insect (III, 2).

Lewes's use of the term 'moral anatomy' is indicative of how the practice of dissection, so important in the history of scientific discovery, provided him, and later George Eliot, with a way to talk about the diagnosis of social and moral ills. Compare this apparently Swammerdam-inspired passage from her 'Notebook for an Unwritten Novel' (c. 1877):

> The transformations of insects, what nature can do in the way of turning a small pulpy grub that you are liable to eat with your salad into a winged creature of marvellous frame & instincts, is a worthy theme of wonder, poetry & science; but so are the metamorphoses of men.[15]

These notes, dating from around 1877, anticipate the textual communication with Lewes so evident in *Impressions*. This passage reveals Eliot's thinking about the metamorphoses of insects as a controlling metaphor to present the development of human character, and asserts as well the 'worthiness' of development in the natural world as a 'theme' for poetry and science, echoing the motto of *Daniel Deronda* (Chapter 1), in which she compares 'Science, the strict measurer' with '[h]is less accurate grandmother poetry'. Throughout *Impressions*, Eliot applies scientific methods of dissecting bodies — anatomies under the microscope as well as in the public, anatomy 'theatres' — to examine the development of human character in the 'medium' of late nineteenth-century English culture.

II

> '... character is not cut in marble — it is not something solid and unalterable. It is something living and changing, and may become diseased as our bodies do'.
> (George Eliot, *Middlemarch*)

One chapter in *Impressions*, 'The Too Deferential Man' (V), presents a particularly complex example of how Eliot's coded communication with Lewes culminated at the end of her career. It also illustrates, through the verbal invocation of visual art, Eliot's and Lewes's shared sense of the

---

[15] Jerome Beaty, 'George Eliot's Notebook for an Unwritten Novel', *Princeton University Library Chronicle*, 18 (1957), 177.

inextricability of art and science in their culture. Comparing the examination of human character to the scientific practice of dissection (with the author in the place of the anatomist) had become common in both Lewes's and Eliot's writing by 1878. Consistent with its interrogation of the meaning of 'character' in *Impressions*, Eliot's Theophrastus carries the idea of development further than either she or Lewes previously had: what is a character who does not 'develop'? Theophrastus answers: not a human being at all.

The way Eliot goes about layering the meanings of 'development' is characteristic of *Impressions*: cryptic, allusive, and elusive. The chapter modernizes a character whom the ancient Theophrastus, in his book of *Characters*, called 'The Flatterer'. The ancient Theophrastus tells us that 'The Flatterer' is one who will say or do anything to gain favour. Eliot's Theophrastus tells us of a man called 'Hinze'. His family comes from Alsace, a province which is a mixture of French and German cultures and an emblem of historically shifting national affiliations (it had recently been annexed by Germany in 1871 following the Franco-Prussian War). Hinze's ambiguous ethnic identification is further complicated by the fact that he is an immigrant settled in England. An Alsatian-English gentleman cannot be judged immediately in terms of national stereotypes; he can only be typed by what he does, and what he does is behave obsequiously, with embarrassing flattery.

Theophrastus fails to mention, but Eliot must have known, that 'Hinze' is a diminutive of 'Heinrich', the German equivalent of 'Harry' in the English 'Tom, Dick and Harry'. Hinze's German name connects him to no single cultural tradition, but it suggests that he is a stereotypical Everyman. Hinze distinguishes himself only by flattering, which angers Theophrastus:

> I confess to some rage on hearing him yesterday talking to Felicia, who is certainly a clever woman, and, without any unusual desire to show her cleverness, occasionally says something of her own or makes an allusion which is not quite common. (49)

Hinze interrogates and relentlessly praises Felicia, who is trying merely to voice the pleasantries of 'the suitable wife of a distinguished man' and to confirm that she 'has enough regard for formulas to save us from shocking outbursts of individualism, to which we are always exposed with the tamest bear or baboon' (50). Her commonplaces about Shakespeare, such as 'a poet may know a good deal about human nature while knowing little of geography', are met by Hinze with adept deference, and he recapitulates her comments, 'weaving them together with threads of compliment': 'As you very justly observed;' and — 'It is most true, as you say;' and — 'It were well if others noted what you have remarked' (52). Theophrastus, calling Hinze 'our complimentary ape', attempts to dissect his character and to discover the motivation for these breaches of well-bred conformities. What he finds is a disturbing lack of motivation: there is nothing to be gained by flattering Felicia, but like every Tom, Dick and Harry, Hinze acts habitually and unthinkingly. Theophrastus observes:

> Few lives are shaped, few characters formed, by the contemplation of definite consequences seen from a distance and made the goal of continuous effort or the beacon of a constantly avoided danger: such control by foresight, such vivid picturing and practical logic are the distinction of exceptionally strong natures; but society is chiefly made up of human beings whose daily acts are all performed either in unreflecting obedience to custom and routine or from immediate prompting of thought or feeling to execute an immediate purpose. (54)

The language here is visual: 'seen from a distance', 'foresight', and 'vivid picturing'. Seeing is intimately bound up with moral character, and Hinze fails to control his life because he fails to act in accordance with foreseen consequences. Throughout *Impressions*, Theophrastus performs the sort of moral anatomy noted even by her contemporary readers of her work. One reviewer of *Middlemarch*, for example, remarked: 'there is something like a medical habit in the writer, of examining her own creations for their symptoms, which runs through her descriptive and narrative art and gives it some of its peculiar manner'.[16] The metaphors of the microscope and of comparative anatomy which underlie the analysis of character in Eliot's earlier 'Study in Provincial Life', are carried further and strikingly literalized in *Impressions*.

Eliot had made associations between the genre of 'character' sketching invented by ancient Theophrastus and the practice of medical examination when she wrote to John Blackwood in 1878 about La Bruyère's *Caractères:* 'There is a sentence of his which touches with the finest point the diseased spot in the literary culture of our time — [...]'.[17] With Hinze, Eliot does not attempt to create an ideal, nor even a realistic figure; rather, she dissects his character with a self-conscious, diagnostic precision and finds that, unlike the chrysalis, Hinze does not 'develop'.

Dissection and the failure to detect development provide a sub-text in 'The Too Deferential Man', offering clues to its otherwise mysterious characterizations. Hinze inquires of Felicia: 'What, may I ask, is your opinion as to the state of Art in England?' She replies: 'I think it suffers from

---

[16] [Sidney Colvin] *Fortnightly Review,* 19 January 1873.

[17] *The George Eliot Letters*, 9 vols, ed. by Gordon S. Haight (New Haven: Yale University Press, 1954-78), VII, 11.

two diseases — bad taste in the patrons and want of inspiration in the artists' He mistakes her banter for profundity, replying: 'That is true indeed [...] You have put your finger with strict accuracy on the causes of decline. To a cultivated taste like yours, this must be particularly painful' (51). Not only does this language recall Eliot's letter to Blackwood about La Bruyère's Theophrastus — who 'touches with the finest point the diseased spot in the literary culture of our time' — it also foreshadows the pre-eminent joke in the chapter, bringing together the examination of diseased bodies and moral characters in a testimony to a well-known visual representation of the anatomist at work. Art in England suffering from two diseases, the invocation of patron and artist, Felicia putting her finger on the causes of decline, and the decline being 'particularly painful', are all hints pointing to the subsequent description of the mysteriously named object of Hinze's most exalted deference. This man is 'Tulpian', whose Latinized name appears consistent with others in *Impressions*, such as Minutius Felix (I) or Lentulus (IV). *Impressions* as a whole directs us to look for an analogue in history or in art for the shadowy figure of 'Tulpian'.

Theophrastus tells us nothing about Tulpian, so we must start with the word itself. 'Tulp' means 'tulip' in Dutch. Nineteenth-century English readers might well be familiar with at least one famous 'Tulp' — Dr Nicolaes Tulp (1593-1674), a prominent citizen and physician in seventeenth-century Amsterdam. His Dutch name was 'Claes Pieterszoon', and the professional name Tulp, which he assumed for himself, may derive from his family's connection to the sale of tulips. An additional association of Theophrastus with tulips can be found in the modern addition by La Bruyère to his own translation of Theophrastus' *Caractères* — the very work that Eliot called diagnostic of a diseased culture, and which she was clearly reading in 1878 as she wrote her own book of 'Characters'. In the section on 'fashion', he condemns the character of his own invention, a tulip-worshipper: 'God and nature are not in his thoughts, for they do not go beyond the bulb of his tulip. [...]'.[18]

The original Dr Tulp (also known as Tulpius) wrote in Latin on the subject of human anatomy, and he was the first patron in Amsterdam to commission a painting from the young Rembrandt. In 1866, when Eliot finished writing *Felix Holt*, she and Lewes travelled to Holland, Belgium and the resort of Schlangenbad. Lewes wrote to his sons on 22 June 1866:

---

[18] La Bruyère, *The Characters* (London: 1885), p. 378.

> We stayed three days at the Hague [...]. The picture gallery was also an immense attraction; not only from the great beauty of the pictures but from the comfortable style in which we were enabled to study them.[19]

While this letter shows that Eliot and Lewes did visit The Royal Cabinet of Paintings (Mauritshuis), his unpublished journals further demonstrate the attention they gave to Rembrandt's 'Anatomy of Dr Nicolaes Tulp' (1632), then on display at the Royal Cabinet. On 15 June 1866, he wrote the following account in his journal:

> Rembrandt's 'School of Anatomy' surpasses all expectation. It is a solemn picture treated in the highest style. Except the lefthand figure who is looking away — to show the spectator his profile — all the heads are not only magnificent portraits of living breathing thinking men, but are expressively & effectively presented. The fair haired man who listens but does not look, and the stouter man who looks more than he listens are wonderful types.[20]

What this description reveals is that Lewes and Eliot examined and discussed the individual portraits comprising Rembrandt's painting and thought about each individually. Lewes's remark that it is a 'solemn picture treated in the highest style' indicates his reverence for the work, but also introduces the potential for an irreverence not recorded until Eliot wrote the painting into *Impressions* as an emblem of the confluence of art and science.

George Eliot's enigmatic 'Tulpian' can be interpreted only with knowledge of her impressions of Rembrandt's Dr Tulp. Rembrandt's 'Anatomy' shows the distinguished Dr Tulp extending with his right hand the tendons in the left forearm of a partially dissected cadaver while he lectures to a small group of privileged viewers (see Illustration 3, p. 57). In his journal entry, Lewes notes:

> The corpse is also very affective, not only in its foreshortened legs (in shadow) but in its unrepulsive yet truthful indications. I question the correctness of the distended thorax. Toulp the anatomist [is a] singularly fine figure. (Beinecke *Ms*)

Theophrastus notes that Tulpian has 'considerable interest at his disposal'. This would be true of Dr Tulp in two senses. In the painting, he has everyone's interest, and he was wealthy enough to commission a painting with himself as the centre of attention. As Theophrastus describes Tulpian, his language grows more precise, almost as if he were looking at a fixed image:

---

[19] *The Letters of George Henry Lewes*, 2 vols, ed. by William Baker, English Literary Studies Monograph Series (Victoria, B C: University of Victoria, 1995), II, 95.

[20] I am very grateful to Rosemary Ashton for drawing my attention to ths reference. This and the subsequent passage from Lewes's journal are published by kind permission of Jonathan G. Ouvry and the Beinecke Rare Book and Manuscript Library, Yale University.

3. Rembrandt's 'The Anatomy Lesson of Dr Nicolaes Tulp'

> Tulpian is appealed to on innumerable subjects, and if he is unwilling to express himself on any one of them, says so with instructive copiousness; he is much listened to, and his utterances are registered and reported with more or less exactitude. (53)

As the verbal portrait of Tulpian is filled in, it looks more and more like the visual portrait of Rembrandt's Dr Tulp. The occasion of the painting is both a dissection and a lesson. Rembrandt has portrayed the observers as almost comical hangers on to Tulp's every word. One figure in the background appears to be registering Tulp's lecture, but the page in his hand contains a roll call of the men in the painting written over an anatomical sketch — perhaps the source of Theophrastus's comment that Tulp's words are 'reported with more or less exactitude'. Theophrastus's language here seems significant, but his choice of words only makes sense when we realize that, starting with the phrase 'interest at his disposal', Theophrastus has initiated a shameless chain of puns:

> But Hinze is especially fervid in his desire to hear Tulpian dilate on his crotchets, and is rather troublesome to bystanders in asking them whether they have read the various fugitive writings in which these crotchets have been published (53).

Without the image of Dr Tulp, these words suggest that Tulpian dilates (expounds) on his crotchets (his personal, perhaps eccentric ideas). Once we have connected Tulpian with Tulp and have Rembrandt's painting in view, we can see the doubleness of the language. 'Dilate' also means to extend — what Tulp is doing to the muscles in the arm of his cadaver. 'Crotchet', in addition to being a personal view, is a surgical instrument, corresponding to the one Tulp holds in the hand with which he is dilating. Fugitive writings may suggest the unidentified tomes lying open at the feet of the corpse (not visible here), or it may refer to Tulp's eclectic and, by the nineteenth century, obscure publications.[21]

From Theophrastus's description, it is not clear whether Hinze is a figure in the painting. More likely, he is a 'Hinze', an Everyman paying his money to watch the dissection of a common body, a *corpus vile,* in the spectacle of the seventeenth-century Dutch anatomical theatre. Here Hinze would have the opportunity to impress bystanders with this knowledge of Tulpian's writings, 'teas[ing] them with Tulpian's guesses', using his superficial knowledge and his brushes with the great or near great to make others feel inferior and excluded. For the nineteenth or twentieth-century reader familiar with this

---

[21] His major work, *Observationum Medicarum* (1641), was written in Latin and translated into Dutch and French in the late seventeenth and early eighteenth century.

painting, Hinze's Tulpian becomes Rembrandt's Dr Tulp, and Theophrastus invites us, not to worship, but to see the characters with a comic irreverence that opens the painting to interpretation and allows viewers to recognize as absurd the deference of the listeners and the pomposity of the speaker. This sketch of Tulpian refers not only to Rembrandt's 'Anatomy' but also to Eliot and Lewes's shared experience of viewing the painting. Similarly, Eliot's Vorticella is a reference to an earlier time and an earlier joke, and her character presents a similar theme: both examples of mindless flattery combine the discourses of science and art. 'Characters' from Lewes's writings on natural science are re-anthropomorphized by Eliot and turned into authors: Volvox flatters Vorticella; scientific men represented in a painting done 'in the highest style' are turned into exaggerated illustrations of excessive deference.

Before introducing Vorticella in 'Diseases of Small Authorship', Eliot's Theophrastus writes: 'Authors are so miscellaneous a class that their personified diseases, physical and moral, might include the whole procession of human disorders, led by dyspepsia and ending in madness — the awful Dumb Show of a world-historic tragedy' (120). Theophrastus's playfulness with disease as metaphor elsewhere in *Impressions* invites an extended reading of this chapter. Felicia's comment that 'Art in England' suffers from two diseases, leads Hinze to comment that she has put her finger on the causes of decline. Much has been made of the particular lesson on the human hand which Dr Tulp is giving to his pupils in Rembrandt's painting.[22] He has separated and extended the tendons which operate the left hand. He is gesturing with this own left hand, as if to demonstrate himself the function of these tendons. In 'The Too Deferential Man', Theophrastus refers ironically to 'the matter in hand' (48), and to Hinze's flux of reverence for what is 'third-hand'. Theophrastus also comments: 'A man is bound to know something of his own weight and muscular dexterity [...]' and that Hinze 'has not the stuff in him to be at once agreeably conversational and sincere [...]' (55).

These cryptic and comic associations between her work and Lewes's reveal traces of an ongoing intertextual conversation spanning their entire careers. This complex set of allusions to Rembrandt's 'Anatomy' recollects a trip the two of them made together; it deflates the pompous professional man of

---

[22] See William Schupbach, *The Paradox of Rembrandt's 'Anatomy of Dr Tulp'* (London: Wellcome Institute for the History of Medicine, 1982). On the anatomical theatres and the history of their representation, see William S. Heckscher, *Rembrandt's 'Anatomy of Dr Nicolaas Tulp', An Iconological Study* (New York: New York University Press, 1958).

science; and it invokes the seventeenth-century Dutch school of anatomy, which included Jan Swammerdam and Dr Tulp. Interestingly, Swammerdam too might have been known to Lewes as a 'deferential', even flattering character. He produced a color plate of the female reproductive system in 1671, and dedicated it to (who else?) his contemporary, the influential Dr Tulp.[23] To complicate this association, the historian F. J. Cole in his *History of Comparative Anatomy* claims that the only portrait of Swammerdam (published in the English translation of Michelet's *L'Insecte*) is not, in fact, a portrait of Swammerdam, but rather a 'forgery' based on one of the pupils in Rembrandt's 'Anatomy'.[24] Given that issues of plagiarism, borrowing and originality are central to *Impressions*, it is possible that in their observations of Rembrandt's painting, Lewes and Eliot recognized a similarity between the fawning anatomy pupils and the ingratiating Swammerdam. It is certain that Eliot, through Theophrastus, was laughing with Lewes about the multi-national habit of embarrassing flattery.

Eliot and Lewes joked with each other in print throughout their twenty-four years together, but they did so under the self-protective cover of a private language which has succeeded in eluding readers and critics. It would be impossible to recognize all of their allusions and puns. What we can ask is, first, what it means to speak privately in public, and what the habit tells us about Eliot's and Lewes's attitudes toward their audience and toward posterity. Secondly, we can recognize how far intertextual readings of their writings might clarify, or decode, previously inaccessible, unknowable aspects of their lives and work. Eliot and Lewes have left these traces of private joking between themselves as a form of laughing with (or is it at?) their future readers. Having destroyed evidence which would reveal the intimacies of their life together (such as letters to each other) and refused to cooperate in the publication of biographies, they nonetheless made their private language present but invisible, almost inviting, especially in *Impressions*, misinterpretation and misunderstanding.

Watching their relationship develop in print, we can at least begin to get a sense of their 'taste in jokes'. In July 1857, Lewes published Part II of 'The

---

[23] Later republished in Tulp's *Miraculum Naturae* (1673), Tab. III.

[24] F. J. Cole, *A History of Comparative Anatomy, from Aristotle to the Eighteenth Century* (London: Macmillan & Co., 1944). Cole says of Swammerdam: 'He belonged to a type which, whilst humbly but loudly proclaiming its own ignorance, arraigns without mercy the ignorance of others' (304). See also Dr A. Schierbeek, *Jan Swammerdam (12 Feb 1637-17 Feb 1680): His Life and Works* (Amsterdam: 1967). Schierbeek claims there are three fake portraits of Swammerdam.

Scilly Isles' section of 'New Sea-Side Studies' in *Blackwood's Magazine*. Here, he writes about the excitement of scientific inquiry generally and his own satisfactions in particular: 'To discover a *new* animal is surely a legitimate pride' (11). He goes on to talk about the difficulty of classifying the *Sagitta bipunctata*. He describes its alimentary canal, on either side of which lie the ova and which cavities hold and issue the spermatozoa: 'It has not inaptly been named a "crystal arrow" by Mr Kingsley [...] but the name would less aptly designate the Scilly species, which has only a faint resemblance to an arrow' (13). This Scilly species is one Lewes believed himself to have discovered. He does not name it in his article, but when he revised the 'New Sea-Side Studies' for publication in a single volume with Blackwood's, he made some notable changes. At the point where he had previously invoked Kingsley's name for the *Sagitta bipunctata*, he now refers to: 'My species, which I have christened *Sagitta Mariana*' (268) and directs us to a figure — one of the illustrations (see p. 62) added to the volume, which did not appear in the serialized essays. Not surprisingly, Lewes includes a picture of this discovery of which he is so proud. The description of the plate reads:

> **Plate V, Fig. 2**: *Sagitta Mariana*, greatly magnified; natural size quarter of an inch. I believe this to be a new species, and I have named it the *Mariana*. The ova are seen on each side of the alimentary canal; and in the lower half of the body are the cells containing spermatozoa, which issue from the orifices in the fin near the tail. (414)

The in-joke, added as an afterthought and in nose-thumbing disregard for the scientific seriousness of Lewes's contributions at that time, is intimate innuendo. The *Sagitta Mariana* is hermaphroditic, both male and female. 'She' is slyly implied to be Lewes's discovery, but, as an hermaphrodite, she is self-contained and self-sufficient. The new species is also cunningly prophetic of the new Marian: 'sagitta' — wise Mariana, sharp, arrow-pointed Mariana (even Sagittarius Mariana, her birthday falling under that sign) — recently metamorphosed into a novelist. Between the simultaneous publication of *Sea-Side Studies* and the anonymous, 'Scenes of Clerical Life' in *Blackwood's*, 'Mariana' had become 'greatly magnified', and by 1858, when Lewes added *Sagitta Mariana* to the book version of his first scientific publication, she had also become 'George Eliot,' the female author disguised by the same name (in part) as *George* Henry Lewes.[25]

---

[25] Ashton notes the importance of *Sea-Side Studies* to both Eliot and Lewes, quoting Eliot's letter to Bessie Rayner Parkes (19 August 1859) calling *Sea-Side Studies* 'a pet book of mine: there is so much happiness condensed in it', and also Lewes's recollection of the work in a letter to Alexander Main as 'the book of all my books which was to me the most unalloyed delight' (187).

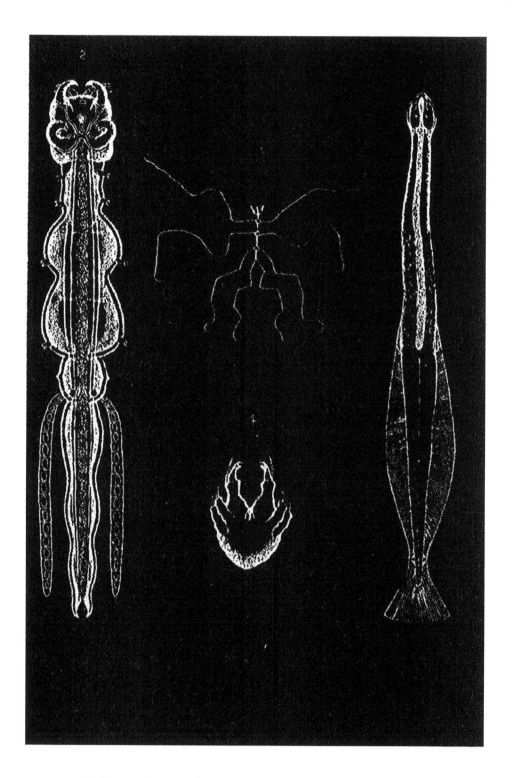

4. *Sagitta Mariana* from G. H. Lewes, *Sea-Side Studies*

The completeness of the new species 'Mariana' is symbolic of a Romantic 'oneness' in which Lewes believed, along with his model poet-scientist, Goethe. As she emerged from her chrysalis state to become the author George Eliot, Lewes began developing as a scientist who filled his scientific writings with poetry, just as Eliot filled her fiction with scientific language, metaphors, and facts. Shortly after *Sea-Side Studies*, Lewes wrote *Studies of Animal Life*. Among the poets he quotes to supplement his observations is Shelley (of whom he had once intended to write a biography): 'Nothing in this world is single | All things, by a law divine, | In one another's being mingle' (180).[26] It may have been this type of Romanticism, this philosophic and literary humanism, that colored his interpretations and blocked his entrance into the ranks of professional scientists. *Sagitta Mariana* marks a habit of textual exchange, which was continuous throughout both of Eliot's and Lewes's writing lives. The jokes were most evident in these early days of enthusiastic, mutual discovery, and again at the end, when success and failure, criticism and flattery, humour and illness, brought them together in retrospective and immediate intimacy. The personalized puns and allusions in *Impressions* look back to the time of *Scenes* and *Sea-Side Studies*, possibly because those were years of forward-looking potential, and because with Lewes's impending death, communication in disguise, but in print, seemed a reassurance of an idealized and lasting unity.

---

[26] Taken from 'Love's Philosophy', the last next line, left out by Lewes is 'Why not I with thine? —'.

Chapter Five

The Miserable Marriages in *Middlemarch, Anna Karenina,* and *Effi Briest*

Barbara Hardy

This essay is a study in affinities, not sources and influences, but those affinities are not simply a matter of a reader's impressions. Leo Tolstoy and Theodor Fontane read George Eliot, in English, and admired her. Tolstoy lists George Elliot (*sic*) as one of the authors who made a 'Great' impression on him, between the age of thirty-five and fifty. (The only novelists to make a greater, an 'Enormous' impression, were Dickens in *David Copperfield* and Victor Hugo in *Les Misérables*.)[1] He picked out *Scenes of Clerical Life* and *Felix Holt* for special praise, and unlike Fontane, he felt sympathetic towards George Eliot's inheritance of the English puritan tradition.[2] Fontane spent several years in England, in the forties and fifties, knew the work of Scott and Dickens well, was a journalist who made a special study of the English press — just when Marian Evans was at the height of her journalistic powers, though writing anonymously — and reported on English culture as part of his official responsibility to the *Zentralpressestelle* and the German ambassador. Since I first read *Effi Briest* I have felt sure that he read and was influenced by George Eliot, and this is confirmed by Charlotte Jolles, in her M.A. thesis for the University of London, 'Theodor Fontane and England: A Critical Study in Anglo-German Literary Relations' (1947), which quotes a reference to George Elliot (*sic*) in which Fontane praises her for combining 'detail' with 'Komposition', though he anticipates Henry James in complaining that the details are too many and too minute. David Malcolm, in his Ph.D. thesis, 'Contemporary and Radical Themes in George Eliot's and Theodor Fontane's

---

[1] *Tolstoy's Letters*, ed. by R. F. Christian, 2 vols (London: Athlone Press, 1978), II, 486.

[2] *Tolstoy's Letters*, I, 128-9, and II, 377.

Fictions' (London, 1981) tells us that this is Fontane's one reference to her, in a letter of 10 June 1862.[3] Like Thackeray's influence on Fontane, which Jolles discusses, George Eliot's remains a matter of speculation, particularly since Fontane would have responded to her not only directly, but indirectly, through other European novels. The known links with the greatest Russian and the greatest German realist of the century make a comparative reading especially interesting.

I am concerned with these three novelists' presentation of the loveless marriage and its social implications. *Anna Karenina* and *Effi Briest* — like two other earlier novels by Fontane, *Beyond Recall* and *The Woman Taken in Adultery* — share an interest in marital infidelity, but I want to read them side by side with *Middlemarch*, which is not about adultery, and to omit what may seem obvious connections with Goethe's *Elective Affinities* and Flaubert's *Madame Bovary*, in order to shift the theme from adultery to unhappy marriage. I want also to extend the theme and consider the novels' presentation of marriage as part of their scrutiny of a nineteenth-century woman's representative life in history.

The three novels, products of different cultures, are all triumphs of what is still called European nineteenth-century realistic fiction, but are by no means confined to realism, as they deal with the social constriction and construction of a woman's life, and develop a critique of the institution of marriage. They are novels about the loveless marriage, but what is politically interesting is not the lovelessness, which is what George Eliot might call 'an extreme image' of a defective institution, but the implications for a critique of marriage in certain European societies. It is this aspect of their subject-matter — together with some related themes and formal features — on which I want to focus attention, suggesting that the critique, tangentially in Eliot and Tolstoy, and most noticeably and boldly in *Effi Briest*, involves not only an analysis of the conditioned life but some attempt to imagine also — what can only be fantasised — the unconditioned life.

The first two novels are close in time: *Middlemarch* was published in 1871-2, *Anna Karenina* in 1874-6; *Effi Briest* was twenty years later in 1895. Fontane was born in 1819, the year of Eliot's birth, Tolstoy in 1828. The first two are multiple actions, though in each the woman's life is central. All three are remarkable for psychological complexity, dramatised, analysed, and implied, and for social grasp.

---

[3] Theodor Fontane, *Briefe*, 5 vols (Munich: Hanser, 1979), II, 69.

After Barbara Bodichon read the first published part of *Middlemarch* (which ends with Dorothea leaving for her wedding journey to Rome) 'all in a day' and 'as hard as she could', 'to take in the whole impression', she wrote a remarkable letter to the author, probably on the tenth of December, 1871:

> My dearest Marian,
>
>   I have read your new book and I think it the most interesting subject you have ever given us and I think it is only too happy and beautiful a book for the horrid things coming after in her life. I feel intensely about it [...]. I dread the unfolding and feel quite certain there is a horrible tragedy coming [...]. I hear people say it is so witty amusing and lively so it is but all is shadowed by the coming misery to me. I can't help feeling it desperately. I am very sorry for the poor thing just as if she were alive and I want to stop her. She is like a child dancing into a quick sand on a sunny morning and I feel a sort of horror at your story as if it were all real and going on at this moment. I do not know if you meant to produce this sort of terrible foreshadowing of inevitable misery.[4]

'Horrible', 'misery' and 'terrible': one of the fascinating aspects of the sensitive response of this creative and emancipated woman is her recognition of the novel's tragic element. Unlike *Anna Karenina* and *Effi Briest*, to whom all Bodichon's words also apply, *Middlemarch* is not about adultery, and it is not a tragedy. Of its four interlaced narratives, only Lydgate's story ends in death, and though the death is a significant mark of his wasted life, it is not presented as a tragic consequence of that waste, or as part of a tragic causality. Dorothea's story, though explicitly refused an ideal ending, ends with a second marriage, offspring, and moral approval and affirmation. In her earlier fiction George Eliot had shown women destroyed by the social constraints and cruelties of class and poverty, but she chose to deal differently with Dorothea, as with her predecessor, Esther Lyon, in *Felix Holt*, and her successor Gwendolen Harleth, in *Daniel Deronda*. An anonymous reviewer of *Anna Karenina* in the American journal *Critic*, 10 April 1986, calls Tolstoy 'a kind of double' of George Eliot, and sees Anna as 'lovely but miserable' like Gwendolen.[5]   *Middlemarch* is not a tragic novel, but Bodichon's sensibilty was sound: Dorothea is tragically married to Casaubon. Her survival of that tragedy — a word which Eliot uses as she describes Dorothea's misery on her wedding journey in Rome, 'that element of tragedy which lies in the very fact of frequency' — scarcely blunts the point. What happens to her, in her young hope and brilliance, is horrible, terrible, and

---

[4] *The George Eliot Letters*, ed. by Gordon S. Haight, 9 vols (New Haven and London: Yale University Press, 1954-78), IX, 33-4.

[5] *Tolstoy: The Critical Heritage*, ed. by A. V. Knowles (London: Routledge & Kegan Paul, 1978), p. 340.

miserable, as George Eliot implied in the subtle foreshadowings of that first Book. It was one of the weaknesses in the BBC film of 1994, that Dorothea's health, radiance, and physical energy were not strongly presented, and the tragic potential Bodichon writes about was missing. Such force and energy was presented — and felt — most strongly in the serial form of fiction, where the isolation of episodes made it emphatic, and left the reader to dwell on premonitions. George Eliot chose not to write a marriage-tragedy, like Tolstoy and Fontane, but the three novels about conventional and loveless marriage reveal close affinities. Dorothea lives to make a better second marriage, and is rescued by her author from the fate of Anna and Effi, but her life with Ladislaw, as the wife of a member of the first reform parliament, is left vague, and scrupulously admitted not to be ideally or totally fulfilling. In her first miserable marriage, she is, like Anna and Effi, a suffering wife, and for similarly generalisable social reasons.

The beginnings of the marriage-tragedies, *Anna Karenina* and *Effi Briest*, perfectly fit Bodichon's account of the young Dorothea, like a child, dancing, and in scenes which are happy and beautiful. Tolstoy's heroine bursts upon us in full bloom and vitality some time after she has been married to Karenin, and after they have had a child, but both she, and the merry virginal Effi, impress the reader on their first appearance as Dorothea impressed Bodichon. They are young women tragically destined for conventional marriages, especially horrifying as passive, sacrifical figures, because of their full endowment of mind, creativity, and health. All three burst upon the reader as young, attractive, blooming, and physically active. When we meet Dorothea we see her fine hand and wrist, and are told that 'most men' find her 'bewitching on horseback' and that 'when her eyes and cheeks glowed with mingled pleasure she looked very little like a devotee' (Ch. 1).[6]

But she makes her most radiant appearance soon after her return from the marriage journey:

> She was glowing from her morning toilette as only healthful youth can glow; there was gem-like brightness on her coiled hair and in her hazel eyes; there was warm red life in her lips; her throat had a breathing whiteness [...]. (Ch. 28)

Anna's vitality is first seen through the response of Vronsky:

> Vronsky had time to notice the suppressed animation which played over her face and flitted between her sparkling eyes and the smile curving her red lips. It was as though

---

[6] Unless otherwise indicated quotations are from *Middlemarch*, ed. by W. J. Harvey (Harmondsworth: Penguin Books, 1965).

> her nature were so brimming over with something that against her will it expressed
> itself now in a radiant look, now in a smile. (Pt 2, Ch. 18) [7]

and

> He pressed the little hand offered to him, and the energetic grip with which she boldly
> and vigorously shook his filled him with joy, as if it were something special. She
> walked rapidly away, carrying her rather full figure with extraordinary lightness. (Ch.
> 18)

These physical details are not just the rendering of his attraction, but continue
to be registered by others, Kitty for instance, just before Anna is seen as
dancing, in the ballroom scene:

> She saw the quivering, flashing light in her eyes, the smile of happiness and excitement
> that involuntarily curved her lips, and the graceful sureness and ease of the movements.
> (Ch. 23)

Effi is first seen, out of doors and on a sunny noon, as irrepressibly physical,
jumping up from the patchwork altar-cloth she is making with her mother — a
symbolic object like almost every thing in the novel — to do Swedish
gymnastics, playing 'Tig' with her friends, and planning to climb a mast, with
yard-arms and ropes, which her father will build for her. Her mother tells her
she should have been a circus rider. She is dressed in a short loosely-belted
smock for freedom of movement, and her mother decides that she should not
change for the interview with Innstetten, who has asked for her hand:

> [...] looking at the ravishing young creature who was standing there, a picture of health
> and gaiety, still flushed from the excitement of her game. (Ch. 2)[8]

Her games with her friends are given resonance in a famous episode in that
same chapter, where they call to her through an open window, just as her
middle-aged suitor 'approached her with a friendly bow': 'Come on, Effi!'
('Effi! komm!'), a phrase symmetrically and ironically repeated towards the
end of the novel in a telegram inviting her to her parents' home in the same
words.[9] Each novelist takes care to show the woman as young and healthy,
strong and active, self-delighting, clearly wrong for marriage to an older man.
Sexuality is ripe, but the picker of the fruit is withering. These glowing and

---

[7] Quotations are from *Anna Karenin*, trans. by Rosemary Edmonds (Harmondsworth:
Penguin Books, 1978) but in my text I use the old form 'Karenina'.

[8] Quotations are from *Effi Briest*, trans. by Douglas Parmée (Harmondsworth: Penguin
Books, 1967).

[9] This is comparable, structurally and thematically, with the variations on Dorothea's
'Think what I can do' and 'What should I do?', a pattern I discussed in *The Novels of George
Eliot* (London: Athlone Press, 1959), Ch. 5.

active appearances prepare the story of mismatching and frustration, leading to misery or death.

For Dorothea, misery and not death. George Eliot had personal reasons for not writing a marriage-tragedy. The tragic novel was the genre in which she was adept. She had written four stories of a woman's life, ending in death, two *Scenes of Clerical Life*, 'Amos Barton', in which Milly Barton is worn out and wasted by childbirth and miscarriages, and 'Mr Gilfil's Love Story' in which Caterina is killed by class-separateness and childbirth, *Adam Bede* in which Hetty is tortured, and her child destroyed, by class-separateness and the sexual double standard, and her greatest tragic novel, *The Mill on the Floss*, in which Maggie is destroyed, from a complexity of social and psychological causes, including sexual convention and restriction. Her last four novels show women suffering greatly from being women in their time and culture, but surviving. None of these novels has a heroine in any danger of committing adultery.

Their author was herself guilty of adultery. Her personal circumstances, in which she lived unmarried with George Henry Lewes, who was married to Agnes Lewes and unable to get a divorce because of his condonation of her adultery with Thornton Hunt, would have inhibited a central treatment of adultery. Her two portraits of the adulteress, Mrs Transome in *Felix Holt*, and Lydia Glasher, in *Daniel Deronda*, though marvellously individuated and sympathetic, are not portraits of a heroine, and compress the narrative of motive and desire. But apart from her own sex and personal circumstances, there was also the cultural difference, which inhibited the representation of adultery in English Victorian fiction, as both Thackeray and Henry James complained. An English novel's heroine as sympathetic as Edith Newcome or Dorothea — or an American one as sympathetic as Isabel Archer — could not be led or driven to adultery, but she could be in Russian and German novels.

Middlemarch devises a way of including adultery, by displacing it, locating it within Ladislaw's imagination in a brilliantly oblique suggestion of desireless anticipated possibility:

> Will felt inexpressibly mournful, and said nothing. Rosamond had that morning entreated him to urge this step [leaving Middlemarch] on Lydgate; and it seemed to him as if he were beholding in a magic panorama a future where he himself was sliding into that pleasureless yielding to the small solicitations of circumstance, which is a commoner history of perdition than any single momentous bargain. (Ch. 79)

Despite this displacement and absence, *Middlemarch* can be bracketed with its bolder cross-Channel successors, as a novel profoundly exploring the social construction and destruction of women's lives, and a model for later novels about conventionally and miserably married women.

Shown first in physical health and radiance, the suffering heroines, Dorothea, Anna and Effi have many other things in common. They are sympathetic, well-born, intelligent, creative human beings, under-educated, untrained, taught a few superficial accomplishments and manners, dressed and cultivated, with marriage in mind, a marriage to someone of their own or a better class, a marriage with money. They are all brought up in a culture where marriage is what is expected of them and is all that is expected of them. The horror and misery of such a system is demonstrated in marriages with men who are old enough to be their fathers, who have little in common with them, and who in various ways fail in sexuality and love. Casaubon is over forty-five, Dorothea nineteen; Karenin is twenty years older than Anna; Innstetten, who has been in love with her mother, who 'of course' chose a safer match, with another older man, is thirty-eight, Effi seventeen. The Casaubon marriage is childless; Anna has a son by her husband, and a daughter, Anni, by her lover; the Innstetten marriage produces one child, also called Annie; Dorothea has two children, by Ladislaw, a son about whom a few details are given, a daughter about whom nothing is said, her sex barely indicated by the process of elimination. George Eliot reticently uses the suggestions of fact and metaphor to tell what is probably the untold story of an unconsummated marriage. Tolstoy shows Karenin desiring his undesiring wife. Fontane implies that Innstetten is low in libido, in one or two bedroom scenes where Effi is left alone, and in one or two of her observations about his lack of demonstrativeness, and after the couple have one child, it is said that no others are expected. Her mother makes a fascinating response to Effi's innocent desire to have a red bedside light, 'lovely and poetic', 'reality is different and it's often a good thing, instead of a red glow, to have it quite dark' (Ch. 4).

Each novel makes the social critique explicit. After appearing in the first editions of *Middlemarch*, the separately published parts (1871-2) and the first edition in four volumes, (Edinburgh and London: William Blackwood and Sons, 1872), the following passage was taken out, perhaps as too boldly radical, in subsequent editions:

> Among the many remarks passed on her mistakes it was never said that such mistakes could not have happened if the society into which she was born had not smiled on propositions of marriage from a sickly man to a girl less than half his own age — on modes of education which make woman's knowledge another name for motley ignorance — on rules of conduct which are in flat contradiction with its own loudly-asserted beliefs. While this is the social air in which mortals begin to breathe, there will

be collisions such as those in Dorothea's life, where great feelings will take the aspect of error, and great faith the aspect of illusion. (Finale)

This was followed by the sentence which was retained in later editions: 'For there is no creature whose inward being is so strong that it is not greatly determined by what lies outside it.' George Eliot makes her social generalisation, in both versions, the strong and the mild, through the voice of her omniscient narrator.

In *Anna Karenina* the bitter social diagnosis is voiced by the experienced, worldly, and affectionate Oblonsky, who says to his sister with wonderful directness: 'I'll begin at the beginning. You married a man twenty years older than yourself. You married him without love, or without knowing what love was'(Pt 4, Ch. 21). Dorothea's marriage is seen as 'made' by society's acquiescence, though in the novel it is her own choice. Anna's match, like Effi's, is made for her by her elders. The novel shows the sexual double standard in several ways, including the contrast between social responses to Vronsky and Anna, and by showing both brother and sister discontented with their marriages. Though Tolstoy makes it clear — right at the start of the novel — that Oblonsky's wife Dolly suffers bitterly from her husband's infidelity, it is not to have tragic consequences, but is seen as an ordinary marriage, with ordinary unhappiness. In spite of Tolstoy's epigraph, 'Vengeance is mine, | And I will repay', Anna is presented not as a sinner but as a social victim — and so are Vronsky and Karenin.

Fontane makes Effi articulate her own judgement at the end, and she says, devastatingly, though with an admirable steadiness and lack of self-reproach, directed by a less didactic but perhaps more politically alert author than Dorothea or Anna, that she had married a man incapable of love: 'as fine a man as one can be who doesn't really love'. Her sense of social reality is also expressed by her parents, intelligent victims of the same marriage-market economy, as they ask, 'Whether we ought not to have brought her up differently [...] whether she wasn't perhaps too young?'. As her father, von Briest , a character with a slight resemblance to George Eliot's Mr Brooke but involved in marriage and family life as Brooke managed not to be — 'It *is* a noose, you know' — repeats his usual evasion at the end, 'Too big a subject' ('ein zu weites Feld'), his irony and accuracy help to keep conclusions open. These are characters who may plausibly consider their own responsibility but scarcely make the social diagnosis and generalisation George Eliot made in the words of her omniscient narrator, and then cautiously modified, to a less boldly radical conclusion. It is too big a subject for them to go into. They are not socially conscious novelists.

Of course the novels are novels, and act out these statements and insights. They show upper-class women who are ignorant and uneducated, though a lack of knowledge is much stronger in the English and German stories. Unlike Eliot, Fontane does not despise woman's accomplishments, and shows Effi's music — and later on, her amateur painting, as real resources, more creative than Innstetten's superficial and affected cultivation of literature and painting. Like Dorothea, and like Effi's predecessor Melanie in Fontane's *The Woman Taken in Adultery*, Effi von Innstetten goes to Italy with her husband, and her letters home complain of his indefatigable museum-going and her aching feet. Both Eliot and Fontane wring the utmost irony from the romance of Italy and of Italian art, as the cold Casaubon and the enthusiastic Innstetten take their young wives to the galleries. In *The Woman Taken in Adultery* Melanie goes to Venice with her husband — who is culturally 'inferior' though he knows enough to buy a copy of the theme-picture by Tintoretto, with a laboured and implausible prescience, then goes to Rome with her lover — eventually her second husband, in this unusual happily-ending adultery-novel — with whom she visits the Farnesina, mentioning the Cupid and Psyche frescoes discussed by Casaubon and Dorothea, and used symbolically by both novelists. Both Effi and Dorothea deplore their own lack of education, though the candid no-nonsense Effi sympathetically admits being bored by the museums, while the earnest Dorothea works hard at understanding art.

The sterility, low libido and emotional deficiency of the husbands is reinforced by their affectation or failure in artistic feeling. Casaubon can only quote the educated opinion of Raphael, Innstetten's enthusiasm is a bit of a joke, Karenin is said to read the literary journals but to affect an interest in literature and the arts. The aesthetic failure, like the sexual, is an affective failure. As Effi comes to know, Innstetten cannot love. (But one of the novel's ironies is that he has loved — her own mother — when they were both young and passionate, but before he was a good match. Like Casaubon, he has outlived, or not lived, his passions.)

The husbands are all professional men, with enough status and money to make them good matches for young women, so socially approved in spite of their middle age. They are very much identified with their careers, and though they are by no means equally successful — Casaubon is a failure as a scholar, Karenin is a fairly good civil servant who does not get to the top of his tree, and the highly ambitious and successful Innstetten's promotion turns to dust — their careers are an item in their authoritative, possessive and destructive marriages. They stand for an establishment and an order.

Casaubon represents landed gentry, wealth, the Church of England, and sterile scholarship — a configuration of synecdoches like that expressing his descendant, D. H. Lawrence's landed gentleman, industrialist, technologist, and stream-of-consciousness novelist Sir Clifford Chatterley. Karenin is an ambitious but not a high-flying official, of impeccable position, but mediocre. Innstetten is an able provincial governor, smiled on by Bismarck, an ideal servant of Prussian law and order. This institutional representation of the husbands both images and compounds an affective sterility or reluctance, a dryness or coldness, an excessive compliance with order and convention, an inhumane systematisation. The psyches, physiques, and occupations of the lovers are constructed to provide the finest contrast with these wintry husbands. All of them, however, are in one way or another allowed qualities, or moments, of warmth which attract sympathy and understanding: Casaubon is moved, once, to be gentle to Dorothea; Karenin forgives Anna and accepts her daughter; and Innstetten grows in stature to become a sympathetic character. It is marriage which is attacked, not men, who are victims also.

Criticising Ladislaw, as other critics have done, Henry James said what Dorothea needed after Casaubon was a trooper, and Tolstoy and Fontane anticipated his judgement, since a soldier is precisely what they supply for the satisfaction of their frustrated women, in Colonel Vronsky, and Major von Crampas. There are a number of novels, (discussed in *The Appropriate Form*, 1964) in which a romantic rescuer, like Ladislaw, is supplied for an emotionally and socially imprisoned woman, for instance for Meredith's Diana, Aminta, and Carinthia, for D. H. Lawrence's Connie Chatterley, and for the heroines of E. M. Forster's Italian novels: out of this group, only Meredith is making a radical critique of the institution of marriage. Will Ladislaw is a more interesting rescuer than is often suggested, but he is presented romantically rather than sexually, as the contrast with Tolstoy and Fontane makes clear. But the variations are not predictable. Vronsky is a splendidly young, healthy and handsome foil to Karenin, and less phony in his pursuit of the arts, but he is condemned for a certain dilettantism, especially in his painting. Crampas is wonderfully presented, as a womaniser, a bit flashy, no longer young, whose affair with Effi is predictable. I disagree with the translator, Douglas Parmée, who says, in his Introduction to the Penguin edition, that their encounter is the product of chance: any incident would do to start the affair, which is inevitable from the moment he turns up, as the only eligible man for the role. His interest in poetry and acting, together with the way he talks about the subjects with Effi, is genuine and felt. But Fontane is tough and realistic in his refusal to romanticise the affair, and one of the ironies of the action — as important as the long gap of time between the affair and its discovery — is Effi's relief when chance takes her away from Kessin and her lover. She is clear about not loving him:

> Honour, honour, honour [...] and then he shot that poor man, whom I didn't even love, and whom I'd forgotten because I didn't love him. (Ch. 33)

One of the effects of reading Effi as a descendant of Dorothea, is to appreciate her amused, relaxed, and shrewd sense of reality. Fontane demystifies and deromanticises the rescue into love, and Effi is his brilliant spokesperson. Will writes to remonstrate with Dorothea for her moral intensities and aesthetic inhibitions, to urge on her 'a sturdy neutral delight in things as they are'. In spite of Will's criticism, and the narrator's splendid articulation of his meanings, it is Fontane, not Eliot, who creates characters capable of savouring this sturdy neutral delight. The novel's *raisonneur*, Wüllersdorf, Instetten's second, discusses the need to make the best of life's second-best. When Innstetten admits that he takes no pleasure in his promotion, has lost his interest in life, and realizes that he has been stupidly complicit with the Prussian code of honour and order, his friend advises:

> The best thing is to hold the fort until you drop. But first of all, to get the most out of the small things, the very small things of life, and to have an eye for violets in bloom or the Luise Monument decked out in flowers or little girls skipping in long lace-up boots. (Ch. 35)

Fontane finds good phrases for the stuff of survival, Innstetten's 'miniature delights' and Wüllersdorf's architect friend's 'makeshift constructions'.

But it is Effi whose life most fully demonstrates this untragic grasp of survival, and in *Effi Briest*, though tragic, Fontane centrally and actively develops the idea of sturdy neutral delight as Eliot herself never does. It remains as a brilliant insight, in *Middlemarch* and elsewhere, but her intensity and idealism never allowed its development in a novel. It is the strength of Fontane's imagination that he does make room for it, and though his novel is technically tragic, since Effi's loneliness, losses, confinements and exposures seem to be contributory causes of her death, the novel's conclusion is as heartening as it is critical.

Like Beatrice's ideal husband, in *Much Ado About Nothing*, Effi is a heroine for working-days as well as Sunday best. Her survival shows first of all in her eventual acceptance of the marriage, after they move to Berlin — like her mother's acceptance before her — but this is overtaken by the discovery of her affair with Crampas. Later, it is a survival which reveals the relativity of human content; as she enjoys the thought of a flat of her own, after the boarding-house; as she enjoys Roswitha's company, but wants more to do; as she learns painting and finds '[h]er poor life [...] less poor' (Ch. 32), longs to see her child but is disappointed, then at last comes home, and even then, has her lot further improved by the companionship of the dog Rollo, thanks to Roswitha. Fontane wonderfully imagines this small-scale series of improvements in miniature delights and makeshift constructions.

Effi ends with a response to the small things around her, the open air, watching trains, smelling the rape and clover, looking at larks, listening to cowbells, eating an apple, and looking at the summer shooting stars from her window. Like many women, including Dorothea, she looks at the world from a window, but it is significant that what she sees is no expansive vision of labour and duty, like Dorothea's in Chapter 80 of *Middlemarch*, only beautiful nature, with no symbolic resonances. Looking at the night sky, in the final chapter, does make her think of heaven, from which 'perhaps' we come, and to which we may go, but though she longs, she is a realist who does not 'know' and does not 'want to know' and is finally killed — on behalf of her author, also a realist — by the dangerous night air.

Innstetten, like Casaubon and Karenin, in demonstrating his author's sense of a man's social disadvantage, in an analysis which is far from taking a separatist attitude to sexual politics, rejects his constructed gender role, as custodian of honour and order, regrets that he killed the man who cuckolded him, and wishes he had not divorced his wife. Erich Heller, in an Introduction to *The Woman Taken in Adultery* and the comic attack on class and rank, *The Poggenpuhl Family*,[10] says that Innstetten's insistence 'on the necessity of the social order being protected by the power of established morality' of that order represents Fontane's own 'ineradicably "Prussian" ' part. But Innstetten does not stay with this belief, acting from it almost automatically and coming to articulate an awareness that his beliefs and actions are imposed by history. So he grows to speak, imaginatively, for the creatures of history who know what has made them, and joins, across their division, Effi's sense of wasted, but comprehensible, lives.

Instetten's, Wüllersdorf's, and Effi's sense of reality is shared by an important character in the novel, the servant Roswitha. Before *Middlemarch*, the idea of Ladislaw's sturdy neutral delight or Innstetten's miniature delights, is articulated, on the fringe of action, by one of Eliot's best servants, Denner, in *Felix Holt*, a remarkable minor character. In the novel's first chapter, her

---

[10] *The Woman Taken in Adultery* and *The Poggenpuhl Family*, ed. by Erich Heller (Chicago and London: The University of Chicago Press, 1979).

mistress, Mrs Transome, whose guilty past she knows all about, asks her what her pleasures are, and the answer includes these:

> Why, if I've only got some orange flowers to candy, I shouldn't like to die till I see them all right. Then there's the sunshine now and then; I like that, as the cats do. I look upon it, life is like our game at whist, when Banks and his wife come to the still-room of an evening. I don't enjoy the game much, but I like to play my cards well, and see what will be the end of it. (Ch. 1)[11]

In *Middlemarch* the sub-plot of Tantripp, Dorothea's maid, and Pratt, Casaubon's butler, is nicely done: when Tantripp wishes his master buried in the 'caticoms' of his books, Pratt is amused, liking his master well, but liking Tantripp better, and eventually we learn that they are to marry. A love-story takes place downstairs, while the gentry court, marry, fall sick, die, and survive. Fontane does even better than George Eliot, enlarging the strengths of Denner and Tantripp to place his maidservant on an equal footing with her masters and mistresses. Tantripp loves her mistress, and her density of life is brilliantly compressed and implied, but Roswitha is a major character. She has had her love-tragedy, been seduced, threatened, had her baby taken away, served for small return, and been rescued from death-wishing desolation by Effi's need. There is something comic in her repeated story of the blacksmith father chasing her with a hot iron, but also something terrible. Her story is fully told and felt, and her relationship with Effi is a womanly bonding: she is the good nurse, who looks after Effi's baby but also sleeps in Effi's room, to avert the ghost (*der Spuk*) who is both the image of fatal love and a trick in a man's rule of fear. She is also the spokesperson for freedom, for the sturdy acceptance of things as they are, as she joins Effi after the divorce, when her parents are too conventional to take her in, and when she writes to ask Innstetten for the dog Rollo, in a letter which quietly but clearly criticises Innstetten and the social ethic in a way he and Wüllersdorf are ready to comprehend and re-articulate.

Instetten moves from the subject of his own depression to her letter, with its simple telling sentence, quoted from Effi, 'That's the advantage of animals, they don't worry about things too much' (Ch. 35), and Wüllersdorf knows what is in his mind, 'Yes ... she's worth more than we are'. Innstetten's recognition of his historical burden is provoked by 'those simple words with their deliberate or perhaps accidental accusation'. She does more than speak: her actions are beneficial, and both she and Rollo, in different ways outside the social order, speak for the unconditional, the natural, and the free, through

---

[11] *Felix Holt*, ed. by Peter Coveney (Harmondsworth: Penguin Books, 1972).

love, silence, common-sense, and ignorance. Their affinity is made clear on their first meeting, when Rollo immediately takes to her, when she observes that he has an exotic name, like her, and when she compares herself to a faithful dog. Effi's father, the councillor von Briest, recognizes Rollo's freedom at the end, as the dog mourns by Effi's stone: 'Ah yes, Luise, the beasts of the field. That's what I'm always saying. We're always talking about instinct. All in all, it's the best thing' (Ch. 36).

When Roswitha ignorantly addresses Innstetten, on her envelope, as 'Baron' and 'Esquire', Fontane is not simply letting her make a likely error, but using her apt subversion of rank and order. And if the class-implications in the relations of mistress and servant are offensive to our modern political sensibility, we can value Fontane's important recognition that the intelligent servant has what her mistress may lack, a job to do, certain skills, a training, a something outside the self.

Dorothea has her maid and her dog, Monk, but they do not quite achieve the imagined representation of a natural freedom and uninstitutionalised affection, like Fontane's. This is making big claims for a pet and a servant, but they are justified. There is something similar in *Anna Karenina*, dramatised but not conceptualised, in the hunting scenes and the mowing episode which bring Levin out of society, into freedom and nature, in a holiday experience and a symbolic action. But Tolstoy assimilates his pastoral freedom into the moral and social action, as part of Levin's vision and development. Part too, of his vision of purpose and ideal and meaning, which he shares with Dorothea, who is also allowed her vision. Unlike Effi, who achieves something which is at least as valuable, and more accessible, an acceptance of unideal existence.

As well as a benevolent affirmation, the novels have their shadow side. The women are all haunted, miserably, horribly and terribly, and the realistic novels which embody their characters and experience suggest or dramatise the haunting in forms of fantasy. The most obvious ghost is the last, the ghost of the Chinaman who haunts Effi's married dwelling, making the sound of rustling in the room above, frightening Effi when she sleeps alone, explained by Crampas as part of Innstetten's mystifying technique for keeping his wife in awe. There is another connection too, with the imagery of love, since like Effi the Chinaman was an alien imprisoned in a strange society, love-lorn and destroyed, and both he and Effi are buried in unlikely places, his grave an unconsecrated patch among the sand-dunes where lovers embrace, hers in the private garden where she used to play. The ghost walks, indeed frightening

Effi, in her bed and in her husband's absence.   And as a comic touch, Innstetten is rather proud of having a ghost in the house.

Anna is haunted by the premonition of her death, which tautly connects the novel's beginning to its end, across its great spaces and pages.   The fused image of the watchman killed on the occasion of her first meeting with Vronsky, and taken by Anna as a bad omen, is merged with a nightmare figure of an old man 'doing something dreadful to her with the iron', and a little peasant with a bag, to haunt her dreams and Vronsky's, and the repeated '*Il faut le battre — le fer: le broyer, le pétrir*', which neither dreamer can understand, comes in and out of the characters' minds and experiences, and in and out of the novel's fantasy, to return at the end when the iron crushes Anna (I have discussed this aspect of the novel in some detail in *The Appropriate Form*, 1964).

The least obvious supernatural apparition is the first, the ghost which haunts Middlemarch.   Reading *Middlemarch* with *Anna Karenina* and *Effi Briest* brings out the undercurrent of fantasy in Eliot's realistic novel. (This is the influence of later novels on earlier, as readers move to and fro, subverting chronology.)   Eliot used fantasy in *The Lifted Veil*, but there is a ghost-story acted out in the imagery of *Middlemarch*.   The ghost of Casaubon is first present through a simile in his self-description, when he first dines at Tipton Grange:

> I live too much with the dead. My mind is something like the ghost of an ancient, wandering about the world and trying mentally to construct it as it used to be, in spite of ruin and confusing changes. (Ch. 2)

In the sub-text or the story told by the imagery, Dorothea marries a ghost and enters a haunted house, with an 'air of autumnal decline', dark, small-windowed, with neglected gardens and sombre yews.   In the last scene of her liberation her husband's ghost seems to haunt his place, the brown library, a catacomb, a monument, a place of the dead.   Tragedy often needs ghosts, and George Eliot's ghost — a ghost of a ghost — intensifies our sense of a tragic enclosure and close relationship which are, to recall Bodichon's words, miserable, horrible and terrible.   Casaubon dies before Dorothea can answer the request for a widowhood devoted to his work and memory, and he appears to stay for an answer. (In Chapter 7, Innstetten tells Effi, 'To tell the truth, if I were to die, I'd prefer to take you with me. I don't want to leave you behind for anyone else. What do you think about it?' and she says, 'I must think it over.')   In Chapter 54, Dorothea feels that she cannot receive Will in the library and chooses the more 'neutral' drawing-room and on a later occasion, in Chapter 83, when she thinks of going out to meet him in the grounds, the weather grows turbulent. She is kept inside by rain but also by an undefined reluctance, associated with the symbolic weather:

> The sky was heavy, and the trees began to shiver as at a coming storm. Besides, she shrank from going out to him.

In a fine nuance the storm's menace is noticed after she feels that 'her husband's prohibition seems to dwell' in the library. The storm rouses the lovers — like Dido and Aeneas in their cave — to a declaration, but it is by no means simply erotic. As she thinks defensively about her love, before Will comes in, she thinks of herself speaking 'to some imagined audience in the library', later on she sees a lightning flash as 'the terror of a hopeless love', and the lovers look out together, despondent and hopeless, at 'the drear outer world' until they kiss, and,

> The rain was dashing against the window-panes as if an angry spirit were within it, and behind it was the great swoop of the wind.

'As if an angry spirit': the library's former inhabitant tried to keep his widow in the labyrinth of books and notebooks, and wrote a will to prohibit this love, with his 'Dead Hand'. The storm subsides, and the lovers sit down and hold hands. After reading *Effi Briest*, with *Middlemarch*, I noticed another strand in the ghostly sub-text, another implication of the metaphorical and actual fantasies, the theme of primitive sacrifice. Though primitive, it is used in Fontane, and perhaps in Eliot too, for a contemporary feminist emphasis. It is barely noticeable in *Middlemarch*, and after first recognising the reference I was puzzled by its purpose, which is elucidated by an episode when Effi and Innstetten go on holiday to Rügen, near lake Hertha. Everything conspires to bring back Crampas, guilt, and premonition: Effi comes across a village oddly named after her lover, 'Crampas' so having to be shunned. And the holiday is shadowed by blood-sacrifice. When they find a guide who 'looks as if had been at the very least an assistant in the old rites of Hertha worship', Effi remarks that the still, dark lake looks 'ready for the cult of Hertha', he points to 'the stones that are still there to remind us of it', she asks 'What stones?', he replies, 'The sacrificial stones', and they come to

> a number of smooth stones [...] leaning, each slightly hollowed out, with downward-sloping grooves:
> 'And what are they for?'
> 'So that it would flow away more easily, ma'am.'

Effi has never 'seen anything' in her life which has made her 'feel so miserable' (Ch. 24).

The comparable episode in *Middlemarch* comes in one of the repeated library scenes. (Houses, rooms, and objects are less conspicuously symbolic in George Eliot and Tolstoy than in Fontane, but the symbolism is there.) Casaubon's first heart-attack comes on in the library, and the novel has made it clear that it is his place, sombrely lit, with brown books, and the suggestions of labyrinth and catacombs. Will thinks of him as growing 'grey crunching bones in a cavern luring a girl into his companionship' for 'the most horrible of virgin-sacrifices' (Ch. 37); when he talks to her in the library in the same chapter he thinks of 'beautiful lips kissing holy skulls and other emptinesses ecclesiastically enshrined'; Tantripp makes that joke about caticoms, and the omniscient narrative adds images of prison, narrow spaces, and darkness. Dorothea has to return to the library because Casaubon cannot be left in possession, and must be exorcised:

> So by the end of June the shutters were all opened at Lowick Manor, and the morning gazed calmly into the library, shining on the rows of notebooks as it shines on the weary waste planted with huge stones, the mute memorial of a forgotten faith. (Ch. 54)

This seems to be an ingenious reference to Stonehenge, which George Eliot did not see until 1874, though she would have seen paintings and photographs. The primary emphasis is on the waste land of past faith, Casaubon's out-of-date research and Dorothea's lost faith in him, but there may be some magnetism of symbol from Will's imagery of 'virgin-sacrifices'. My reading is probably influenced not only by Fontane's sacrifice theme, but by the Stonehenge scene at the end of *Tess of the D'Urbervilles*, another novel of the nineties, where the sacrifice of a woman's life is even clearer than in *Effi Briest*. The image joins Will's 'most horrible of virgin-sacrifices' to make Casaubon's metaphorical haunting, and his attempts at restriction, both more 'horrible' and more feminist.

Effi Briest begins with a casual, romantic schoolgirl's mention of sacrifice, when Effi light-heartedly tells her friends the story of her mother's marriage, beginning 'A story that ends in self-sacrifice is never *bad*', but her own story ends with a discovery that it was not a matter of self-sacrifice, and that sacrifice can be bad. *Middlemarch* ends by imagining women whose lives 'may present a far sadder sacrifice than that of the Dorothea whose story we know' (Finale). The theme of sacrifice not only intensifies the misery and horror of the marriage, but also generalises the woman's story. The transformation of Casaubon's books into the stones of Stonehenge is not only a good metaphor for what he wants to do with his widow, but an example of actual sacrifice which makes the metaphor at the end more substantial.

At the end of the three novels there is idealisation, with some grasp of reality. In *Middlemarch*, Dorothea is placed historically, far from 'ideal' in her determining acts. Eliot preserves Dorothea, by killing Casaubon and marrying her to Ladislaw, and allows her, after her usual sunset views from the boudoir, the east-facing sunrise, from her marriage bedroom, lighting images of human endurance — the man with a bundle, the woman with a baby, and perhaps a shepherd with his dog. But at the end Eliot makes it clear that life is imperfect, with no grand significant achievement. Like Anna's and Effi's, Dorothea's life demonstrates wasted powers. What the narrator calls her absorption 'into the life of another', and her being 'only known in a certain circle as a wife and mother', do not allow an outlet for a potential Saint Theresa.

We first see her at the beginning, working hard, in study and practical application, at plans for good rural housing, and having to execute the plans through a man, Sir James Chettam. We see her hoping for education and service in her marriage, and finding even fewer channels for work and idealism than before marriage. We find her disappointed in widowhood because she can not afford to found a small ideal community and must diffuse ideas and energies in little personal acts, like her movements of sympathy for Lydgate and Rosamond. She has imagined what Daniel Deronda recommends to Gwendolen, an interest in something outside the self:

> [...] some real knowledge would give you an interest in the world beyond the small drama of personal desires. It is the curse of your life — forgive me — of so many lives, that all passion is spent in that narrow round, for want of ideas and sympathies to make a larger home for it. Is there any single occupation of mind that you care about with passionate delight or even independent interest? (Ch. 36)[12]

Work and social activity is found with Vronsky by Anna, and they do create something like a good small local community, with educational and medical facilities admired by Dolly, but fatally outside society, a putting-down of local roots which still leaves them fatally *déracinés*. But the activity outside self is found, mildly and belatedly by Effi, in art, nature, and small domestic creativities in her parents' house.

The three novels are significantly named, one after a provincial town, with symbolic resonance, the others after their heroines. But the first book of *Middlemarch*, 'Miss Brooke', retains the title George Eliot originally planned for the novel she eventually made only a part of the more expansive project of *Middlemarch*. We do not know whether she would have kept the name if the novel had concentrated on the woman — and if so, why — but it is interesting that she placed Miss Brooke in an action which extended the theme of social frustration to men as well as women. However, Dorothea begins the novel,

---

[12] *Daniel Deronda*, ed. by Barbara Hardy (Harmondsworth: Penguin Books, 1967).

engrossing the reader for a long stretch of narrative, and we tend to call her Dorothea Brooke even though she becomes Mrs Casaubon and Mrs Ladislaw. Perhaps we pine for her independence, like the novel, or at least like those at its end who regret that 'so substantive and rare a creature should be absorbed into the life of others', as wife and mother, but who are unable to say what else she could do.   Anna's name is given to 'her' novel even though she shares its large and multiple action with the story of a man, Levin, and the fact of her remaining married is a key to the tragedy in both the marriage and Karenin's refusal to divorce. It is in keeping with the self-awareness and self-articulateness of Effi Briest that she chooses the name for her tombstone — and so for the novel — placing herself with that earlier eponymous heroine whose maiden name proudly, accurately, and ironically names the story, Richardson's Clarissa Harlowe. Effi's is a choice of the maiden name, of independence, erasing her made marriage, and importantly also erasing the mark of rank, taking out the 'von' from the Briest, as earlier, when she writes to the Minister's wife about seeing her child, she signs herself 'Innstetten' without her husband's 'von'.   We can see a development in political consciousness as Effi's choice takes in class as well as gender. Dorothea is in fact more explicitly class-conscious, radically criticising the gentry and privilege, and George Eliot's first, excised comment emphasized the structure of society rather than gender. But her novel, unlike Tolstoy's and Fontane's, and unlike her first project, does not make the point through an act of naming. In spite of the cultural and historical differences, the novels can be read together, the juxtaposition bringing out new emphases or confirming old ones. These products of midland provincial and county England, aristocratic Moscow and St Petersburg, Prussian aristocracy, middle class commerce, and officialdom, all cause us, as Bodichon says, to feel for their fictitious women, and men, in similar dilemmas, as if they were 'real'.

Each concludes with a movement beyond fiction, an expansive opening and questioning. After the height of her east-facing vision, of the family, labour, and a world beyond her property, there is a descent to the ordinary world, of her personal life, her lack of achievement, and their historical implications. After Dorothea's story is scrutinised, the last sentences applaud and derive hope from her diffused and 'unhistoric' achievement, for its benevolence and hopefulness, and 'she' is pluralised, in a way which can remind us of Carlyle's belief that history is composed of innumerable biographies:

> Certainly those determining acts of her life were not ideally beautiful. They were the mixed result of a young and noble impulse struggling amidst the conditions of an imperfect social state [...]. But we insignificant people with our daily words and acts

are preparing the lives of many Dorotheas, some of which may present a far sadder sacrifice than that of the Dorothea whose story we know. (Finale)

After the last cruel breakdown and devastation of Anna's imagination and sense of self, and the appropriate but chilling dismissal of Vronsky to war, Levin remains to assert an affirmative religious and social vision, but it is a qualified vision. His expectation of an exalted communication of life's meaning to his wife, and a transformed existence, is diminished by domestic reality, Kitty raising the question of furniture in a guestroom — 'See if they've put the new washstand in' — to take us from the heights to the quotidian world. Levin and Tolstoy, like Dorothea and George Eliot before them, interrogate and qualify, but articulate a romantic meliorism, while Fontane moves, understandably — at the *fin de siècle* — to Effi's stronger sense of reality, which speaks for his radical discontents. In spite of her consumption — a perfect metaphor for the wasted life — her independence, quietism, matter-of-factness, stoicism, self-assertion, her miniature delights and makeshift constructions, make it an exhilarating novel, as she tolerates and accepts her own life and death, and this satisfactory and unsatisfactory earth, the very world in which we have to live, while actively, articulately questioning its limits and our dissatisfactions.

Chapter Six

Mr Dagley's Midnight Darkness: Uncovering the German Connection in George Eliot's Fiction

Nancy Cervetti

In a letter to Sara Sophia Hennell in 1849, Eliot explained how reading other writers helped her to make 'new combinations':

> I wish you thoroughly to understand that the writers who have most profoundly influenced me [...] are not in the least oracles to me. It is just possible that I may not embrace one of their opinions, that I may wish my life to be shaped quite differently from theirs. For instance it would signify nothing to me if a very wise person were to stun me with proofs that Rousseau's views [...] are miserably erroneous [...]. It is simply that the rushing mighty wind of his inspiration [...] the fire of his genius has so fused together old thoughts and prejudices that I have been ready to make new combinations. [1]

Distancing herself from any particular writer, Eliot understood the possibility of reshaping and recombining past and present discourses. In her fiction she transposed diverse philosophic systems of thought. The medium of her intellect blended narration, dialogue, philosophy, and irony into novels where she not only represented but also challenged conventional attitudes regarding gender, race, and class.

We often discuss Eliot in relation to other writers, to Milton, Spinoza, Walter Scott, Auguste Comte or Wordsworth, for example. Bernard Semmel in *George Eliot and The Politics of National Inheritance* narrates Eliot's intellectual biography as though she embraced one belief system after another – first, Evangelical Calvinism, then freethinking followed by determinist phrenology, then Comtean Positivism followed by Feuerbachian humanism,

---

[1] *The George Eliot Letters,* ed. by Gordon S. Haight, 9 vols (New Haven: Yale University Press, 1954-78), I, 227-8. Further references to the *Letters* are given in the text.

and finally, the traditional politics of inheritance of Burke and the conservatives.[2] Semmel evokes an either/or paradigm here, but my general approach differs. Rather than the fragmented either/or paradigm, I prefer a fluid both/and paradigm, a process of selecting and fusing from a variety of sources. This essay examines the German influence on Eliot's thinking and writing, especially that of Ludwig Feuerbach and David Strauss, and the subsequent common ground Eliot may have shared with Karl Marx. Yet, it is necessary to keep in mind that in terms of influence, no one influence dominated her thought.

Eliot did considerable amounts of reading in German higher criticism and philosophy. She translated Strauss's *Life of Jesus, Critically Examined* in 1844-46 and Feuerbach's *The Essence of Christianity* in 1853-54. In 1854 she left for Germany with George Henry Lewes. A sizable portion of the George Eliot-George Henry Lewes Library (approximately 2,400 items) is housed at Dr Williams's Library in London. Around twenty-five percent of these titles are in German, and William Baker writes that the books illustrate their 'preference for and immersion in Continental and especially German thought'.[3] From these various experiences in reading, translating, research, and travel, Eliot assimilated the key concerns of contemporary German intellectual activity.

In 1835 Strauss published his *Life of Jesus, Critically Examined,* one of the century's most important texts. Horton Harris writes that nineteenth-century theology was split in two by its publication, and that Strauss became a notorious celebrity overnight, everywhere regarded as the arch-fiend of the true Christian faith.[4] A detailed scientific inquiry into the historicity of the Gospels, *The Life of Jesus* gave shape to the discipline of biblical criticism, and through its influence on the left-wing Hegelians and Marx, it altered the course of European and world history. Harris explains that Strauss 'remorselessly exhibited the discrepancies, contradictions and mistakes in the Gospel narratives and made the supernatural explanations appear weak and untenable. The [...] rationalistic interpretation fared even worse'.[5] Called

---

[2] Bernard Semmel, *George Eliot and The Politics of National Inheritance* (New York: Oxford University Press, 1994).

[3] William Baker, *The George Eliot – George Henry Lewes Library: An Annotated Catalogue of Their Books at Dr. Williams's Library* (London and New York: Garland Press, 1977), p. xxviii.

[4] Horton Harris, *David Friedrich Strauss and His Theology* (Cambridge: Cambridge University Press, 1973), p. 41.

[5] Harris, p. 42.

antisocial, immoral, heretical and cynical Strauss's work and was seen as a serious threat to the existing political order. According to Marilyn Massey, conservatives thought that such biblical criticism made way for political criticism and opposed a principle that allowed every objection against a system to be printed and made public. This theological quarrel over the relation of human reason to the Gospels was also a political quarrel over freedom of expression and freedom of the press.[6]

Throughout the work Strauss's serious tone is sometimes marked by satire, sometimes biting satire, and was thus criticized as irreverent. Irony is the text's dominant rhythm. Inverting what had been considered reality, Strauss argued that what had appeared to be historical truth, was, in fact, a product of human consciousness. He unmasked the activity of the religious consciousness of Jesus's age without substituting a 'real' history of Jesus; thus, 'the unmasking of the activity of collective consciousness as the subject of the study was itself the act of recovering the substantial'.[7] Yet, disproving the historicity of the evangelical narratives was not new; Strauss's real contribution was his theory that events and acts recorded in the Gospels were meant to glorify Jesus and were deduced from the Old Testament, thus fulfilling the Old Testament prediction and descriptions of a Messiah.

The Life of Jesus begins by explaining the mythical principle informing the entire text, followed by three sections discussing in great detail the birth and childhood of Jesus, his public ministry, and his passion, death and resurrection. Presenting three possible interpretations of each event in Jesus's life — the supernatural, the rationalistic, and, finally, his own mythical interpretation — Strauss relinquishes the historical reality of the sacred narratives in order to preserve an absolute inherent truth regarding the real existence of spirit. Strauss explains that in myth, the source of inspiration is not immediate divine agency, but the spirit of a people or community, and, thus, the Christ of the Gospels is a product of that particular historical period.

Understanding this change in focus from Jesus to the community can free readers from submission to a past which exalted individual and past consciousness to a recognition of the human potential for agency in the present. Massey comments, 'the Young Germans, and many of the left-wing Hegelians, including Marx, had sought literary forms to express visions of a democratic society and to effect change. *The Life of Jesus* gave them such a

---

[6] Marilyn Chapin Massey, *Christ Unmasked: The Meanings of 'The Life of Jesus' in German Politics* (Chapel Hill: University of North Carolina Press, 1983), p. 47.

[7] Massey, p. 77.

form in theology'.[8] Because belief in the orthodox Christ and support for the hereditary monarchy were held to be intertwined, herein lies the threatening nature of Strauss's text — common people rather than the exalted individual leader create meaning and interpret history. In this radical democracy, humanity takes the place of Christ; the true Christ is the human species. For Strauss, humanity is the proper subject to the predicates which the Church assigns to Christ.

For Eliot, Strauss's ideas concerning the divinity of Jesus had been thoroughly anticipated by her reading of Charles Hennell's *Inquiry Concerning the Origin of Christianity* and made little further change in her views. Because of Strauss's shift from the individual to the group, however, his influence emerges in the problematic nature of hereditary wealth and power as seen in the Donnithornes in *Adam Bede,* for example, and the Cass family in *Silas Marner,* Mr Brooke in *Middlemarch,* and Grandcourt in *Daniel Deronda.* Rather than the aristocrats, middle to lower-class characters like Adam Bede and Felix Holt and marginalized characters like Ladislaw and Daniel Deronda grow and develop through the narratives to assume positions of power in the end. In 1868 a writer for *The Daily News* commented on Eliot's characters: 'No one in our day has given more adequate expression to the sentiments of persons who, though born in a lowly station and playing their part therein with cheerfulness and success, are yet endowed with the qualities which suffice for occupying more prominent places on the world stage'.[9] In addition to this class consciousness, the notion that 'Jesus' was a product of a historical community both those Old Testament writers who predicted his coming and the disciples who fulfilled the prediction — reveals the importance and the connectedness of individuals, the human web, in creating history and culture. Herein lies one source of Eliot's emphasis on sympathy, duty, and community. Actions, no matter how insignificant they appear, affect others and shape the future. In 1853 Eliot wrote, 'I begin to feel for other people's wants and sorrows a little more than I used to do. Heaven help us! said the old religions; the new one, from its very lack of that faith, will teach us all the more to help one another' (*Letters*, II, 82). Acquiring a social consciousness which includes understanding and appreciation of others becomes one of the most important aspects of human development.

Like Strauss's *Life of Jesus,* Feuerbach's work *The Essence of Christianity* was viewed as subversive, heretical, and dangerous. The author was

---

8 Massey, pp. 78-9.
9 Review of Felix Holt, *Daily News*, 3 January 1868, p. 4.

condemned by the majority of his contemporaries, and the work's 'inopportuneness had the effect, if not of sending his own skin off to market, at least of sacrificing his academic "career" immediately and irrevocably'.[10] In the Preface Feuerbach wrote, 'Briefly, the "Idea" is to me only faith in the historical future [...] it has for me only a political and moral significance; for in the sphere of strictly theoretical philosophy, I attach myself, in direct opposition to the Hegelian philosophy, only to *realism,* to materialism [...] ' [original emphasis] (xxxiv). Feuerbach saw and expressed the need to transfer the emphasis from some external Sovereign Being to human beings and their social interaction. Rather than emphasizing the spirit, he constructed humans as 'species-beings', that is social beings: 'Only where man has contact and friction with his fellow-man are wit and sagacity kindled; hence there is more wit in the town than in the country, more in great towns than in small ones. Only where man suns and warms himself in the proximity of man arise feeling and imagination' (83). This attitude toward the country is, obviously, not Romantic.

A passage in *Middlemarch* regarding Mr Brooke's visit to Mr Dagley, the tenant farmer at Freeman's End, demonstrates how Eliot translated Feuerbach's attitude toward the country into novelistic discourse:

> It is true that an observer, under that softening influence of the fine arts which makes other people's hardships picturesque, might have been delighted with this homestead called Freeman's End: the old house had dormer-windows in the dark-red roof, two of the chimneys were choked with ivy [...] the mouldering garden wall with hollyhocks peeping over it was a perfect study of highly-mingled subdued colour [...]. The pauper labourers [...] the scanty dairy of cows [...] the very pigs and white ducks seeming to wander about the uneven neglected yard as if in low spirits from feeding on a too meagre quality of rinsings—all these objects under the quiet light of a sky marbled with high clouds would have made a sort of picture which we have all paused over as a 'charming bit', [...]. Mr Dagley himself made a figure in the landscape, carrying a pitch-fork and wearing his milking-hat.
>
> Some who follow the narrative of his experience may wonder at the midnight darkness of Mr Dagley; but nothing was easier in those times than for an hereditary farmer of his grade to be ignorant, in spite somehow of having a rector in the twin parish who was a gentleman to the backbone, [...] a landlord who had gone into everything, especially fine art and social improvement, and all the lights of Middlemarch only three miles off [...]. Poor Dagley read a few verses sometimes on a Sunday evening, and the world was at least not darker to him than it had been before. Some things he knew thoroughly, namely, the slovenly habits of farming, and the awkwardness of weather, stock and crops, at Freeman's End—so called apparently by

---

[10] Ludwig Feuerbach, *The Essence of Christianity,* trans. by George Eliot, intro. by Karl Barth (New York: Harper & Row, 1957), p. xi. Further page references to this edition are given in the text.

way of sarcasm, to imply that a man was free to quit it if he chose, but that there was no earthly 'beyond' open to him. [11]

This passage disrupts the Romantic trope of the beauty and contentment of simple people in rural settings. Going behind the scenes, Eliot uses irony to criticize a tendency to make poverty and hardship picturesque, and she points out class injustices and the pathetic misfortune of being illiterate. This realistic treatment of poverty and exploitation in conjunction with Eliot's German translations invites a comparison with Marx.

Eliot was born in 1819 and died in 1880; Marx was born in 1818 and died in 1883. In August of 1849 Marx sailed for London and lived there for the remainder of his life. In 1851 Eliot also made London her permanent home. During most of 1851 and 1852 she lived at 142 Strand, the home and literary headquarters of John Chapman, editor of the *Westminster Review*, and in 1852 Eliot became assistant editor of the journal. Scientists like T. H. Huxley and Richard Owen, and political refugees like Mazzini and Ferdinand Freiligrath gravitated to 142 Strand, which was, according to Haight, London's 'centre of enlightened radicalism'.[12] Finally, Eliot and Marx are buried near one another in Highgate Cemetery. Such coincidence would be no great matter if it went no further, but the physical proximity suggests a more profound intellectual link.

From 1836-1838 Marx studied philosophy, law, history, English, and Italian at the University of Berlin. As one of the young Hegelian radicals, he also read and praised Feuerbach, and in 1845 Marx wrote his 'Theses on Feuerbach'. When Engels published the 'Theses' in 1888, he referred to it as 'the brilliant germ of the new world outlook'. It is this 'new world outlook', this materialism, immediately seized upon by Eliot and Marx that makes a comparison of the two significant, for both writers extracted from Feuerbach major premises regarding God and religion, identity, and social relations that would influence their later thinking.

Both Eliot and Marx referred to religion as the opiate of the people. In religion people can limit themselves to self-consciousness and self-discovery, devoted primarily to the goal of personal salvation. The positive value of earthly suffering is commonplace in religious rhetoric; that is, material deprivation enhances spiritual intensity. Feuerbach wrote that 'the most genuine Christians have declared that earthly good draws man away from

---

[11] George Eliot, *Middlemarch*, ed. by David R. Carroll (Oxford: Clarendon Press, 1986), pp. 384-8. All subsequent references in the text will be to this edition.

[12] Gordon S. Haight, *George Eliot: A Biography* (New York: Penguin Books, 1968), p. 99.

God, whereas adversity, suffering, afflictions lead him back to God, and hence alone are suited to Christians' (185); the 'more limited a man's sphere of vision, the less he knows of history, Nature, philosopy — the more ardently does he cling to his religion' (216); 'Faith is the opposite of love [...]. It was faith, not love, not reason, which invented Hell' (257); '*In faith there lies a malignant principle*' [original emphasis] (252); and 'Faith necessarily passes into hatred, hatred into persecution' (260). I provide these particular statements to display the intensity of Feuerbach's attack on Christianity. The English words are Eliot's, of course, carefully chosen during translation, and in 1854 she stated: 'With the ideas of Feuerbach I everywhere agree' (*Letters*, II, 153). From Feuerbach and Eliot's perspective, the negative consequences of religion vary from self-absorption and alienation to the justification of oppression and persecution of others.

In 1860 in a letter to the feminist activist Barbara Smith Bodichon, Eliot wrote:

> I have faith in the working-out of higher possibilities than the Catholic or any other church has presented, and those who have strength to wait and endure, are bound to accept no formula which their whole souls – their intellect as well as their emotions – do not embrace with entire reverence. The highest 'calling and election' is to *do without opium* and live through all our pain with conscious, clear-eyed endurance [original emphasis]. (*Letters*, III, 366)

In 1843 in his 'Contribution to the Critique of Hegel's *Philosophy of Right*: Introduction', Marx stated: 'Religion is the sigh of the oppressed creature, the sentiment of a heartless world, and the soul of soulless conditions. It is the *opium* of the people' [original emphasis].[13] Both Marx and Eliot used and emphasized the word 'opium' in describing the effects of religion, underscoring religion's thoughtless attraction and seduction and the nature of their objection.

Eliot foregrounds this theory of religion in *The Mill on the Floss* in the concluding chapter of Book Four where the text marks Maggie as thirteen. At this point Bob Jakins brings her Thomas à Kempis's *The Imitation of Christ*, and only nine pages later, the text marks Maggie as seventeen. In these nine pages, pages that mark the passing of four years in a book that lasts for a total of eleven years, the narrator moves quickly from the specifics of Maggie's static relationship with Thomas à Kempis to speak generally about the connection between religion, attending church services, and class structure –

---

[13] Friedrich Engels and Karl Marx, *The Marx–Engels Reader*, ed. by Robert C. Tucker (New York: W. W. Norton, 1978), p. 54. Further page references to this edition are given in the text.

to explain how religion can be misused. This social critique, this point of view toward wealt⊦ and religion, is one of several places in *The Mill* where Marx and Eliot's philosophies intersect. The *Mill's* narrator contends that,

> in writing the history of unfashionable families one is apt to fall into a tone of emphasis which is very far from being the tone of good society where [...] no subjects being eligible but such as can be touched with a light and graceful irony. But then, good society has its claret and its velvet-carpets, its dinner-engagements six weeks deep, its opera and its faëry ball-rooms; rides off its ennui on thoroughbred horses, lounges at the club, has to keep clear of crinoline vortices, gets its science done by Faraday, and its religion by the superior clergy who are to be met in the best houses: how should it have time or need for belief and emphasis? But good society, floated on gossamer wings of light irony, is of very expensive production; requiring nothing less than a wide and arduous national life condensed in deafening factories, cramping itself in mines, sweating at furnaces, grinding, hammering, weaving under more or less oppression of carbonic acid [...]. This wide national life is based entirely on emphasis – the emphasis of want [...]. Under such circumstances, there are many among its myriads of souls who have absolutely needed an emphatic belief [...]. Some have an emphatic belief in alcohol [...] but the rest require something that good society calls 'enthusiasm,' something that will present motives in an entire absence of high prizes [...].[14]

The class structure described in this passage consists of a few fashionable families living off the labor of the majority; the expensive reproduction of good society — the velvet carpets and thoroughbred horses — requires the exploitation of workers and their families. This relation between good society and poverty requires religious enthusiasm to reproduce itself — requires that selfless and resigned state of mind that looks to life after death as the reward for earthly suffering. Only in the institutionalized space of the Church do the two classes meet; the workers to take their opium and the bourgeoisie to valorize the taking. What the narrator calls religious 'enthusiasm' is the price tag of 'good society', a society that by definition requires hunger, ignorance, and sickness for great numbers of the population.

The relations of production between capitalist and worker also emerge at the level of plot and character between Mr Tulliver and Mr Wakem. The lawyer Mr Wakem is in the upper circles of St. Ogg's society, and he knows 'the stepping-stones that would carry him through very muddy bits of practice' (219). Wakem is a man 'who had made a large fortune, had a handsome house among the trees at Tofton, and decidedly the finest stock of port-wine in the neighbourhood' (219). When he attends church, he sits under 'the handsomest of mural monuments erected to the memory of his wife'

---

[14] George Eliot, *The Mill on the Floss*, ed. by Gordon S. Haight (Oxford: Clarendon Press, 1980), pp. 254-5. All subsequent references in the text will be to this edition.

(221). After Tulliver's bankruptcy, the narrator ironically explores Wakem's motivation in buying the mill: 'He had once had the pleasure of putting an old enemy of his into one of the St Ogg's alms-houses, to the rebuilding of which he had given a large subscription; and here was an opportunity of providing for another by making him his own servant' (220). Once Maggie's father loses the mill and works for a wage, an exploitative relation develops between him and Wakem, and it is this change — 'the unhappy-looking father [...] the childish, bewildered mother; the little sordid tasks that filled the hours' — that directly causes Maggie to embrace Thomas à Kempis. Thus, the narrative demonstrates how depression and despair can lead one to take up a position of religious renunciation and self-abasement. Feuerbach explains: 'Pleasure, joy, expands man; trouble, suffering, contracts and concentrates him; in suffering man denies the reality of the world; [...] he is absorbed in himself, in his own soul. The soul thus self-absorbed, self-concentrated, seeking satisfaction in itself alone, denying the world, idealistic in relation to the world [...] — this soul is God' (185-6). Feuerbach hoped to change heavenly citizens into world citizens, believers into thinkers, and theologians into anthropologists, and it is difficult to imagine two philosophies as contradistinct as those of Thomas à Kempis and Feuerbach.

As well as their common Feuerbachian inheritance, Eliot and Marx moved beyond Feuerbach's materialist humanism in similar ways to develop and share two additional ideas. Both Eliot and Marx stressed the danger of conceptualizing people in terms of self-consciousness, the individual ego, or the (innate) self, and again we see the influence of Strauss. In his polemic against the ego, 'On the Jewish Question', Marx stated:

> Human emancipation will only be complete when the real, individual man has absorbed into himself the abstract citizen; when as an individual man, in his everyday life, in his work, and in his relationships, he has become a *species-being;* and when he has recognized and organized his own powers [...]. as *social* powers so that he no longer separates this social power from himself as *political* power [original emphasis]. (46)

Several of Eliot's characters like Adam Bede, Dorothea, Ladislaw, Romola, Felix Holt, and Daniel Deronda enact this movement from 'self' to social being with varying degrees of success. The emphasis Eliot and Marx placed on the power of language to construct and reconstruct conventions of personality and experience was quite forward-looking, and in this attitude toward language and 'self', they had little in common with the traditional Victorian attempt to uncover and develop the buried self. In terms of both religion and egotism, Marx and Eliot asked that people look outside their personal dreams and desires, to historical, political, and social relations as cause and cure for pressing social problems.

Both Eliot and Marx embraced a materialist point of view. Marx and Engels tersely asked, 'Does it require deep intuition to comprehend that man's ideas, views, and conceptions, in one word, man's consciousness, changes with every change in the conditions of his material existence, in his social relations and in his social life?' (489). In 'The Natural History of German Life' (1856), Eliot stated that the 'selfish instincts are not subdued by the sight of buttercups, nor is integrity in the least established by that classic rural occupation, sheep-washing. To make men moral, something more is requisite than to turn them out to grass', and 'there is an analogous relation between the moral tendencies of men and the social conditions they have inherited'.[15] In these quotations we do not see an internal or transcendent spirit expressing itself through the world; rather, we see that 'spirit' is constructed by social and material conditions. To achieve 'good people' we must provide a decent, just and equal culture in which people can grow to goodness.

In her essay 'The Influence of Rationalism' (1865), Eliot focused on the ability to recognize these changes in material existence and thus consciousness. She defined 'external Reason' as a material force determined by physical science and causing the rejection of the miraculous. This 'cultivated Reason', this rationalism, is

> the sum of conditions resulting from the laws of material growth, from changes produced by great historical collisions shattering the structures of ages and making new highways for events and ideas [...]. No undiscovered laws accounting for small phenomena going forward under drawing-room tables are likely to affect the tremendous facts of the increase of population, the rejection of convicts by our colonies, the exhaustion of the soil by cotton plantations, which urge even upon the foolish certain questions, certain claims, certain views concerning the scheme of the world, that can never again be silenced. No séances at a guinea a head for the sake of being pinched by 'Mary Jane' can annihilate railways, steamships, and electric telegraphs, which are demonstrating the interdependence of all human interests [...].[16]

Human consciousness is an effect of specific historical conditions, and progress issues from the transformation of a historically produced self-consciousness to an historically produced social consciousness. Improved conditions result from an alteration in material existence, not from prayer, suffering, or sacrifice.

---

[15] *George Eliot: Selected Essays, Poems and Other Writings*, ed. by A. S. Byatt and Nicholas Warren (New York: Penguin Books, 1990), pp. 110 and 128.

[16] *Essays of George Eliot*, ed. by Thomas Pinney (London: Routledge and Kegan Paul, 1963), p. 402.

Marx and Engels summarized the upheaval in German thought — 'the putrescence of the absolute spirit' — in 'The German Ideology':

> The decomposition of the Hegelian philosophy, which began with Strauss, has developed into a universal ferment into which all the 'powers of the past' are swept [...]. Principles ousted one another, heroes of the mind overthrew each other with unheard-of rapidity, and in the three years 1842-45 more of the past was swept away in Germany than at other times in three centuries [...]. When the last spark of its life had failed, the various components [...] began to decompose, entered into *new combinations* and formed new substances [emphasis added]. (147)

Eliot's personal movement from Evangelical Calvinism to radical skepticism paralleled the general upheaval Marx and Engels outlined here. Her translation of Strauss and Feuerbach, her association with the *Westminster Review* and first years in London, and her decision to live with a married man constituted radical acts; yet, she experienced compelling but contradictory needs — to earn money, to participate in the literary practices and tradition of her time, and to speak her mind. Novelistic discourse, irony, and a male pseudonym were the vehicles through which she could negotiate her financial needs, philosophy, style of living, and ambition.

In describing Eliot's first years in London, A. S. Byatt writes that it was 'an immense increase of freedom and life. She mixed with others of her own kind — the Insurgents; like herself, they were not part of the established social and religious hierarchy, but were liberal, questioning, free-thinking, interested in reform' (xi). Eliot went on to achieve great fame during her life, and in 1880 after her death, Herbert Spencer and others sent telegrams and collected signatures to urge the Dean to admit her to Westminster Abbey. Spencer wrote T. H. Huxley for his support, and Huxley's response reveals an attitude then current:

> MY DEAR SPENCER - Your telegram which reached me on Friday evening caused me great perplexity [...]. Westminster Abbey is a Christian Church and not a Pantheon, and the Dean thereof is officially a Christian priest, and we ask him to bestow exceptional Christian honours by this burial in the Abbey. George Eliot is known not only as a great writer, but as a person whose life and opinions were in notorious antagonism to Christian practice in regard to marriage, and Christian theory in regard to dogma. How am I to tell the Dean that I think he ought to read over the body of a person who did not repent of what the Church considers mortal sin, a service not one solitary proposition in which she would have accepted for truth while she was alive?
>
> You tell me that Mrs. Cross wished for the funeral in the Abbey. While I desire to entertain the greatest respect for her wishes, I am very sorry to hear it [...]. One cannot eat one's cake and have it too. Those who elect to be free in thought and deed must not hanker after the rewards, if they are to be so called, which the world offers to those who put up with its fetters.

Thus, however I look at the proposal it seems to me to be a profound mistake, and I can have nothing to do with it. [17]

One could say that Huxley's tone and Eliot's exclusion from Westminster mark the extent of her radical life and views. However, the writer of *The Daily News* article quoted earlier calls the 'Address to Working Men, By Felix Holt' a 'Tory manifesto' and *Blackwood's Magazine* a magazine 'which has steadfastly adhered to the fortunes of the recognized leaders of the Tory party' (4). In what ways, then, was Eliot radical?

For the purposes of the discussion, I have described Eliot and Marx as Feuerbachian siblings, emphasizing a common background in German philosophy in order to spotlight a common philosophy sometimes neglected in critical approaches to Eliot's fiction, but there are important differences as well. As early as 1856, through her review of Riehl in 'The Natural History of German Life', Eliot argued for social policy founded on the study of people as they are, on 'the Natural History of social bodies' – rather than on abstract democratic and socialistic theories. The study of a fragment of society, the small group of Parisian proletarians or English factory-workers, cannot be the basis for a universal social policy except on paper and 'can never be carried into successful practice. The conditions of German society are altogether different from those of French, of English, or of Italian society'.[18] Also, later in her life, Eliot does not seem to be the same kind of radical Hale White described when he wrote to the *Athenaeum* in 1885 'to correct an impression which Mr. Cross's book may possibly produce'. White, who lived in Chapman's house while Eliot lived there, wrote:

> To put it very briefly, I think he [Cross] has made her too 'respectable'. She was really one of the most sceptical, unusual creatures I ever knew, and it was this side of her character which to me was the most attractive [...].
>
> I can see her now, with her hair over her shoulders, the easy chair half sideways to the fire, her feet over the arms, and a proof in her hands, in that dark room at the back of No. 142, and I confess I hardly recognize her in the pages of Mr. Cross's—on many accounts—most interesting volumes. I do hope that in some future edition, or in some future work, the salt and spice will be restored to the records of George Eliot's entirely unconventional life. As the matter now stands she has not had full justice done to her, and she has been removed from the class—the great and noble church, if I may so call it of the Insurgents, to one more genteel, but certainly not so interesting. (*Letters*, I, xv-xvi.)

---

[17] Leonard Huxley, *Life and Letters of Thomas Henry Huxley* (New York: D. Appleton, 1900), pp. 19-20.

[18] Byatt, pp. 129-30.

If the older Eliot were significantly different from this image of a young radical, the completion of *Felix Holt, The Radical* in 1866 may have heralded the change. This change may have been caused by a complex set of factors, including, perhaps, Eliot's special sense of her audience, pressures from her editor John Blackwood, social ostracism, financial success and fame, and 'marriage' to Lewes and the mothering of his sons. Two texts in particular capture the differences between Marx and Eliot, the 'Manifesto of the Communist Party' and the 'Address to Working Men, By Felix Holt'.

The Manifesto, commissioned by the Communist League, was first published in English in 1850 in the *Red Republican.* At Blackwood's request, just after the second Reform Bill in 1867, Eliot wrote the 'Address to Working Men', published as the opening article in *Maga* in 1868. Although eighteen years separate these texts, they seem to respond directly to one another, thus reflecting the dominant sides in the debate. Both texts identify and discuss the masses, class struggle, the unions, and the importance of history; however, they differ in terms of their ideas regarding consequences and solutions.

Whereas Marx and Engels state that the 'ruling ideas of each age have ever been the ideas of its ruling class' and 'Communism abolished eternal truths, it abolishes all religion, and all morality, instead of constituting them on a new basis; it therefore acts in contradiction to all past historical experience' (489), Felix states,

> But it would be fool's work to batter down a pump only because a better might be made, when you had no machinery ready for a new one: it be wicked work, if villages lost their crops by it. Now the only safe way [...] is not by any attempt to do away directly with the actually existing class distinctions and advantages, as if everybody could have the same sort of work, or lead the same sort of life (which none of my hearers are stupid enough to suppose), but by the turning of Class Interests into Class Functions or duties.[19]

Felix's attitude is what Marx and Engels would describe as conservative or bourgeois socialism:

> The Socialistic bourgeois want all the advantages of modern social conditions without the struggles and dangers necessarily resulting therefrom. They desire the existing state of society minus its revolutionary and disintegrating elements [...]. In requiring the proletariat to carry out such a system [...] it but requires in reality, that the proletariat should remain within the bounds of existing society, but should cast away all its hateful ideas concerning the bourgeoisie. (496)

---

[19] *Essays,* p. 421.

For Felix, the need to cast away anger rests on the need to preserve 'the common estate of society', what he calls 'that treasure of knowledge, science, poetry [...]. This is something distinct from the indulgences of luxury and the pursuit of vain finery; and one of the hardships in the lot of working men is that they have been for the most part shut out from sharing in this treasure' (425). This exclusion is the tragedy of Mr Dagley's darkness – his exclusion, except for those few Biblical verses on Sunday, from participating in the give-and-take of culture and the construction of history.

But, Marx and Engels seem to respond: 'That culture, the loss of which he laments, is, for the enormous majority, a mere training to act as a machine', an opportunity to 'sell themselves piece-meal', to become 'an appendage of the machine', 'slaves of the bourgeois class' (478-9), and, finally, the 'proletarians have nothing to lose but their chains. They have a world to win' (500). In contrast to this call for revolutionary action, Felix calls for reform born of social responsibility and education.

Eliot's family, according to Haight, 'would have been surprised to know how thoroughly conservative Marian had become. The revolutionary sentiments of those years in the Strand were gone forever'.[20] Still, I am uncomfortable with charting Eliot's movement as a linear movement from radical to conservative. In her essay 'Margaret Fuller and Mary Wollstonecraft' Eliot objected to an essentialist approach to women's nature, writing that 'some of the best things she [Fuller] says are on the folly of absolute definitions of woman's nature and absolute demarcations of woman's mission. "Nature", she says, "seems to delight in varying the arrangements, as if to show that she will be fettered by no rule; and we must admit the same varieties that she admits" '.[21] Eliot will be fettered by no labels. In her subsequent writing she transposed and orchestrated multiple and diverse ideologies into novelistic discourse where conflicting social and political voices speak and respond to one another. Subverting the very essence of labels like 'conservative', 'radical', 'wife', 'mother', and 'writer', Eliot seemed to delight in varying the arrangements as she struggled to disrupt and expand the effects of discourse and broaden participation in culture and the possibilities of experience.

---

[20] Haight, *George Eliot*, p. 395.
[21] Byatt, p. 335.

Chapter Seven

George Eliot and the Germanic 'Musical Magus'

Delia da Sousa Correa

The 'musical Magus' who so suddenly widens the horizons around Gwendolen's 'small musical performance' in *Daniel Deronda* is, of course, Julius Klesmer. Associations between Eliot's account of Klesmer and German Romantic literature suggest ways of connecting some of the very disparate critical responses which his portrayal has provoked. Comments on Klesmer range from seeing him as an unimpeachable manifestation of serious European culture, guardian of the privileged discourse of music, to noting how strange a figure he is and how he forms part of the rather sinister coercive patterning through which Deronda and Grandcourt double one another in their relation to the novel's heroine. I believe that Klesmer fits not either, but both these extremes.

The portrayal of Eliot's most important musician figure is without doubt crucial to the novel's scrutiny of aesthetic and moral value. A 'felicitous combination of the German, the Sclave, and the Semite', Klesmer provides, as Alexander Welsh has pointed out, 'a persistent reminder of English cultural impoverishment among the classes who can afford better'.[1] Simultaneously, he is a slightly uncanny and disturbing musical maestro in a novel where music's association with extremes of sympathetic communication, coincidence and insight forms part of its patently experimental quality, disturbing notions of 'realism'.

In this paper, I will outline what might be termed the 'pedigree' for Klesmer's stature as the representative of Germanic, musical culture. I will

---

[1] George Eliot, *Daniel Deronda* [1876], ed. by Graham Handley (Oxford: Clarendon Press, 1984) p. 41. Subsequent references to this edition are given in the text. Alexander Welsh, *George Eliot and Blackmail* (Cambridge, Massachusetts and London: Harvard University Press, 1985), p. 300.

then go on to draw a literary parallel with E. T. A. Hoffmann's creations and explore the analogies between our experience of Klesmer as uncanny, and the German romantic tradition.

The figure of Klesmer indicates the significance of allusions to music within *Daniel Deronda* where Eliot explores music as both aspect and symbol of cultural life. Music plays a role in her contrast of English with European (particularly German) and Jewish culture. Through her analysis of the status of music and of the professional musician, Eliot probes the interaction of social, commercial and artistic activity in English society, proposing alternative standards of evaluation for individual and national achievement.

In her essay on Heine, Eliot extolled the cultural achievements of Germany as the country which:

> has fought the hardest fight for freedom of thought, has produced the grandest inventions, has made magnificent contributions to science, has given us some of the divinest poetry, and quite the divinest music in the world.[2]

If we look at Klesmer as an ambassador for serious Germanic culture, we find that Eliot presents him both as a true artist and a heroic personality. A comparison with Mendelssohn indicates that Klesmer represents the music of the German Romantic school (222). Mendelssohn's reputation in Britain was extremely high. He was admired as much for his moral integrity as for his music.[3] Eliot had read his letters in 1870 and praised 'the sense they give of

---

[2] Eliot, 'German Wit: Heinrich Heine', [*Westminster Review*, 65 (1856), 1-33] reprinted in *Essays of George Eliot*, ed. by Thomas Pinney (London: Routledge and Kegan Paul, 1963), pp. 222-3.

[3] The posthumous adulation of Mendelssohn features in Elizabeth Sara Sheppard's novel of 1853, *Charles Auchester*. Her hero is a romanticised portrait of the composer. The novel, extolled by Disraeli and highly successful at the time, diametrically opposes music to all commercial and theatrical entertainment. Disraeli wrote to Sheppard of his conviction that 'No greater book will ever be written upon music', quoted by Nicholas Temperley, Introduction to *The Romantic Age*, Vol. V of *The Athlone History of Music in Britain*, ed. by Temperley (1981), p. 22. Temperley discusses *Charles Auchester* (a useful index of 'middle class attitudes to art music') alongside his account of the sterilising effect which Mendelssohn's music had on British composition when it was approached with a 'middle class romanticised view of the artist' as 'hermetically sealed from society'; he cites Parry as a composer initially influenced by his reading of the novel, although eventually able to find it 'foolish and mistaken' and to develop his own musical aspirations differently, *The Romantic Age*, pp. 22-3; for further comments on the appreciation of Mendelssohn in Britain see also pp. 306, 403, 419, 502.

communion with an eminently pure, refined nature, with the most rigourous conscience in art'.[4] A performer, composer and thinker, Klesmer is:

> as versatile and fascinating as a young Ulysses on a sufficient acquaintance—one whom nature seemed to have first made generously and then to have added music as a dominant power using all the abundant rest, and, as in Mendelssohn, finding expression for itself not only in the highest finish of execution, but in that fervour of creative work and theoretic belief which pierces the whole future of a life with the light of congruous, devoted purpose. (222)

Klesmer's elevated Germanic status is explicitly pitted against superficial Italianate music, as his response to Gwendolen's singing of an aria by Bellini makes clear. His list of the qualities lacking in the music of Bellini reads like a manifesto of German Romanticism: 'deep, mysterious passion', 'conflict', a 'sense of the universal' (43). It evokes the passion, turbulence and sense of the infinite praised in E.T.A. Hoffmann's account of Beethoven's music.[5]

> [T]hat music which you sing [Klesmer proclaims] is beneath you. It is a form of melody which expresses a puerile state of culture—a dandling, canting, see-saw kind of stuff—the passion and thought of people without any breadth of horizon. There is a sort of self-satisfied folly about every phrase of such melody: no cries of deep, mysterious passion—no conflict—no sense of the universal. It makes men small as they listen to it. Sing now something larger. And I shall see. (42-3)

Gwendolen with her *bel canto* Bellini, like Lush, with his penchant for Meyerbeer and for the *opera buffa*, and like the so-called 'jealous baritone' Grandcourt (676), takes part in a lesser social opera against which Klesmer assumes heroic Germanic stature.

'We shall so like to renew our acquaintance with Klesmer whom we met at Weimar in '54!' wrote G.H. Lewes at the prospect of their dining with Anton Rubinstein. This was in 1876, whilst Eliot was finishing *Daniel Deronda*.[6] Numerous German musicians are alluded to in her portrait of Klesmer. The plethora of possible models emphasizes how important is the figure of the Central-European musician as a medium of German Romantic aesthetics within Eliot's negotiation of musical and cultural value. Rubinstein was

---

[4] Eliot to the Hon. Mrs Robert Lytton, 8 July, 1870, *The George Eliot Letters*, ed. by Gordon S. Haight, 9 vols (New Haven and London: Yale University Press, 1954-78), V, 107.

[5] E. T. A. Hoffmann, 'Beethoven's Instrumentalmusik': *Poetische Werke*, 12 vols (Berlin, 1957), I, 46; trans. in R. Murray Schafer, *E. T. A. Hoffmann and Music* (Toronto and Buffalo, 1975), pp. 84-85; see also *E. T. A. Hoffmann's Musical Writings: Kreisleriana, The Poet and the Composer, Music Criticism*, ed. by David Charlton and trans. by Martyn Clarke (Cambridge: Cambridge University Press, 1989), pp. 97-8.

[6] George Henry Lewes to Mrs F. Lehmann [8 May, 1876] *Letters*, IX, 176-7.

Jewish, Slav (Russian), and German by name.[7]   Eliot was originally introduced to him by Liszt and she also describes Klesmer as 'not yet a Liszt' (220).   Klesmer, whilst broadly Germanic, is, as was Liszt, a thoroughly cosmopolitan figure.[8]   Like Liszt also, whose playing enraptured Eliot, he performs his own compositions.   Eliot's journal records her response to Liszt's personality and musicianship:

> My great delight was to watch Liszt and observe the sweetness of his countenance, and his manners are in perfect harmony with it. [...]
> Then came the thing I had longed for—Liszt's playing. [...] For the first time in my life I beheld real inspiration—for the first time I heard the true tones of the piano. He played one of his own compositions—one of a series of religious *fantaisies*. There was nothing strange or excessive about his manner. His manipulation of the instrument was quiet and easy, and his face was simply grand.[9]

Certainly Klesmer's playing of his own 'fantasia' in *Daniel Deronda* is recognized by Gwendolen as embodying 'real inspiration'.   Still smarting from Klesmer's devastating criticism of her Bellini performance, Gwendolen, 'in spite of her wounded egoism, had fulness of nature enough to feel the power of this playing, and it gradually turned her inward sob of mortification into an excitement which lifted her for the moment into a desperate indifference about her own doings' (43).   Klesmer's fantasia *Freudvoll, Leidvoll, Gedankenvoll* is probably derived from a Liszt setting of Goethe (43).[10]   In his study of Liszt, Alan Walker comments:

---

[7] See Gordon S. Haight, *George Eliot: A Biography* (Oxford: Clarendon Press, 1968), pp. 489-90. Eliot met Rubinstein in Weimar in 1854 where he was preparing a production of his own opera *The Siberian Huntsman* and also presented several of Wagner's operas including those which Eliot heard; Haight, *George Eliot,* p. 156.

[8] This, together with his embodiment of a 'felicitous combination of the German, the Sclave, and the Semite' makes Klesmer a counterpart to Mordecai's vision of 'separateness with communication', Eliot, *Daniel Deronda,* p. 673.

[9] Eliot, *Journal,* 10 August, 1854, *Letters,* II, 170.

[10] Franz Liszt, 'Freudvoll und Leidvoll', (Goethe) song for mezzo-soprano and piano, (Raabe, 579) dedicated to A. Scheffer. It was first performed on 25 June, 1844 (published Vienna, 1847, revised version published 1860). See *Franz Liszts Musikalische Werke,* ed. by F. Busoni, P. Raabe et al. (Leipzig, 1907-36), VII, 1, 110-17 (original plus additional setting) and VII, 2, 66-7 (revised version). Beethoven also wrote a setting for soprano and orchestra as part of his incidental music to *Egmont* (Opus 84). 'Freudvoll und Leidvoll' was composed 1809-10 and first performed on 15 June 1810 (published 1810, 1812); see *Musik zu Goethes Trauerspiel 'Egmont'* in *Ludwig van Beethovens Werke* (Leipzig, 1862-1888), Serie 2, 12, pp. 50-52. Eliot could have had either or both these settings in mind (or neither Liszt nor Beethoven, but only Goethe, although this seems unlikely as she went to considerable trouble over selecting musical references). Klesmer is explicitly associated with Liszt, whom Eliot heard playing 'one of his own compositions – one of a series of religious *fantaisies*'; see

simply to read the words that Eliot puts into the mouth of Klesmer is surely enough. His ideas on talent, genius, musicality, and priest-like devotion to work are basically the ideas of Liszt, and Eliot had opportunity enough to hear them expounded many times by him during her nine-week stay in Weimar.[11]

Klesmer's scornful views on bourgeois misapprehensions about artistic talent 'could not have been better phrased by Liszt himself' states Walker: 'indeed, it is not impossible that George Eliot took them down from Liszt *verbatim*'.[12]

Both Liszt and Rubinstein were promoting Wagner's works during Eliot's time in Weimar. Representative of advanced musical culture, Klesmer is clearly also to be associated with Wagner's 'music of the future'(93).[13]

Eliot, *Daniel Deronda* [1876], ed. by Graham Handley (Oxford: Clarendon Press, 1984), p. 220; *Journal*, 10 August 1854, in *Letters*, II, 170. However, Eliot was also inordinately fond of Beethoven. Beethoven's music offered a Wordsworthian 'speech of men' unlike the difficulties of Wagner; see Eliot, *Essays*, p. 103. Music by Beethoven features frequently in the letter and journal records of concerts which the Leweses attended. In *Daniel Deronda*, Mirah sings three Beethoven songs; see Eliot, *Daniel Deronda*, pp. 344, 524, 720. Beethoven also featured in the repertoire of Rubinstein, another 'original' for Klesmer, when Eliot heard him play in 1876; see G. H. Lewes, *Diary*, 15 May, 1876, in Eliot, *Letters*, VI, 251, n. 3.

The original scoring of either Liszt's or Beethoven's 'Freudvoll und Leidvoll' settings does not necessarily serve as an indicator of which Eliot had in mind since both piano versions of songs and piano reductions of orchestral scores were common. (The British Library holds several copies of Beethoven's *Egmont* setting arranged for piano accompaniment and dating from 1812 onwards.) The potential double reference serves of course to add extra emphasis to Klesmer's credentials as the representative of German Romanticism.

[11] Alan Walker, *Franz Liszt*, 2 vols (London: Faber and Faber, 1989), II, *The Weimar Years 1848-1861*, p. 250, n. 74.

[12] Walker, *Franz Liszt*, II, 250, n. 74. Klesmer's rebuttal of the businessman Bult, to which Walker refers, is quoted below. To the extent which Klesmer is a portrayal of Liszt, he forms a counter-balance to the depiction of Liszt in Marie d'Agoult's novel *Nélida* (1845), where Liszt's former lover pilloried him in the guise of the painter Guermann, see Walker, I, *The Virtuoso Years: 1811-1847*, pp. 396-401. Liszt used his transformation into a painter to joke that d'Agoult was really criticising her current admirer, the painter Lehmann — a joke which he repeated to Eliot when *Nélida* was discussed during her visit to Weimar: Eliot, *Journal*, Weimar, 10 August, 1854, *Letters*, II, 169. Alan Walker points out striking similarities between *Nélida* and George Sand's novel *Lucrezia Floriani* (1846) which satirises Chopin: Walker, I, 401, n. 47. It is therefore possible to see in Klesmer some reference to a tradition of *romans à clef* based on real musical characters (including of course Elizabeth Sheppard's novel *Charles Auchester*, see note 3 above).

[13] Klesmer's criticism of Bellini is implicitly placed in the context of the battle 'between the declamatory and melodic schools of music' which Eliot had discussed in 1854 in her early essay about Wagner's music; see Eliot, 'Liszt, Wagner, and Weimar', [*Fraser's Magazine*, 52 (1855), 48-62] reprinted in *Essays*, pp. 96-122, p. 100.

Eliot's interest in evolutionary development endorsed Wagner's progressive organicist aesthetic.[14]   Klesmer's condemnation of Gwendolen's choice of Bellini reiterates the correlation between states of musical and social evolution alluded to in Eliot's 1855 essay 'Liszt, Wagner and Weimar'.[15]

The puerile state of development which enjoys Bellini's music is satirised further in Gwendolen's conversation with an admirer whose only response to Klesmer is to deride his eccentric appearance, dismissing his judgement of Gwendolen's singing with: '[i]t is not addressed to the ears of the future, I suppose.   I'm glad of that: it suits mine' (93).   (This, by the way, is a caricature of Eliot's own self-conscious resistance to Wagner's music as expressed in *Liszt, Wagner, and Weimar*, where she suggests that her musical taste was insufficiently evolved for her to appreciate his 'music of the future' as much as she admired his ideas.[16]) '[Y]oung Clintock' prefers Gwendolen's singing to Klesmer's 'tip-top playing' (43).   '[D]epend upon it' he assures her, 'croquet is the game of the future'.   'I shall study croquet to-morrow' replies the self-mocking Gwendolen, 'I shall take to it instead of singing' (44).

Klesmer's illustrious heritage lends weight to his criticism of English culture.   In his advice to Gwendolen when she considers a professional musical or stage career, he combines eulogy of the artistic vocation with blistering criticism of English amateurism.   Inexacting standards of education and dedication lead Gwendolen to imagine that because her talents are admired from 'the drawing-room *standpunkt*' (237), she can don the life of an artist 'as a livery' (236).

Condemning society's poor estimation of art and the artist, Klesmer makes a Romantic claim to equal status with legislators.   He establishes himself as the representative of cultural standards in the broadest sense whilst also endorsing the aesthetic hierarchy central to German Romanticism, in which music occupies the highest pinnacle.   Responding to a comment from Bult, a

---

[14] Eliot, *Essays*, pp. 96-122.

[15] See Eliot, *Essays*, pp. 101-4. Nonetheless, Eliot herself did not entirely despise Bellini and enjoyed attending a number of his operas, see Eliot to Sara Sophia Hennell, 30 April 1847, *Letters*, I, 233; Eliot to Cara and Charles Bray, 24 May 1852, *Letters*, II, 28; Lewes to Charles Lee Lewes, [26 April, 1871], *Letters*, V, 144. In 'Liszt, Wagner, and Weimar' Eliot appeals to the concept of evolution to explain the nature of her own musical taste, suggesting that her personal stage of development means that she requires music to be melodic, *Essays*, p. 103.

[16] Eliot, *Essays*, pp. 102-3.

successful man of business and politics, that he appears to have 'too much talent to be a mere musician', Klesmer retorts:

> No man has too much talent to be a musician. Most men have too little. A creative artist is no more a mere musician than a great statesman is a mere politician. We are not ingenious puppets, sir, who live in a box and look out on the world only when it is gaping for amusement. We help to rule the nations and make the age as much as any other public men. We count ourselves on level benches with legislators. And a man who speaks effectively through music is compelled to something more difficult than parliamentary eloquence. (224)

Mr Bult, has 'hardly regarded [Klesmer] in the light of a serious human being who ought to have a vote' until surprised by his eloquence against 'the lack of idealism in English politics' (223). Klesmer also objects to commodification of art and the artist. A suitor of Catherine Arrowpoint's, Bult 'did not mind Miss Arrowpoint's addiction to music any more than her probable expenses in antique lace' (223).[17]

Like E.T.A. Hoffmann's persecuted Kapellmeister Johannes Kreisler, Eliot's chimingly named Julius Klesmer performs amid uncomprehending Philistines.[18] After suffering Gwendolen's lamentable singing, Klesmer plays his own set of variations (43). Kreisler is 'content to play the piano for hours, elaborating the most curious themes'.[19] In the story 'Kapellmeister Johannes Kreisler's Musical Sorrows', he plays Bach's Goldberg variations adding his own inspired improvisation. This follows an occasion when the talentless daughters of his patrons have been persuaded to sing: 'although she often sang a quarter of a tone flatter than the piano', he writes of one of them, 'she had such a pretty little face and such rosy lips that in the end one could put up with it'.[20] Like Klesmer in Catherine Arrowpoint, Kreisler finds only one truly musical exception amongst the young women to make society bearable.

---

[17] Cf. Eliot, *Middlemarch* [1871-2], ed. by David Carroll (Oxford: Clarendon Press, 1986), p. 567: 'it was clearly worthwhile for Rosamond to take pains with her music and the careful selection of her lace'; see also Eliot's definition of a philistine critic being one who persistently adopts a lower scale of reference than that required by the work under scrutiny ('the personification of the spirit which judges everything from a lower point of view than the subject demands'), Gisela Argyle, *German Elements in The Fiction of George Eliot, Gissing and Meredith*, (Frankfurt am Main, Berne, Las Vegas: Lang, 1979), p. 72.

[18] Shirley Frank Levenson points out that the name means 'musician' in Yiddish, 'The Use of Music in *Daniel Deronda*', *Nineteenth Century Fiction*, 24 (1969), 317. It seems to have been a term of reasonably wide currency to describe groups of Jewish musicians.

[19] Hoffmann, *Kreisleriana* I, *Poetische Werke*, I, 26; trans. by Charlton, p. 80; see also Schafer, p. 114.

[20] Hoffmann, 'Johannes Kreislers des Kapellmeisters Musikalische Leiden', *Poetische Werke*, I, 29-30; trans. by Schafer, p. 122; see also Charlton, p. 82.

I would like to suggest Kreisler as a possible literary forbear of Klesmer. Not only was Eliot familiar with Hoffmann's work,[21] but Hoffmann's stories, many of them translated by Carlyle, enjoyed considerable popularity in Britain. There are numerous parallels between Julius Klesmer and Johannes Kreisler apart from their shared initials and the assonance of their names. More general affinities with elements in Hoffmann's writing also exist: Hoffmann's fiction dwelt on the elevation of the artist and aimed merciless satire against the Bourgeoisie, their amateurism and their failure to distinguish artistic and commercial value. Moreover, as Freud noted in his 1919 essay on 'Das Unheimliche', 'Hoffmann is the unrivalled master of the uncanny in literature'.[22] Reading Eliot's novel alongside Hoffmann's fiction throws light on some of the more uncanny aspects of her musical maestro in a novel where music evokes strange coincidence and insight.

Today, Hoffmann's Kapellmeister Kreisler is probably most frequently associated with Schumann's *Kreisleriana* piano cycle. According to Murray Schafer, Kreisler rates as 'the most influential fictional hero of his time' — he 'informed the world of the artist's dreams, torments and hopes'.[23] Brahms later styled himself 'Johannes Kreisler Jnr'. Kreisler became symbolic of the spirit of music. He is, Schafer notes, the 'archetype of a new social order in which musicians are distinguished from dilettantes and true musicians disinherited from society'.[24] Kreisler was created before the days when such universally worshipped musical heroes as Liszt or Mendelssohn were proclaimed. Nonetheless, there is an analogy between Hoffmann's account of Kreisler's idealist spirit clashing with German bourgeois society and Eliot's view of England in the 1870s.

Like his successor, Kreisler is given to public pronouncements on the state of musical culture: 'true Italian music has disappeared' he proclaims one day — a parallel of sorts to Klesmer's disparagement of Bellini.[25] Similarly proud and insolent in the face of bourgeois obtuseness, Kreisler's behaviour is

---

[21] A familiarity also indicated in *Middlemarch* where Eliot's comment about the perspective of 'Murr the cat' is surely an allusion to E. T. A. Hoffmann's novel *Kater Murr*, of which Kreisler is also the hero (the Clarendon Edition of *Middlemarch* [p. 36, n.m.] glosses 'Murr' as a 'Scots dialect form of purr'!).

[22] Sigmund Freud, 'The "Uncanny"', in *Art and Literature: Jensen's 'Gravida', Leonardo da Vinci and Other Works*, Vol. XIV of *The Pelican Freud Library*, ed. by Albert Dickenson (London, 1985), p. 355.

[23] Schafer, p. 119.

[24] Schafer, p. 119.

[25] Hoffmann, *Kreisleriana* I, *Poetische Werke*, I, 25; trans. by Schafer, p. 113; see also Charlton, p. 79.

always extravagant. When happy, 'roguish irony spice[s] his conversation'; at other times he is given to 'bizarre outbursts'.[26] 'What is it that rustles so miraculously, so strangely around me?' he exclaims above a chord of A flat major on the piano.[27] Confounding Bult, Klesmer's 'mysterious wind-like rush backwards and forwards on the piano' as he proclaims: 'I am the wandering Jew' seems an especially Kreisler-like antic (224).   Whatever echoes there may be of Eliot's grave account of Liszt in Klesmer's playing, a Hoffmanesque element has also crept into his characterisation.   One could hardly claim that 'There was nothing strange or excessive about [Klesmer's] manner'.[28]

Describing Klesmer's appearance, Eliot dwells on the incongruity of his hat (92).   Kreisler has been sighted wearing two hats on top of each other: a clear sign of madness.[29] Klesmer's physical appearance is at odds with the 'perfect nullity of face and perfect tailoring' of English gentlemen (92).   His animated speech and un-English melodramatic gestures disturb also.   One of the ways in which Klesmer is uncanny is simply that his manner and appearance disturbs what is familiar to those around him.   This uncanniness is integral to the challenges with which his art confronts them.

Whilst the brunt of authorial satire is aimed at the uncultured audience, both musicians are comic figures.   Klesmer's behaviour and appearance have an element of the grotesque which is central to Hoffmann's portrayal of Kreisler. Eliot does not shy away either from occasional gentle satire on Klesmer's lofty Romantic status (and the obfuscating tendencies of German thought in general) as when, having dismissed Bellini's degenerative melody, his own composition is described as: 'an extensive commentary on some melodic ideas not too grossly evident' (43).[30]

---

[26] Hoffmann, *Kreisleriana* I, *Poetische Werke*, I, 26; trans. by Schafer, p. 114; see also Charlton, p. 80.

[27] Hoffmann, 'Kreisler's Musikalisch-Poeticischer Klub', *Poetische Werke*, I, 353; trans. by Schafer, p. 146; see also Charlton, p. 132.

[28] See Haight, *George Eliot*, p. 156.   Eliot's account of Liszt's playing is quoted above.

[29] Hoffmann, *Kreisleriana* I, *Poetische Werke*, I, 26; trans. by Schafer, p. 114; see also Charlton, p. 80.

[30] Hoffmann's *Kreisleriana* describes Kreisler 'elaborating the most curious themes with elegantly contrapuntal devices and imitations and highly ingenious passage work': 'ideas not too grossly evident' perhaps? *Kreisleriana* I, *Poetische Werke*, I, 26; trans. by Charlton, p. 80; see also Schafer, p. 114.   Interestingly, Hoffmann's review of Beethoven's song settings for *Egmont* including of 'Freudvoll und Leidvoll' with which Klesmer's composition is associated (see note 10 above) criticises them as 'much too elaborate'; trans. by Charlton, pp.

Obviously, Klesmer is not as extreme a romantic portrait as is Hoffmann's Kapellmeister with his morbid hypersensitivity and incipient madness. Whereas Klesmer is 'one whom nature seemed to have first made generously and then to have added music as a dominant power' (222), the unhappy genius Kreisler appears, according to his friends, to be a failed experiment of nature.[31]   Eliot incorporates some of the enhanced stature of historical German musicians into her portrait of Klesmer. He seems a Kreisler figure appropriated into her more polemical narrative and given heroic stature and a considerable corrective power.

More significant even than these specific similarities between the musicians Kreisler and Klesmer is the way in which Eliot's portrayal of Klesmer's musical powers accords with some of the distinctive traits of Hoffmann's fiction more generally. For Klesmer has uncanny powers of perception and his effect on Gwendolen is that of a magician who can suddenly shift horizons. His mastery over the piano displays 'an imperious magic in his fingers that seemed to send a nerve-thrill through ivory key and wooden hammer and compel the strings to make a quivering lingering speech for him' (43). His influence over Gwendolen is both salutary and frightening, suggestive of mesmeric power. He is last glimpsed in Hans Meyrick's letter where he features as an eastern 'genius', showering Mirah with 'oriental gifts' and so completing his magician-like appearances in and disappearances from the text. (Kreisler, we are told, simply disappears one day without trace.)

Klesmer is one of a line of magnetic musical maestros running from Hoffmann's Kreisler to Du Maurier's Svengali — literary counterparts to the mythologisation of the powers of historical musicians such as Paganini and Liszt. Gisela Argyle has suggested that the name 'Klesmer' is intentionally rhymed with 'Mesmer' to convey the influence of Klesmer's judgement.[32] Certainly Klesmer's extraordinary powers of vision have special significance in a novel preoccupied with second sight and near telepathic powers of empathy. They make him reminiscent not merely of Kapellmeister Kreisler, but of a whole range of mesmeric effects and magnetic characters which

---

346, 348. The review, which Eliot is not known to have read, first appeared in the *Allgemeine Musikalische Zeitung*, XV: 21 (July 1813), 437-81.

[31] Hoffmann, *Kreisleriana* I, *Poetische Werke*, I, 25; trans. by Schafer, p. 113; see also Charlton, p. 79.

[32] Argyle refers specifically to Klesmer's unveiling of the philistinism of British culture. She connects this association with 'Mesmer' with a consequent rhyme: 'mésalliance' which exposes further 'philistine prejudices' when applied to the marriage of Klesmer and Catherine Arrowpoint; see Argyle, pp. 79-80.

populate Hoffmann's fiction including 'The Magnetiser', 'The Automaton' and 'The Uncanny Guest'. Hypnotic powers in Hoffmann's tales are signalled by piercing eyes or burning gaze. 'Fire' shows in Klesmer's glances, (92) and the effect of his eloquence is of 'fireworks accidentally ignited' (223).

Hoffmann's interest in mesmerism accompanied his obsessive pre-occupation with eyes and optical instruments, most famously in 'The Sandmann'. Klesmer's peculiar visionary powers are emphasized by the glinting spectacles (450) of 'that wide glancing personage, who saw everything and nothing by turns' (104). 'That young lady is musical, I see!' he asserts of Mab Meyrick, striking her as 'a dreadfully divining personage' and prompting her mother to conclude that '[h]e has magic spectacles and sees everything through them, depend upon it' (453, 455). Mirah agrees with Klesmer that it is better to sing 'vor den Wissenden'.[33] Clearly, Klesmer is 'knowing' in more senses than one (453).

Eliot's preoccupation with the potential lifting of normal barriers of perception gives her writing a particular kinship with that of Hoffmann despite obvious differences in their prose styles. This interest is most obviously manifest in 'The Lifted Veil', yet 'conceptually and rhetorically', as Nicholas Royle comments, it 'pervades and even dominates her work'.[34] 'Indications on claire-voyance witnessed by a competent observer are of thrilling interest and give me a restless desire to get at more extensive and satisfactory evidence,' she commented in 1852.[35] By the time of *Daniel Deronda*'s publication, a systematic study such as she advocated was about to take place. Among the Leweses' acquaintance was F.W.H. Myers, who was preparing to investigate the phenomena he christened 'telepathy', a term which largely came to replace what Eliot's contemporaries knew as 'sympathetic clairvoyance'.[36]

Music invariably features in Hoffmann's narratives as a powerful agent of enhanced apprehension. In *Daniel Deronda*, the 'deep, mysterious passion',

---

[33] Literally 'before those who know'.

[34] Nicholas Royle, *Telepathy and Literature* (Oxford: Blackwell, 1991), p. 86.

[35] Eliot to George Combe, 22 April 1852, *Letters*, VIII, 45.

[36] Accounts of research by Myers and his colleagues are presented in the *Proceedings of the Society for Psychical Research*, 5 vols (1882-1889); see also note 46 below. Eliot's literary experiments in *Daniel Deronda* preceded the experiments in telepathy and other psychical phenomena conducted by the Society for Psychical Research. However, both Myer's interest in psychical phenomena and that of Edmund Gurney, whom Eliot also knew, dated from the late 1870s. They attended spiritualist meetings but soon felt disenchanted with spiritualism as an appropriate subject of scientific investigation and turned their attention to the more promising phenomena of thought-transference and hypnotism.

'conflict ', and 'sense of the universal' attested by Klesmer prepare the reader to think of allusions to music as signalling a heightened level of perception (43). As Deronda rows on the Thames, singing the Gondolier's song from Rossini's *Otello*, he experiences a transcendent sense of identity with the surrounding landscape and a clairvoyant apprehension of Mirah (174). Later, Klesmer's playing opens a telepathic level of communication between Gwendolen and Deronda. The 'torrent-like confluences of bass and treble' (522) become emblematic of their fervent empathy: music not as a mere substitute for conversation but as Hoffmann describes it: 'a higher mode of expression than normal speech can provide'.[37]

The cumulative and combined influence of Klesmer's gaze and of his playing, along with the coincidence of visual and musical effects in Eliot's novel more generally, accords well with the synaesthetic identification, especially pronounced in Hoffmann's writing of visual and aural imagery. A synaesthetic coincidence of influences is often an especially potent 'lever' for effecting a transcendent plane of vision in his work. In 'The Golden Pot', the transition from ordinary vision to creative insight takes place as a combination of light and musical sound. A mellifluous blend of chiming bells, whispers, strange melodies and murmuring lulls the hero into a mesmerist trance in which he achieves poetic vision.[38] For Mordecai, leaning on a bridge, the river and oncoming boats are a symphony of blended sound and colour anticipating the moment when Deronda will row out of the haze, the embodiment of his proleptic visionary power.

By contrast with the beauty of this vision, Klesmer's uncanny powers can be frightening as well as prophetic, as when he turns Gwendolen's tableau of *The Winter's Tale* into a moment of authentic terror, dramatically proving his musical magicianship to be more than metaphorical. At Paulina's 'Music, awake her, strike! [...] [d]ear life redeems' the original Hermione.[39] Klesmer's 'thunderous chord' causes a panel in the room to fly open presenting Gwendolen with the terrifying apparition of a figure fleeing from a corpse, predictive of her future implication in Grandcourt's death (54).

---

[37] '[D]as Bedürfnis eines höhern Ausdrucksmittels, als die gewöhnliche Rede gewähren kann' (my translation); Hoffmann, 'Der Dichter und der Komponist', *Die Serapionsbrüder I*, *Werke*, V, 102. A translation of this story is included in Charlton, pp. 188-209.

[38] 'Der Goldne Topf: Ein Märchen aus der Neuen Zeit', *Poetische Werke*, I, 215-17. The story is translated in *The Golden Pot and Other Tales*, trans. by Ritchie Robertson, The World's Classics (Oxford: Oxford University Press, 1992), pp. 1-83.

[39] William Shakespeare, *The Winter's Tale* [1623], V. 3. 98, ed. by J. H. P. Pafford (1963), p. 159.

Gwendolen has previously ordered this panel to be kept locked: the incident chimes precisely with Schelling's definition, as quoted by Freud, of the uncanny as that which 'ought to have remained [...] secret and hidden but has come to light'.[40] 'Unheimlich' it is in a more literal sense as well, disturbing Gwendolen in the very heart of home. The incident certainly involves her crossing a new threshold of vision, for it 'showed Gwendolen in an unforeseen phase of emotion' and '[h]ow it came about was at first a mystery (54)'.

Gwendolen undergoes 'a change of expression [...] terrifying in its terror' becoming 'like a statue into which a soul of Fear had entered' (54). She gives every sign of a mesmerised trance: 'her pallid lips were parted; her eyes, usually narrowed under their long lashes, were dilated and fixed' (54). Her uncle soon identifies the vibrations from Klesmer's playing as the medium of Gwendolen's mortification (55), but Klesmer's role is none the less uncanny for this explanation and its force in bringing her to a state of 'spiritual dread' (57) is even enhanced by the gentle mockery of spiritual*ism* which the 'mystery' facilitates meanwhile:

> 'It is very mysterious. It must be the spirits.'
>   'But there is no medium present.'
>   'How do you know that? We must conclude that there is when such things happen.'(55)

A more prosaic 'medium' (55) transpires to have been Gwendolen's younger sister, Isabel, who had earlier failed to re-lock the panel over the painting. But it is Klesmer who causes it to fly open. 'Only the composer who knows how to use harmony to work on the human soul has truly mastered its secrets,' asserts Kreisler.[41] In Hoffmann's literature of terror, Kreisler's playing can reveal the Devil himself, as it does at the conclusion of his story 'Kreisler's Musical-Poetical Club'.[42]

Ironically, Klesmer is initially described as being in 'one of his placid silent moods' (53) and his agreeing to accompany Gwendolen's tableau

---

[40] Freud, 'The "Uncanny"', p. 345. Freud here traces transitions in the meaning of 'heimlich' from 'homely', thus 'private', thus 'hidden', until it denotes its opposite: 'secret' and 'unheimlich'. See also 'The Uncanny' in Andrew Bennet and Nicholas Royle, *An Introduction to Literature, Criticism and Theory: Key Critical Concepts* (London, 1995), p. 37.

[41] Hoffmann, 'Beethoven's Instrumentalmusik', *Poetische Werke*, I, 51; trans. by Schafer, p. 88; see also Charlton, p. 102.

[42] Hoffmann, 'Kreisler's Musikalisch-Poetischer Klub', *Poetische Werke*, I, 355; trans. by Schafer, pp. 147-148; see also Charlton, pp. 134-135.

performance on the piano is depicted as simply a 'good-natured' act (54). The terrifying, if improving, effect of his intervention suggests otherwise — or is his the silent passivity of the medium? Klesmer is an 'Uncanny Guest'. The original *Unheimliche Gast* also immobilises the story's heroine (by confronting her with a pair of mesmerising eyes).[43] Gwendolen's humiliation at Klesmer's original judgement of her singing and the subsequent influence of his magical playing are depicted as lifting her above egotism. Here, his corrective influence transforms a contrived performance into a moment of genuine drama. Klesmer shows Gwendolen the prophetic picture of her future husband's drowned face and her own flight from it. He extends the broadening of her perceptual horizons to new extremes of uncanniness.

Hoffmann's work illuminates much in *Daniel Deronda*. It highlights how Klesmer, the apparently unassailable manifestation of serious cultural value is as unstable a construction as everything else in the novel. Everything about him is ambiguous. Klesmer, we are told, brings his own 'locus' with him. Eliot leaves us undecided as to whether this is the classical 'locus amoenus' or a more uncanny 'locus suspectus' which Freud cites as the Latin equivalent of 'Das Unheimliche'.[44]

In Hoffmann's writing, music discloses an unknown world where a vision of the infinite is attained. Eliot's resistance to egotism and solipsism emphasizes a connection between moments of uncanny apprehension and increased powers of sympathy. Her dominant metaphors are of expansion rather than of vertical transcendence. The quality of sympathetic vision emphasized in *Daniel Deronda* may ultimately be most akin to Wordsworth's 'eye made quiet by the power [o]f harmony' by which '[w]e see into the life of things' and apprehend 'the still, sad music of humanity'.[45]

Nonetheless, the degree to which musical figures and figurative music are involved in uncanny effects, which pressure the usual boundaries of perception and communication, also gives Eliot's writing a particular affinity with Hoffmann's work. We can see her elaboration of sympathy in the novel

---

[43] Hoffmann, 'Der Unheimliche Gast', *Die Serapionsbrüder III, Poetische Werke*, VII, 126. The story is translated in Alexander Ewing, *The Serapions Bretheren*, 2 vols (1886), pp. 96-149, see p. 118.

[44] Freud, 'The "Uncanny" ', p. 341.

[45] William Wordsworth, 'Lines written a few miles above Tintern Abbey' (1798), 48-50, in *Lyrical Ballads and Other Poems, 1797-1800*, The Cornell Wordsworth, ed. by James Butler and Karen Green (Ithaca and London, 1992), p. 17.

as a new manifestation of the uncanny: a dramatisation, as Nicholas Royle has proposed, of 'sympathetic clairvoyance'.[46]

E. T. A. Hoffmann's artist seeks only escape. George Eliot's 'comes into the world to make new rules' (94). Eliot's devotion to sympathy guarantees her commitment to the performative value of art: or does it? Her equivocal artist-legislator, the musical magician, vanishes. Deronda's Zionist enterprise evokes another Hoffmanesque archetype of the artist's escape: that of Atlantis. Coincidence, clairvoyance, expansion, dissolution: the uncanny makes us uncertain. Klesmer is a starting point; Hoffmann shows that the uncanny pervades Eliot's text as well as helping us to understand her 'musical Magus'.

---

[46] Royle, *Telepathy and Literature*, p. 4; see also note 36 above. The psychologist James Sully linked Eliot's personal power of sympathy with clairvoyance, writing that 'George Eliot enfolded her auditors in an atmosphere of discriminative sympathy. She had a clairvoyant insight into mind and character, which enabled her to get at once into spiritual touch with a stranger [...]', *My Life and Friends: A Psychologist's Memories* (1918), pp. 263-4.

Chapter Eight

Daniel Deronda and Allegories of Empire

Derek Miller

The political focus of both *Felix Holt* and *Middlemarch* is the 1832 Reform Bill. Getting rid of electoral abuses and extending the franchise were useful images for personal struggles in the novels, and for larger themes of social and individual redemption. There is, however, little sign in *Daniel Deronda* of the discussion in the 1860s of the provisions that were to double the electorate in the 1867 Reform Bill. The political allegories here are in tune with the thematic scope of the novel, less to do with reform than with the violence needed for the recovery of lost places and for national formation: the American Civil War, the Risorgimento in Italy, Bismarck's battles for an imperial German identity, and above all, perhaps, the mediaeval upheavals connected with the crusades.

I have chosen two topics to illustrate these allegories: the First Crusade and the double plot.

To remind us of what was going on between Gwendolen and Grandcourt, we might start with some of the language of their coercions. In the early stages of the novel, the reader learns of Gwendolen's desire for dominion — what St. Augustine called '*dominandi libido*'[1] — to be later subdued by the larger force of Grandcourt's imperial sway. In Leubronn she walks along Obere Strasse (Upper Street) past the *Czarina* hotel. 'No one had disputed her power or her general superiority'[2] says the narrator. She is 'the princess in exile', with a 'power of inspiring fear' in the interests of her 'domestic empire' (71). She is enticed into his own 'empire of fear' (479) by a man who

---

[1] *The City of God against the Pagans*, in Latin with English translation by William M. Green (New York: Harvard University Press, 1978), p. 208.

[2] *Daniel Deronda*, ed. by Barbara Hardy (Harmondsworth: Penguin Books, 1986), p. 70. Further page references to this edition are given in the text.

might have 'won reputation' had he been 'sent to govern a difficult colony' where he 'would have understood that it was safer to exterminate than to cajole superseded proprietors' (655) — a colony like Jamaica, perhaps, where, in the uprising of October 1865, in Grandcourt's view 'the [...] negro was a beastly sort of baptist Caliban' (376). The uprising was suppressed by Governor Eyre with the shooting of eighty-five of the ex-slaves without trial, and the execution of three hundred and fifty-four by order of courts-martial.

After seven weeks of marriage 'the belief in her own power of dominating was utterly gone [...] her husband had gained a mastery [...]. Gwendolen's will had seemed imperious' but in Grandcourt 'she had found a will like that of a crab or a boa-constrictor' (477). Grandcourt, with his languid ways, is also a lizard, 'of a hitherto unknown species, not of the lively, darting kind' (174). Gwendolen, at breakfast with him, 'lifting a prawn before her, looked at the boiled ingenuousness of its eyes as preferable to the lizard's' (649). It is difficult to take a moral position against an animal for tearing, squeezing, or snapping, when this is in its nature to keep itself alive, and in this sense Grandcourt seems to be exempted from what Herbert J. Levine calls the novel's demonization of English materialism.[3] What distinguishes him as a non-animal, a human and an individual, is his speech.

Just before he proposes marriage, Grandcourt says these three sentences to Gwendolen:

> 'You will tell me now, I hope, that Mrs Davilow's loss of fortune will not trouble you further. You will trust me to prevent it from weighing upon her. You will give me the claim to provide against that.' (347)

The 'you will', the force of its repetition, the placing of 'now' and 'me' combine to suggest a flavour of what J. L. Austin calls a performative utterance, in which the verbs 'tell', 'trust', 'give', although made predictive by the future tense, become themselves a form of enactment. The imperatives, masked also as implied questions to soften Grandcourt's assumption of her obedience, express in their tact his pleasure in the rhetoric of persuasion that triumphs over Gwendolen's 'piteous equality in the need to dominate' (346). No wonder 'she had a momentary phantasmal love for this man who chose his words so well' (347).

Mid-Victorian anthropology would not be violated by the equation: women are to men as savages are to Europeans. Women and savages are allocated qualities that, if allowed by men to enter their own consciousnesses, could

---

[3] Herbert J. Levine, 'The Marriage of Allegory and Realism in *Daniel Deronda*', *Genre*, 15 (Winter 1982), 421-45 (442).

undermine their ability to govern home, city, country, empire. Women and savages are seen as irrational, unpredictable, impulsive, unknowable, spontaneous, instinctual, anarchic. Like horses, they must be curbed to correct their tendencies to social disruption. In a mode less delicate than his prenuptial offer of help for Gwendolen's mother, Grandcourt keeps Gwendolen in check. She had let go her riding whip, giving 'a little scream of distress' (172), on a walk with him during the days of what might be called their courtship. The whip soon passes to Grandcourt after their betrothal: Gwendolen, who had resembled a 'young race-horse in the paddock' (54), is 'brought to kneel down like a horse under training for the arena' (365). When she obeys him by putting on the 'poisoned gems' (407), 'Grandcourt inwardly observed that she answered to the rein' (482). And later, in Genoa, after his impatience with her tears and a discussion about the propriety of her talking to Deronda, Grandcourt feels 'perfectly satisfied that he held his wife with a bit and bridle' (744).

These binary, oppositional relations, on which much of the novel's allegory is based, are abandoned for a moment in connection with a different kind of horse. I would like to bear in mind here, and throughout this paper, the four levels of meaning expected in a mediaeval narrative: the literal, allegorical, spiritual or mystical, and moral.

When Rex's horse fell in the hunt, his knees were broken and Rex's shoulder was put out of joint. Joel Dagge, 'a young blacksmith' (105), following the hunt on foot, put the shoulder back in. 'I see a man with his eye pushed out once — that was as rum a go as ever I see. You can't have a bit o' fun wi'out such sort o'things. But it went in again.' (104) This magical healer is a Vulcan figure, a pagan artisan with a godlike authority, but it is the horse, not the blacksmith, who limps, and it is chivalry, named from the horse, that is crippled.

This tiny episode in *Daniel Deronda*, a free moment outside any evident requirement of the plot, becomes thematically suggestive as the plot unfolds. The allegory, a word deriving from the Greek, meaning to speak other, in public, will prove to exercise its traditional functions: of instruction by simplifying a complicated activity at the literal level, and of making itself available as a moral authority in matters, for example, of battle, satire, and quest. As Angus Fletcher says in his seminal work, 'allegories are the natural mirrors of ideology'.[4]

---

[4] Angus Fletcher, *Allegory. The Theory of a Symbolic Mode* (New York: Cornell University Press, 1964), p. 368.

Chivalry in *Daniel Deronda* has a sounding point in the First Crusade, an enterprise authenticated and triggered by a sermon of Pope Urban II at Clermont in France in 1095. The Holy Land was to be recovered from the infidel. For the Jews, however, history changed. During the next hundred years they suffered massacres in many parts of Northern Europe including, in England: London, Norwich, Bury, Lynn, Dunstable, Stamford, culminating in a mass suicide in York Castle. And in Jerusalem itself, with the arrival of the Christian conquerors, the Jews were burned alive in the chief synagogue; a medieval soul, born again in Mordecai, heard 'the roar of the Crusaders and the shrieks of tortured Israel' (555). Clermont, the hill of light, is remembered in Hebrew as Har Ophel, the hill of darkness.

Reference to the First Crusade is made formally in a remarkable conversation between Gwendolen and Mrs Arrowpoint early in the novel. Gwendolen 'would give anything to write a book!' (75). Mrs Arrowpoint could have made her life of Tasso 'twice the size'. 'I dote on Tasso,' says Gwendolen, tiptoeing dangerously on a fine line between pertness and impertinence. Gwendolen also says, preposterously, 'I know nothing of Tasso except the *Gerusalemme Liberata*, which we read and learned by heart at school' (76). It seems to me that an option is opened here, not only for Tasso's epic poem of the First Crusade to be absorbed into the heart of the novel, but also — 'ah, you are a student of Goethe,' (75) says Mrs Arrowpoint — for the inclusion of Goethe's play about Tasso. The play provokes a comparison, which I mention here parenthetically, between Princess Leonora, the sister of Tasso's patron, described by Mrs Arrowpoint as 'a cold-hearted woman' (76), and one who, according to the play, lost her singing voice — a comparison between this Princess Leonora and Princess Leonora Halm-Eberstein, who also lost her voice, 'like a fit of forgetfulness' (702), and made her son Daniel Deronda feel 'he had to obey that imperious prohibition of any tenderness' (724).

An edition of Tasso's *Gerusalemma Liberata*, in the Eliot–Lewes collection at Dr Williams's library in London, is signed Mary Anne Evans followed by, in Italian, 'Finished July 27, 1841', when she was not yet twenty-two. The work she read describes perhaps the first great imperial adventure undertaken by Christian Europeans, one of a series that 'had at least this excuse', according to the narrator's paraphrase of Klesmer, 'they had a banner of sentiment around which generous feelings could rally: of course the scoundrels rallied too' (283).

Deronda, described by his friend Meyrick as 'something of the knight-errant' (370), is associated by the narrator with Rinaldo, a great Christian warrior in Tasso's account. Like Rinaldo with the Saracen Armida and, archetypically, Aeneas with Dido, Deronda is tempted by Gwendolen towards a truancy from the obligations to his destiny. In his 'Allegory of the Poem', Tasso calls for support for reason against 'the concupiscent faculties' at play in Rinaldo's dalliance with Armida. Such a reorganisation of the psyche is a prerequisite for the delivery of Jerusalem, a city which 'signifies civic felicity'.[5]

As Armida is converted to Christianity by Rinaldo, Gwendolen is to be converted — by Deronda — if she is to be saved. Unlike Rinaldo, Deronda is not a figure of conquest. The mediaevalism of Deronda and Mordecai substitutes the Jew for the knight-errant, the heroism of persecution for that of chivalry. Deronda imagines himself in Cordova in the time of the Hebrew poet Ibn Gabirol, or a Jew on the borders of the Rhine at 'the end of the eleventh century [...] the Hep! Hep! Hep! of the Crusaders came like a bay of bloodhounds; and in the presence of those devilish missionaries with sword and firebrand the crouching figure of the reviled Jew turned round erect, heroic, flashing with sublime constancy in the face of torture and death' (430). This is a new kind of chevalier, whose experience in oppression and suffering prepares him to seek a new, non-Christian redemption.

Tasso's Hydraotes, ruler of Damascus, sends his niece Armida to weaken the military strength of the Franks outside Jerusalem, using her beauty to entice, if not Godfrey himself, then 'the greatest of the others'[6] away from their mission to liberate the city. Similarly, Mr Gascoigne (who changed his name from Gaskin), blinded by his snobbery to Grandcourt's personal unfitness as a husband for his niece, encourages Gwendolen in the match with Grandcourt in terms as political as those that pressed Hydraotes to despatch Armida – like Gwendolen, a sorceress and an archer. It would be 'a sort of public affair [...] it might even strengthen the Establishment' (176). It was, Mr Gascoigne persuaded himself in an expansive mood, 'a match to be accepted on broad general grounds, national and ecclesiastical' (177). Gwendolen's acceptance of Grandcourt's proposal was a matter of 'duty [...] of responsibility' (179). As paradigms for usages of this kind, one thinks of the sacrifices of Jephthah's daughter and of Iphigenia.

Allegory, not an open form of interpretation, heightens the power struggle, and in this instance acts to deepen the commodification of Gwendolen, to

---

[5] Torquato Tasso, *Jerusalem Delivered*, trans. by Ralph Nash (Detroit: Wayne State University Press, 1987), pp. 473, 470.

[6] *Jerusalem Delivered*, p. 426.

expose the way his social interests allow Mr Gascoigne to ignore the ruin of his niece's life, and to provide the terrain for a satire of the first two estates.

The novel is littered with a series of motifs that touch on Tasso and the First Crusade. Both Mab Meyrick and Mirah sing an aria from Handel's *Rinaldo*, a work with a libretto that reads like a soap opera version of Tasso. A Mallinger ancestor 'had killed three Saracens in one encounter' (210); their heads are included in the family coat of arms with three bezants, coins which became debased after the First Crusade. In an unusually sour tone, Mordecai's poverty is compared by the narrator with that of Peter the Hermit, 'who has a tocsin for the rabble' (529). In Tasso, Peter urges Tancred to stay loyal to his service as a knight of Christ, much as Mordecai directs Deronda towards his road to Jerusalem. I think it is worth pointing out here that in Disraeli's *Tancred*, a novel of which Eliot wrote slightingly, the eponymous hero makes a plea for a reversal of the crusades — the Arabian deserts should send to the West their divine truths and great thoughts to bring a new spirit to a Europe besotted with false excitements and the tumult of material progress. Similarly, as Barry V. Qualls says in a discussion of nineteenth century secular pilgrims, Eliot in her capacity as 'sacred romancer' reverses in *Daniel Deronda* the process of religious liberation as seen by the Christians in, for example, Tasso's 'epic paradigm'.[7]

Grandcourt's power over Gwendolen in the Wessex part of the novel has its parallel in Mordecai's power over Deronda in the Jewish part. Grandcourt and Mordecai, at the centres of their respective plots, never meet and are unaware of each other's existence. Deronda acts as the thematic messenger, crossing between them, margin to margin, then closer and closer to the centres until, not immune to the coercive forces he inherits from them, he becomes a successor both to Grandcourt and to Mordecai. In *Some Versions of Pastoral*, William Empson argued that double plots are bound to suggest a magical relationship between the two levels on which these plots are told. Since pastoral is a literature of differences in social, political or spiritual hierarchies, and since the main aim of double plots is to codify such differences, the play of power between courtiers and shepherds can be reversed when the two groups change places. In *Daniel Deronda* there is another element linking the two plots: The belief, which emerged in the Reformation, in England as, in John Lyly's phrase, 'a new Israel, [God's] chosen and peculiar people'.[8]

---

[7] Barry V. Qualls, *The Secular Pilgrim of Victorian Fiction: The Novel as Book of Life*. (Cambridge: Cambridge University Press, 1982), pp. 171-2.

[8] Quoted in Harold Fisch, *The Dual Image: The Figure of the Jew in English and American Literature* (London: World Jewish Library, 1971), p. 43.

Grandcourt's name, of course, particularly fits him for a position on the dignified side of the pastoral divide. 'Grandcourt's importance as a subject of this realm', says the narrator, 'was of the grandly passive kind which consists in the inheritance of land' (644). His land, and that of other gentlemen in Wessex, Sir Hugo and Mr Arrowpoint for instance, distinguishes them from Mordecai as a shepherd figure, 'a poor Jewish workman' (571), and the unidentified, deracinated Jews for whom Mordecai wants to establish a national land of their own. Deronda is out of contention in this pastoral. Although landless in the Wessex world, he has seven hundred a year, the income, says the narrator rather tartly, from 'capital which somebody else has battled for' (225).

Reversing the pastoral, the clown is not hard to find. Gwendolen's first impression of Grandcourt — 'he is not ridiculous' — is governed as much by his freedom from what she expected, 'grimace or solicitious wrigglings', as by the details of his appearance: 'he showed an extensive baldness surrounded with a mere fringe of reddish-blond hair, but he also showed a perfect hand' (145). The tonsure reminds the reader of the incongruities of Chaucer's monk, whose 'heed was balled, that shone as any glas', who found no need to 'swynken [toil] with his handes', and who 'lovede venerie', practiced by Grandcourt in both meanings of the word. 'The line of feature from brow to chin undisguised by beard was decidedly handsome, with only moderate departures from the perpendicular, and the slight whisker too was perpendicular' (145-6). The line of feature and the whisker are in a late Gothic architectural style that started in England in Chaucer's century. The narrator, allowing Gwendolen to refuse to see the absurdity of Grandcourt's appearance, teases the reader into doing so.

Grandcourt's power extends only over his few dependents: Mrs Glasher, Thomas Cranmer Lush, Gwendolen, thus justifying the oxymoron of the French, or Norman meaning of his name — *grandcourt*, a big sway over a tiny constituency. And the legitimacy of the gentile establishment where Grandcourt has a place in England and a metaphorical governorship in the West Indies is questioned by an example the narrator uses against raising prejudice into generalisation: 'It appears that the Caribs, who know little of theology, regard thieving as a practice peculiarly connected with Christian tenets' (246).

Grandcourt's appearance, the smallness of his domain, the casual tone in which one of the biblical commandments can be brushed aside — these are matters in what Empson calls the comic part of the double plot. In the serious part Mordecai, with 'the face of a man little above thirty' (553), the age of

Jesus when he began his ministry, is the dying king or saint who labours for the good of the clowns in their wretched world.

Their world is of the present, of the gratification of appetite, of an imagination fallen into disuse. When members of the party looking round Sir Hugo's converted mediaeval abbey enter the choir, now the stables, Deronda knows the difference between sacred and profane, and removes his hat. ' "Do you take off your hat to the horses?" said Grandcourt, with a slight sneer' (474). For Grandcourt there is no past and therefore no future; Deronda, even before he becomes a Jew with his father's box of papers, enters the morally powerful side of the pastoral with a growing knowledge that he must endlessly rescue memory if he is to know who he is.

This was not always the case. An early commonplace to Gwendolen about gambling — 'our gain is another's loss' (383) — piously recommends an immobility, an economic stasis, the kind of thing that may have persuaded Robert Louis Stevenson to call Deronda 'the Prince of Prigs'.[9] But the major statements about the clownishness of Wessex are focused on Sir Hugo.

The narrator tells the reader that Sir Hugo is 'a Liberal of good lineage, who confided entirely in Reform as not likely to make any serious difference in English habits of feeling' (864). About young Daniel's musing over his identity, Sir Hugo's 'imagination had never once been troubled with the way in which the boy himself might be affected [...] by the enigmatic aspect of his circumstances' (214). After Sir Hugo's complaint to Mr Gascoigne that Grandcourt left Gwendolen in his will 'only two thousand a-year and a house in a coal-mining district', the narrator's deeply sarcastic '[t]hus spake the chivalrous Sir Hugo' (827) excludes the 'banner of sentiment' or 'generous feelings' of the sort that Klesmer identifies as informing the crusades, and that found a warlike form in the Mallinger coat of arms. The evident decencies of clergy and nobility, Mr Gascoigne's responsibilty to family, Sir Hugo's gallantry, mask from themselves the snobbery of the one and complacency of the other. The two estates have this in common: that both are killers of the soul. The novel's attitude to the third English estate seems less clear, but it is worth noting that the admirable Mrs Meyrick, for no apparent reason, is 'half French, half Scotch' (238).

The allegorical antithesis, ultimately between good and evil, will be expressed in some form of power relations in the pastoral situation. Mordecai's vision of a homeland for his people is of a piece with his

---

namesake's rescue of the Jews from widespread massacre in the Book of Esther. His vision comes out of what he calls 'ideas, beloved ideas' (554). In Wessex, however, there is no indication that a way of life might be governed by the mind. The contrast is between, on the one hand, an imagination in which thought, memory, mysticism can change the fate of a people, and, on the other hand, a psyche frozen in its postures, depending on the repetition of its activity for a feeling of being alive.

As an analogue to Mordecai's arguments for a national centre for the Jewish people, Deronda invokes the temporal power of the anti-imperial, educational, prophetic nationalism of Mazzini's movement for the unity of Italy and its liberation from French and Austrian occupiers.

There is a more elaborate historical authentication by the choice of Genoa as the place where Deronda will be freed for his marriage and his quest, and where Gwendolen must start to transcend her solipsism. Genoa is not only the birthplace of Mazzini, but also of Columbus, with whom Mordecai is identified by Deronda and who, in a predictive passage in Tasso, 'will have the daring first to set himself on the unknown course'.[10] Genoa is also the place, in 1860, from which Garibaldi's Thousand Red Shirts sailed for Sicily. And it was the major port for a fleet, Tasso's *liguri navigli*[11], that supplied the First Crusade.   These political themes associated with Deronda and Gwendolen are those of discovery, liberation — and conquest. To drive this home — while Deronda awaits his mother in Genoa, and the interview with her that will change his universe, 'every day was a hurrying march of crowded time towards the world-changing battle of Sadowa' (684). This was a victory in 1866 for the Prussians over Austria in the course of an expansionism that would lead to the formation of the German Empire in 1871. Although Mordecai's message is itself essentially expansionist, the cadences of the announcement, the melodrama of the military activity, are matched by the silence of the response to Mordecai in the world visible to the reader. None of the Jews in the novel will emigrate to a national home.   Klesmer 'looks forward to a fusion of races' (284); Ezra Cohen the pawnbroker will stay with his business and his faulty celebration of the Sabbath; the Jews in The Philosophers Club, Pash and Gideon, have reasons, commercial and assimilationist, to stay in England, perhaps to 'melt gradually into the population we live among' (586). The intended emigrants live elsewhere. The pattern of Deronda's work — 'I am going to the East to become better

---

[10] Tasso, *Jerusalem Delivered*, XV, 31-2.

[11] Tasso, Torquato, *Gerusalemme Liberata* (Paris: Presso La Vedova Thiériot, 1845), V, 86.

acquainted with the condition of my race in various countries there' (875) —
is likely to be that of an emissary, like the Anglo-Jewish philanthropist Sir
Moses Montefiore, who made many well-publicised visits during the years of
the mid-century, including seven to Palestine, to alleviate distress among
Jewish communities in the region.

The prince of the spirit labours for the clowns of Wessex; at the end the
only one exposed to the labour is Gwendolen. The military imagery is of a
scope to place her in a representative position for England: 'The slow
urgency of growing generations turns into the tread of an invading army or the
dire clash of civil war'. The 'mere speck' of poor Gwendolen must now
survive her internal civil war — the antagonism between, on the one hand, her
own imperiousness and that of the Grandcourt name she carries, and, on the
other, a religion 'which is something else than a private consolation'; the
shock of this is 'something spiritual and vaguely tremendous'.

Deronda's 'crouching figure of the reviled Jew' returns: 'The martyrs live
reviled, they die, and no angel is seen [...] the submission of the soul to the
highest is tested' (875-6). This seems to be an enormous task for Gwendolen,
that she should, like the Jew whose spiritual heirs the English are, turn round
'erect, heroic, flashing with sublime constancy in the face of torture and
death' (431).

Her torture? Grandcourt's death? Literal meanings of course are
inescapable, but the vastness of the lesson presented to Gwendolen suggests
that in some way the only meanings that can have any force are those other
than the literal. The realist novelist turns away from the impossible task of
not telling a story to present to the reader meanings only at allegorical,
mystical and moral levels. One might argue that this attempted desertion of
the English novel sets up a criticism of England as profound as any that could
be imagined.

Chapter Nine

'The Interest of Spanish Sights': From Ronda to *Daniel Deronda*

Bonnie McMullen

The only way to get to Ronda in 1867 was by horseback across the mountains from Malaga, Granada or Gibraltar. George Eliot did not go there. Nevertheless, Ronda's name, commemorated in the title of her last novel and the patronym of its hero, raises questions about George Eliot's imaginative and actual involvement with Spain that have never been answered. What David Carroll has called 'the radically new mode in which *Daniel Deronda* is written'[1] has challenged readers since its first publication and eluded most attempts at precise definition. The foregrounding of national and international issues, juxtaposed with an urgent probing of psychological and religious questions, gives it a wider emotional and intellectual field of reference than the earlier novels. These thematic concerns, realized in the novel through a pervasive use of spatial and dramatic devices, take it above and beyond a world in which most readers can feel quite at home. This discomfort is, to some extent, caused by the wider geographical and historical framework the novel employs, which is related to a different concept of personal identity in the characters. The title itself focuses on the relation between person and place in a way that, by its allusive obscurity, presents a challenge to the reader. The road to Ronda was the road not taken, but the imaginative terrain in which it lies constitutes the subject matter of the novel. An examination of George Eliot's apprehension of this *paysage moralisé* may also open an unexplored passage to the world of Daniel Deronda.

For Marian Lewes, Spain was an enthusiasm of middle age. She had just passed her forty-seventh birthday when she wrote to Sara Hennell at the end of 1866:

---

[1] David Carroll, *George Eliot and the Conflict of Interpretations: A Reading of the Novels* (Cambridge: Cambridge University Press, 1992), p. 273.

No, I don't feel as if my faculties were failing me. On the contrary, I enjoy all subjects —all study, more than I ever did in my life before [...] Science, history, poetry—I don't know which draws me most. And there is little time left me for any one of them. I learned Spanish last year but one, and see new vistas everywhere.[2]

So far, however, the 'new vistas' opened by a knowledge of Spanish had not resulted in anything specific. On the contrary, months of work on *The Spanish Gypsy* had left her 'very miserable about my soul as well as body',[3] prompting Lewes to take the manuscript away from her in February 1865. Within weeks her gaze was redirected from inspiring but distant Iberian vistas to the byways and valleys of provincial England which she had already so masterfully claimed in previous fiction. *The Spanish Gypsy* was only postponed, however, and once *Felix Holt* was completed she returned to it with renewed purpose. 'I am swimming in Spanish history and literature' she wrote (*Letters*, IV, 305), somewhat ominously, to John Blackwood on 6 September 1866, hoping, perhaps, that such strenuous immersion would supply the ingredient 'wanting' to give life to 'the right locus and historic conditions' (*Letters*, IV, 301) she had described to Frederic Harrison.

Marian refers to a visit to Spain as 'a long-cherished project' and declares it the country 'which of all others is the one I long to go to', but when Mrs Nassau Senior offered them a house in the south of Spain in December, Marian turned it down. Lewes's health had been poor, and they were forced to review 'the old difficulties', 'the length of the journey, the terribly cold winds on the high lands of central Spain, and the nature of the Spanish cooking etc. — all which had previously frightened us away [...] Mr Lewes would get cold in travelling from St Sebastian to Madrid, and there would be an end of comfort, and a suggestion of oil and garlick in his food would cause him endless gastric miseries' (*Letters*, IV, 317).

The briefest glance at the small body of travel literature on Spain shows that her fears were justified. As a holiday destination, Spain had a not altogether undeserved bad press, which depicted it as offering the gravest dangers to the property and person of the unarmed British traveller. Therefore, even to be thinking of visiting Spain in this period suggested an unusual degree of adventurousness, if not downright foolhardiness. Never part of the Grand Tour, Spain was, in the words of John Pemble, 'unsanctioned by habit and convention' and, even into the early twentieth century, was regarded, along with Greece, as 'vaguely intimidating and even

---

[2] *The George Eliot Letters*, ed. by Gordon S. Haight, 9 vols (New Haven: Yale University Press, 1954-78), IV, 316. Further references to the *Letters* are given in the text.

[3] George Eliot's Journal, 19, 20, 21 February 1865, quoted in *Letters*, IV, 179.

suspect from [...] association with the excesses of Romantic sensibility,' as exemplified by *Childe Harold's Pilgrimage*.[4] John Steegman has written that '[t]he difficulties and discomforts and even the dangers of travelling about in nineteenth century Spain deterred almost everybody'.[5] It is possible, however, that the very challenge that Spain presented to the traveller may have been part of its attraction to Marian Lewes, who had shown courage in crossing other frontiers in her life as a woman and artist.

With no definite itinerary in mind, the Leweses left for Paris and Biarritz in late December, and Lewes recorded in his journal on 10 January that 'Polly [...] opened to me her secret desire of going from Barcelona to Granada. The idea quite fired me and it was *almost* resolved on' (*Letters*, IV, 330). They bought a Spanish grammar and conversation book, and Marian describes in a letter to Mrs Congreve how they prepare themselves: ' [...] while we plunge about in the sand or march along the cliff, George draws out a book and tries my paces in Spanish, demanding a quick-as-light translation of nouns and phrases. Presently I retort upon him, and prove that it is easier to ask than to answer' (*Letters*, IV, 334).

Armed with their Spanish grammar and romantic novels by Fernan Caballero, the Leweses left France for San Sebastian at the end of January. Their itinerary took them by rail across northern Spain to Barcelona, with brief stops in Saragossa and Lerida, and then by steamboat to Alicante and Malaga. From Malaga, they travelled by diligence to Granada, and after a week went to Cordoba and Seville. From Andalucia, they headed north to Madrid, and from Madrid made their way home via France, arriving in London on the 16th of March. Their journey was 'a great loop all round the east and through the centre of Spain', as Marian described it to Mrs Congreve (*Letters*, IV, 349), exactly forty days in all.

The Leweses were well-grounded in history and Spanish literature of the Golden Age. George Henry Lewes's interest went back more than two decades. His book *The Spanish Drama: Lope de Vega and Calderon* of 1846 had originated as an article in the *Foreign Quarterly Review* in 1843. In 1864, between reading William Hickling Prescott's *Ferdinand and Isabella* and studying Spanish grammar, Marian read *Don Quixote* aloud to Lewes, translating as she went along (*Letters*, IV, 165). In addition, Marian probably knew the limited number of Spanish paintings on exhibit in London; she

---

[4] *The Mediterranean Passion: Victorians and Edwardians in the South* (Oxford: Oxford University Press, 1988), p. 48.

[5] *Victorian Taste: A Study of the Arts and Architecture from 1830 to 1870* (London: Thomas Nelson, 1970), p. 246.

praises Murillo for his 'truthfulness' in her essay on Riehl[6] and may well have seen Gustave Doré's engravings of Spain at the Doré Gallery or his illustrated edition of *Don Quixote* of 1863. Then there was Lewes's old friend Owen Jones, architect, designer, and author of *The Grammar of Ornament,* who took charge of the decorations at The Priory in 1863 and often stayed talking till after midnight. Did he share with his friends his detailed knowledge of Moorish art?

For up-to-date practical information, they relied on Henry Blackburn's *Travelling in Spain in the Present Day* (*Letters*, IV, 344). Published in 1866, it describes a journey made by its author in 1864, the year that the railway across Spain was completed. Blackburn exhorts his readers to visit Spain before this modern convenience, which made such a journey feasible in the first place, would 'destroy its picturesqueness, and banish all chivalry out of the land'. 'Each year a visit to Spain is postponed, some of its characteristics will be lost,' warned Blackburn. 'Wherever the tourist goes in 1870 he will find that Manchester has been there before him. The artist has not an hour to lose [...]'.[7] Attention to the body of Blackburn's text might make the would-be tourist reconsider, however, as the author catalogues the seemingly endless perils and discomforts that are an inescapable part of such a journey as he paradoxically urges on his readers. When Marian declined the offer of Mrs Nassau Senior's house, fearing the effects of the climate on Lewes, she may well have been worried by Blackburn's description of 'fierce blasts of cold wind that sweep over the plains of Castile, through the streets, and up the very staircases of the houses [...]'.[8] Spanish travellers, invariably fat, cigar-smoking, and male, will fall asleep on top of you in railway carriages and stifle you with smoke. Confused passengers are 'left behind or sent the wrong

---

[6] 'The Natural History of German Life', in *Essays of George Eliot*, ed. by Thomas Pinney (New York: Columbia University Press, 1963), p. 270. It is a tragic irony that Riehl's ideas, which lay behind George Eliot's famous doctrine of sympathy, were also put to service by Alfred Rosenberg and others to bolster the Nazi ideology of anti-semitism. For a discussion of Riehl's impact on the politics of nineteenth and twentieth-century Germany see Simon Schama, *Landscape and Memory* (London: Harper/Collins, 1995), pp. 112-18.

[7] Henry Blackburn, *Travelling in Spain in the Present Day* (London: Sampson Low & Co., 1866), p. 236. There is no evidence that the Leweses read Richard Ford's more comprehensive *Handbook for Travellers in Spain* (1845). It is curious to note, however, that Eliot's copy of Georg Bernhard Depping's *Histoire Générale de l'Espagne* is signed 'Richard Ford' on the end back cover of each volume. See *The George Eliot – George Henry Lewes Library: An Annotated Catalog*, ed. by William Baker (New York: Garland, 1977), p. 55.

[8] Blackburn, p. 1.

way' at stations and junctions, which 'amuses the officials immensely'.[9] Even benefits to one's health, the usual British pretext for a journey to Spain, were, at best, uncertain. Spain was dirty, reported Blackburn. In Cordoba, 'our bedrooms [...] seemed as if they had never been cleaned since the Moors held possession' of the city.[10] In Cadiz, he noted, 'one hardly ever went abroad without seeing a funeral'.[11]

Fortunately, the Leweses had a more sensitive and reliable guide in the form of the letters about Spain written by Barbara Bodichon, who had recently passed through the country on her way to Algeria. Barbara, as well as being a trusted friend whose impressions Marian valued, presented a picture of Spain that counterbalanced that of the sensationalist and philistine Blackburn. In contrast to the dirt and squalor described by Blackburn, Barbara reassuringly found cleanliness and order. As a painter who preferred the open air, Barbara's real enthusiasm was for the wild and largely uninhabited landscapes, although she also sought out the life of the country as revealed in its arts and traditional crafts, from scenes in a potter's workshop to the glories of Moorish and Christian architecture and the paintings in the Prado. Marian was so impressed by Barbara's letters that she took them with her to France, and it is likely that the delight they aroused tipped the scale on the visit to Spain question. From Bordeaux, Marian wrote to Barbara that she wanted to send the letters to George Smith for publication: 'You have suggested delicious pictures to me. My favourite is that in the potter's workshop, on the Albajcin at Granada — the still life of the pottery and the pans and the moving life of the dance and the music' (*Letters*, IV, 329).

This letter, and one written the following day to Mrs Frederick Lehmann, exemplify the varieties of interest and enjoyment that the journey held for Marian. First, there was the 'perfect weather — blue skies and a warm sun', she wrote to Barbara, 'weather such as makes even me feel as if life were a good even for my own sake', she told Mrs Lehmann (*Letters*, IV, 338-40). The restorative Mediterranean sun, which, although it is February, sheds 'a more delightful warmth than that of an English summer' (*Letters*, IV, 345), would be remembered years later and informs her portrayal of Mordecai, who reports that on the quay at Trieste 'the soul within me felt its former sun'.[12] A slow train enabled the Leweses to savour the exotic landscape, noting the

---

[9] Blackburn, p. 9.

[10] Blackburn, p. 144.

[11] Blackburn, p. 174.

[12] *Daniel Deronda*, ed. by Graham Handley (Oxford: Oxford University Press, 1981), p. 462. Further page references to this edition will be identified in the text.

effects of the elements on 'hills of palish clay washed by the rains into undulating forms' on which 'some slight herbage [...] makes the shadows of an exquisite blue'. The signs of human habitation arise naturally from this scene. 'The land is all pale brown, the numerous towns and villages just match the land, and so do the sheepfolds built of mud or stone'. The people, however, are in dramatic contrast with the 'ashy green' herbage. There is a touch of the operatic in Marian's description of men 'with a great striped blanket wrapt grandly round them, and a kerchief tied about their hair' and a hint of the genre painting in her description of 'the people scattered on the brown slopes of rough earth round the fortress, the women knitting etc. the men playing at cards. One wonderful family group; another of handsome gipsies'. A Victorian preoccupation with race is evidenced in her observation that 'though Aragon was held by the Moors longer than any part of northern Spain, the features and skins of the people seem to me to bear less traces of the mixture there must have been than one would fairly expect'. She reveals her country origins in noting 'the richest red soil' of Catalonia, and 'the abundant fruit crop this land supports', showing that, as her father's daughter, her interest goes beyond the picturesque and scenic (*Letters*, IV, 338-9).

The decentralization of Spain was a strong element of its appeal, and her delight in noting regional differences probably owes as much to the sociological approach outlined in Riehl's books on German society as to her reading of Spanish history.[13] Her dismissal of Barcelona, 'of the class of mongrel towns that one can never care for much' (*Letters*, IV, 341), also suggests Riehl's anti-urban, anti-cosmopolitan bias. Although, like Riehl, she eschewed 'the prejudice of a mind incapable of discerning the grander evolution of things to which all social forms are but temporarily subservient',[14] she nevertheless betrays an emotional bias in favour of the past, and many observations suggest that modernisation need not mean progress. Much of Spain's power over her imagination arises from its continuity with the past, its stability, so that 'famous Pampeluna' looks 'as beautiful as it did ages ago amongst the grand hills', but in Saragossa only a few houses are 'left undesecrated by stucco', and the 'exquisite inlaid work' on the facade of the Cathedral has 'been overlaid hideously' (*Letters*, IV, 338-

---

[13] In *George Eliot: A Biography* (London: Harper/Collins, 1995), p. 418, Frederick Karl argues that George Eliot 'seems unaware [...] of how Spain differs from region to region [...]' and that 'in Spain she observed as a provincial Englishwoman, not as an experienced traveller'. My reading of the letters and other evidence leads to the opposite conclusion.

[14] 'The Natural History of German Life' in *Essays of George Eliot*, ed. by Thomas Pinney (New York: Columbia University Press, 1963), p. 299.

339). Her strongest enthusiasm, however, was reserved for artistic expression which embodied and evoked a sense of the complex, layered quality of Spanish history and culture. The paintings in Madrid and the Cathedral of Seville, the world's largest Gothic church, built on the foundations of a Moorish mosque, were, between them, 'enough to justify Western civilization, with all its faults, and transcend any amount of diaper patterns even if they were coloured as the Moors coloured' (*Letters*, IV, 351).[15]

Although the Leweses clearly read Spanish with ease, it is impossible to know what level of proficiency they attained in speaking it. In any case, there is little to suggest that they had much opportunity, apart from necessary travel arrangements.   In Germany, Italy, and France, the Leweses moved in sophisticated circles that included leading intellectuals and artists, as well as famous ex-patriots.   In Paris, for example, where they had just been, they spent part of every day at the house of Madame Mohl, wife of Jules Mohl, secretary of the Societé Asiatique.   Here, they met Renan and other current leading lights of French philosophy, literature, and politics.   In Spain, however, their main contact with the natives seems to have been with some gypsies in Granada, who entertained them with music and dancing.   While the relevance of this entertainment to Marian's ongoing project is obvious, the meeting seems to have been more anthropological than social in nature.   In short, in contrast with their travels elsewhere in Europe, the Leweses passed through Spain in almost total social isolation, apart from the most superficial contacts, and although this solitude *à deux* may have suited their mood, it meant that their experience of Spain took place on a different level from their engagement with other European countries.

They were spectators, and Spain was the spectacle. The language of their letters makes the experience clear. In her first letter, Marian writes that 'the interest of Spanish sights' is having a beneficial effect on George's health, 'and such sights!' she adds (*Letters*, IV, 338-9).   The very atmosphere of Spain, 'clear skies and warm sun' mentioned in every letter and contrasted with 'the smoky haze of London', provided a perfect medium for looking and seeing (*Letters*, IV, 344).   Marian   praises the slowness of Spanish trains, which means that 'objects remain before the eyes long enough for delight in them' *(Letters*, IV, 340).   They view a 'scene' near the fort at Lerida, and although they can't understand the gypsies' joke at their expense, they have 'the advantage of seeing their [...] white teeth' (*Letters*, IV, 341).   In

---

[15] This quotation, from a letter to Barbara Bodichon, is a direct allusion to Owen Jones, who praised the colour patterns in Moorish art.

Barcelona, they experienced the professional side of the Spanish spectacle, attending the theatre or opera twice a day. In a mystery play, Marian particularly noticed 'a young actor [...] with a head of ideal beauty', and added, 'We watch the audience as well as the actors [...]' (*Letters*, IV, 342). Granada, 'worth a very long, long journey' was 'one of the loveliest scenes on earth, not just for its transcendent memories and transcendent beauty', but for the view it afforded of the surrounding snow-capped mountains and the Vega, 'ready to yield all things pleasant to the eye', and, less transcendently, 'good for food' (*Letters*, IV, 347-8). They themselves are nearly invisible. 'The Spaniards seem to me to stare less [...] than any other nation I have seen' (*Letters*, IV, 341), wrote Marian without irony. The villages they enjoy 'looking at' are, significantly, 'windowless'. In Spain, Marian Lewes could escape George Eliot, who must not, indeed could not, be invisible.

There is no trace of cultural superiority or hidden hegemonic agenda in Marian's approach to Spain (as there is everywhere in her guide, Blackburn, who argues that the world may hope for an improvement in Spanish culture from the increasing presence of English educational materials and English nannies in Madrid). Rather, there is humility in the face of a rich and complex culture, only some aspects of which were accessible to her. The 'windowless villages' which protect the sightseer's anonymity also conceal the lives of those within. Thus the limitations of the mere traveller's vision become a theme that is expanded to cover a wider range of cross-cultural encounters, and becomes a central theme in *Daniel Deronda*. Deronda's 'rambling' in London's East End is 'a process not very promising of particular discovery' (321). The achievement of his goal requires 'the force of imagination that pierces or exalts the solid fact' (322), and the full awakening of Deronda's imagination entails a lesson in humility in the face of difference. His first reaction to the shopkeeping Cohens is 'supercilious dislike' (334), which is replaced by a sense of their dignity when he becomes their guest in the privacy of the room behind the shop. When he realizes that Mordecai is sheltered in a further recess of the house, and eventually comes to understand the nature of the relationship between the two Ezra Cohens, their essential oneness as external and internal manifestations of modern Jewish identity, his attitude becomes one of unqualified respect and total acceptance. The pawnbroker and his family attend Deronda's wedding to rejoice 'in common with' Mordecai (694) and to signify the essential unity of the Jews, but their presence at the wedding also signifies a tentative marriage between the English and Jewish worlds of the novel.

The 'Spanish sights' that impressed Marian were not those of the eye alone and, as she travelled, a complex interplay took place between the passing scene before her and the rich properties of her memory and imagination. Therefore, to her, the most significant aspect of Spain was not what it was, but what it evoked. To Barbara Bodichon, she writes, 'Perhaps if I had been in Africa, I should say as you do that the country reminded me of Africa: as it is, I think of all I have read about the East. The men who look on while others work at Saragossa also seem to belong to the East' (*Letters*, IV, 339). For Mrs Lehmann, she paints a monochrome landscape of 'far-stretching brown plains with brown sheep-folds, brown towns and villages, and far off walls of brown hills' *(Letters,* IV, 341). This 'domaine of difference'[16] in Homi K. Bhabha's phrase, could not be farther from the green and pleasant land of her origins, and Marian, significantly, finds Spain 'more unlike what we think of as European than anything I had seen before. Looking at the brown windowless villages, with a few flocks of sheep scattered far apart on the barren plain, I could have fancied myself in Arabia' (*Letters*, IV, 341*)*. At Alicante, the Leweses walked 'among the palm trees, with the bare brown rocks and brown houses in the back-ground', and took note of a fellow-traveller's assurance 'that the aspect of the country closely resembled Aden, on the shore of the Red Sea' *(Letters,* IV, 348).

It was common in this period for English visitors to the dryer regions of the Mediterranean to associate the landscape with their mental pictures of scenes from *The Arabian Nights*, as John Pemble reports.[17] A deeper and stronger evocation, however, was that of imagined scenes from the Bible, an association that gave travel in these regions the excitement of discovery combined with the nostalgic satisfaction of return. For some, a journey through olive-covered hills could be an emotional pilgrimage, eliciting powerful and complex responses even from those for whom conventional religious dogma no longer had authority. Gethsemane, identified as 'the Mount of Olives' in the Gospel of St. Luke and 'a garden' in the Gospel of St John, is suggested in Marian's description of 'an olive garden' (*Letters*, IV, 341) seen from the fort at Lerida, while her more rapturous description of the land between Monserrat and Barcelona, 'a perfect garden [...] blooms on the plum and cherry trees, olives thick in the hedges' (*Letters*, IV, 339), suggests a scene not far from Edenic. While looking at Spanish 'sights', Marian was

---

[16] *The Location of Culture* (London: Routledge, 1994), p. 2.

[17] *The Mediterranean Passion*, p. 122.

also, in the words of Emily Dickinson, 'looking oppositely| For the site of the Kingdom of Heaven'.[18]

Even without these literary and religious associations, however, the very vastness and relative emptiness of the Spanish landscape, which Marian emphasizes in her description of 'far-stretching' plains, along with the harmonic blending of natural background and human habitation, suggest a space in which the mind can expand to its natural proportions. The intensity of her experience suggests Gaston de Bachelard's formula 'on the correspondence between the immensity of world space and the depth of "inner space"'.[19] It was another world from the claustrophobic England of small fields and complicated rules of property ownership and inheritance which George Eliot had just described in *Felix Holt,* a world where land as well as society should be, as Sir Hugo Mallinger would put it, 'well fenced' (680). It was a pre-urban, pre-industrial world, where the grandeur of the earth itself could be experienced directly. For detached travellers like the Leweses, whose past and present emotional and material well-being was in no way connected to the land they passed through, the direct experience of the Spanish landscape could, paradoxically, be more intense than for a native. Spain was the prototype for what Theophrastus Such referred to as 'those grander and vaster regions of the earth which keep an indifferent aspect in the presence of men's toils and devices'. Although this land of 'eternal snows and stupendous sun-scorched monuments' can never evoke the 'affectionate joy' of 'tree-studded hedgerows' to one brought up in these quieter scenes, it nonetheless commands attention with its own powerful 'speech of the landscape'.[20]

In *Culture and Imperialism,* Edward W. Said asserts that 'there are hardly any exceptions [...] to the overwhelming prevalence of ideas suggesting, often ideologically implementing, imperial rule', and lists as the first of these ideas 'the fundamental ontological distinction between the West and the rest of the world', on which 'there is no disagreement'. He goes on to argue that 'so strongly felt and perceived are the geographical and cultural boundaries between the West and its non-Western peripheries that we may consider these boundaries absolute. With the supremacy of the distinction there goes what Johannes Fabian calls a denial of "coevalness" in time, and a radical

---

[18] 'A loss of something ever felt I', in *The Complete Poems of Emily Dickinson,* ed. by Thomas H. Johnson (Boston: Little, Brown and Co., 1955), p. 449.

[19] *The Poetics of Space,* trans. by Maria Jolas (Boston: Beacon Press, 1969), p. 205.

[20] 'Looking Backward', in *Impressions of Theophrastus Such,* ed. by Nancy Henry (London: Pickering and Chatto, 1994), pp. 22-4.

discontinuity in terms of human space'.[21]   Although the terms 'West' and 'East' are employed by George Eliot as much as by any other writer of her period, her experience of Spain taught her the limitations of this kind of terminology.   In this country at the southern boundary of Europe, a culture had once grown and flourished from the richest influences of Christianity, Islam, and Judaism, although each strain had retained its separate identity. The fertile mixture of Western and Eastern cultures and people in Spain suggested exciting possibilities for the future of European civilization. Although multi-ethnic, multi-confessional Spain represented a cultural experiment that had ultimately failed the test of time, its example may well lie behind Mordecai's vision of 'a community in the van of the East which carries the culture and the sympathies of every great nation in its bosom' (456), a kind of multi-national nationalism.[22]

It is hard to know in what way Marian's visit to Spain helped her in completing the twice-stalled *Spanish Gypsy*. The inspiration for that work came, however, from an Italian painting, and its themes and characters were all worked out before a visit to Spain was ever spoken of. The real impact of George Eliot's Spanish experience, I would argue, is most clearly seen not in *The Spanish Gypsy*, but in the fiction that followed, and especially in *Daniel Deronda*. In *Middlemarch*, Spain is evoked in the allusion to St Theresa, but only to show the impossiblility of an 'epic life' for a woman in Dorothea's circumstances. In this novel, characters move within a clearly defined social world, and their success or failure is determined by their willingness and ability to mark out some personal space within the restrictions it imposes. The English social world of *Daniel Deronda*, although broader in range, is essentially similar to that of *Middlemarch*. Movement from one class to another brings, not the sought-for freedom, but a narrowing of possibilities for action, as illustrated by Gwendolen's marriage. But while Gwendolen moves from the relative liberty of girlhood to the bondage of marriage, Deronda escapes the restrictive pattern in his journey from the cloisters of Topping Abbey towards an indefinable East. Gwendolen's world is one in which action is allocated according to social roles, and she herself, as a star player,

---

[21] *Culture and Imperialism* (London: Vintage, 1994), pp. 129-30.

[22] In 'The Pastoral of Intellect', *Critical Essays on George Eliot*, ed. by Barbara Hardy (London: Routledge & Kegan Paul, 1970), p. 210, John Bayley has written that '*Daniel Deronda*, unlike *Middlemarch*, is [...] a novel which increases in intellectual interest when we reread it and measure it against the growth of our own awareness of historical and cultural developments [...]'. His insight seems tragically pertinent in this dark summer and autumn of 1995.

derives her whole sense of self from her relation to her audience. Thus, she is overcome by horror and near loss of selfhood when she finds, in her marriage, a marriage in which she expected to be 'the heroine of an admired play without the pains of art' (301), that she is playing a role scripted by another for a hostile audience of one. As if to reinforce the point, Gwendolen's life is presented in a series of vividly realized dramatic scenes. Deronda, on the other hand, can conceive no social role for himself because, owing to the mystery of his origins, he doesn't know what role to play. His passion is history, but he is unable, without help, to perform on this vast platform. Thus he lacks self-definition, and literally drifts with the current. His early life is presented in a long narrative retrospect, lacking all dramatic incident until he is forced into a role by his meetings with Mirah and Mordecai and the eventual revelation of his origins.

Spain is a point of reference from the first chapter of *Daniel Deronda*. In the second paragraph, we are told that Gwendolen is 'occupied in gambling' but 'not in the open air under a southern sky, tossing coppers on a ruined wall, with rags about her limbs [...]' (3), and 'Deronda's first thought' in the casino is that 'the gambling of Spanish shepherd-boys had seemed to him more enviable' (5). When Mirah is introduced, we are told that 'any one who had seen delicate-faced Spanish girls might simply have guessed her to be Spanish' (164). One function of these allusions is to take the reader beyond a recognizable locus. Given that Spain was largely unknown to George Eliot's contemporaries, she could write with the certainty that references to 'Spanish shepherd boys' or 'delicate-faced Spanish girls' would evoke images that would conform to no actual knowledge on the part of most readers. Thus, what seems, at first glance, a guiding authorial hand is, in fact, a device for distancing and defamiliarizing. The allusions become even more esoteric when Deronda's quest for Mirah's family in the East End of London is contrasted with an imaginary 'quest of a beautiful maiden's relatives in Cordova elbowed by Jews in the time of Ibn-Gebirol' (320), or when Mordecai explains that his religious fervour arises from the Jewish poetry and philosophy of mediaeval Spain, to which he traces his spiritual ancestry. Most significant, however, is Deronda's name and the novel's title. 'What a delightful name!' says Gwendolen in Chapter One, 'Is he an Englishman?' (9).

When Gwendolen, who has spent most of her life 'abroad', poses this question, she is just about to be recalled home to a house her family are on the brink of losing. So preoccupied is *Daniel Deronda* with thwarted homecomings, that the novel forces a revaluation of the concept of 'home'.

Offendene is 'not the home of Miss Harleth's childhood' (17), but merely a house her mother is renting. Mirah is told that the street of her childhood home is 'all done away with' (188). The newly-married Grandcourt's announcement, 'Here we are at home!' (301) is shortly followed by 'hysterical violence' (303) when Gwendolen comprehends what her new 'home' will be. In contrast with these *unheimlich* houses, Mordecai speaks of a 'lasting habitation' for his people, 'lasting because movable' (453), and finds a ready sympathizer in Deronda, who has already declared that he can bear to leave his boyhood home, 'I carry it with me,' he says. 'To most men their early home is no more than a memory of their early years, and I'm not sure but they have the best of it. The image is never marred. There's no disappointment in memory [...].' (362). This theory of memory relates directly to Mordecai's idea of the 'unchangeable foundation' (453) of the hope of his people. Deronda, through his name, embodies his people's memory of a historical moment of spiritual and cultural achievement and equilibrium, and his life's mission becomes the attempted re-creation of that remembered moment, a recovery of 'home'.

Ronda, the Spanish city from which Daniel's ancestors have been expelled, serves as a locus of memory in the novel, the home and starting-place which can only be revisited through re-creation. Its history, as a centre of Jewish and Muslim culture in the Middle Ages, and its topography, characterized by a deep gorge spanned by a bridge linking the Muslim and Christian quarters, old city and new, make its usefulness for George Eliot obvious. Daniel's challenge is to link his known present to an unknown past, and he is troubled by 'certain facts which had an obstinate reality — almost like the fragments of a bridge, telling you unmistakably how the arches lay' (142). He becomes the bridge between Gentile and Jew, between modern and ancient learning, to replace the 'breaking' bridge of Mordecai's 'narrow life' (428). But the brief equilibrium that once allowed a multicultural flourishing of Christian, Muslim, and Jewish science, art, and philosophy in mediaeval Spain before collapsing in violence and persecution, is not to be replicated in modern Britain. 'Jerusalem' will not be built in this land. Deronda's ambition to give 'a national centre' to his people reflects George Eliot's belief that, in a world of nation-states, no group is secure without its own 'political existence' (688).[23] The ultimate failure of peaceful coexistence of peoples and faiths in

---

[23] Susan Meyer in '"Safely to their own Borders": Proto-Zionism, Feminism, and Nationalism in Daniel Deronda', *ELH*, 60 (1993), 733-58, has argued that 'the novel is rife with anti-semitism'. To sustain this argument, it is necessary to overlook the novel's

Spain, and its tragic aftermath, are reflected in the plight of Deronda. Ronda can only be the place that Daniel is *from,* but at the same time, the name marks him as being from, or belonging to, nowhere else. Hence Gwendolen's 'Is he an Englishman?'.

In her letter to Sara Hennell of 1866 where she writes of the 'new vistas' opened by her knowledge of Spanish, Marian goes on to say, 'I could enjoy everything, from arithmetic to antiquarianism, if I had large spaces of life before me. But instead of that, I have a very small space'. Her experience of Spain, however, gave her a sense of conquering the spatial and temporal limitations that are the human lot. Spain was, in the most literal sense, an expansion of horizons, both physically and culturally. The implications of this experience are reflected in Gwendolen's presentation. Gwendolen's life is a dialectic between 'the narrow theatre which life offers to a girl of twenty' (51) and a 'vastness in which she seemed an exile' (52). The 'drama of personal desires' must always be a 'small drama'(387). The effect of her recognition of Deronda's life-mission is that 'the world seemed getting larger round poor Gwendolen' (688). This radical shift in Gwendolen's perspective is 'bewildering [...] a crisis [...] a shock'. It is also potentially liberating from the self-consciousness that perceives the self only as the object of other eyes, a performer.

For George Eliot, the novelist, the performer in prose, the attention of other eyes was a necessary condition of existence, but Marian Lewes achieved liberation in Spain through engagement with impersonal 'Spanish sights'. Her progress through Spain — a 'succession of delights' (*Letters,* IV, 338) culminating in an experience of transcendence — recalls Robert Frost's definition of poetry, which 'begins in delight and ends in wisdom'.[24] In *Daniel Deronda*, we are presented with a territory between the 'hard unaccommodating Actual' (321) and what Seamus Heaney has recently called 'the domain of the imagined'.[25] The bridge to span this gap is constructed by the process of reading itself. Gwendolen, at the end of the novel, is in a position where she can see, instead of always being seen. She can escape the circumscribed self by looking outward, transcending what Eliot once called 'the vulgarity of exclusiveness'. 'Before all, to make you *see.* That — and no

---

unrelenting criticism of English social and political life, as well as to forget, in Salman Rushdie's phrase, 'the fictionality of fiction'.

[24] 'The Figure a Poem Makes', in *Twentieth Century Poetry and Poetics*, ed. by Gary Geddes (Toronto: Oxford University Press, 1969), p. 463.

[25] *The Redress of Poetry: Oxford Lectures* (London: Faber, 1995), p. xiii.

more, and it is everything', said Conrad of his purpose in writing.[26] Gwendolen's radical accession of vision, for her a bridge to a more fulfilling existence, becomes a type for the reader's experience of *Daniel Deronda,* a novel which, in its resistance to conventional closure, opens 'new vistas' beyond the usual horizons of nineteenth-century realist fiction.

---

[26] Preface to *The Nigger of the 'Narcissus'* (London: Dent, 1963), p. 5.

Chapter Ten

'Animated Nature': *The Mill on the Floss*

Beryl Gray

All George Eliot's works of fiction are the products of a cultivated intelligence made European through travel, translation, and formidably extensive reading. What George Eliot herself called the *'epische Breite'* [1] of the first two volumes of *The Mill on the Floss* is indicative of the scope of her vision for this novel. Her presentation of St Ogg's and its inhabitants depends as much on the implications of her perspectives of the Rhône and the Rhine, on her allusions to Aristotle, Sophocles, and Homer, on her application of Greek and Roman mythology, and on her engagement with the German cultural historian, Wilhelm von Riehl, as it does on the sense of an intimately-recollected past a sense that, in turn, recognizes the abiding spiritual, local presence of Roman, Saxon, and Dane. These allusions and presences permeate the novel, vastly extending its referential world beyond the horizons of those who belong to the tiny, trading society of St Ogg's. They are intrinsic to the 'large vision of relations'[2] which George Eliot invites the reader to share, serving as one of the ways in which 'the small pulse' (II, 6) of the focal organism is linked with 'the world's mighty heart' (II, 6), and unobtrusively substantiating the observations of life which, in *The Mill on the Floss*, means life in all its forms.

In an early chapter of *The Mill on the Floss*, we are told that, to the nine-year-old Maggie,

---

[1] *The George Eliot Letters*, ed. by Gordon S. Haight, 9 vols (New Haven and London: Yale University Press, 1954-78), III, 317.

[2] George Eliot, *The Mill on the Floss*, Cabinet Edition (Edinburgh and London: William Blackwell and Sons, 1878), II, 6. Further references to the novel are to the volumes and pages of this edition, and will be given in the text.

the mill was a little world apart from her outside everyday life. The spiders were especially a subject of speculation with her. She wondered if they had any relatives outside the mill, for in that case there must be a painful difficulty in their family intercourse — a fat and floury spider, accustomed to take his fly well dusted with meal, must suffer a little at a cousin's table where the fly was *au naturel*, and the lady-spiders must be mutually shocked at each other's appearance. (I, 39)

A few chapters later, when the children are at Garum Firs, where Maggie is ostracized for having disgraced herself and disgusted Tom in various ways, Lucy wishes that Maggie were allowed to enjoy the spectacle of Tom plaguing a toad with a piece of string dangled through the area grating. Maggie's presence would enhance the entertainment because she would be certain to find a name for the portly toad, 'and say what had been his past history' (I, 151).

Lucy's certainty is founded on the fact that Maggie is always able to make up stories about the creatures that the children happen to come upon. Maggie had been able to tell, for example, 'how Mrs Earwig had a wash at home, and one of her children had fallen into the hot copper, for which reason she was running so fast to fetch the doctor' (I, 151).

Apart from illustrating the richness of Maggie's interior life, these fantasies are instances in the novel where sub-human animal life is raised to the level of human experience. The social mores and susceptibilities of the arachnid are shown to be as delicate as those of carriage folk, while the anxiety of the earwig is obviously affectingly maternal.

Tom is of course contemptuous both of 'this nonsense of Maggie's' (I, 151), and of all inferior organisms. Naturally, therefore, the earwig is smashed 'at once as a superfluous yet easy means of proving the entire unreality of such a story' (I, 151). But while in their small-scale anthropomorphism these little improvisations and fantasies honourably anticipate the tales of Beatrix Potter, they also reveal that their teller is a natural, natural historian. It is the concentrated observation of the naturalist that preserves Maggie's narratives and make-believe explanations from mawkishness. With their individualizing details, they are convincingly the product of a young imagination — an expression of the way in which, in childhood, Maggie experiences 'animated nature'. Not only do they distinguish her response — and therefore her own nature — from Tom's, but as a manifestation of her quick, inventive curiosity, they counterbalance those influences of the natural world to which she is otherwise so susceptible: the dipping sounds, whisperings, rustlings, and dreamy silences which induce bliss, and the forgetfulness for which she is so often criticized. Incorporated as they are within the omniscient narrative, they are also intrinsic to the author's own account of the natural history of St Ogg's.

These stories of Maggie's carry no moral freight. They seem entirely uninfluenced by Aesop, whose fables are included among Maggie's books. What does hover over the stories, though, is the work from which I have taken the title of this essay: *An History of the Earth and Animated Nature*, by Oliver Goldsmith. It is the work which Maggie recommends to her father's head miller, Luke, by the abbreviated title I have borrowed. She thinks it might be more attractive to Luke than *Pug's Tour of Europe* because it is about 'elephants and kangaroos, and the civet-cat' (I, 40-41) and so forth, rather than what she calls 'the different sorts of people in the world' (I, 40). George Eliot's own sustained pattern of references to the animated nature that inhabits the world of her novel is offered not as an alternative to its 'different sorts of people', but as crucial to their presentation.

It is true that, in *Animated Nature*, Goldsmith offers no anecdotes of spider cousins or harassed mother earwigs, but he does tell us in his Preface that he hopes his work will yield a 'satisfactory History of [the] [...] manners, [...] friendships and hostilities'[3] of any animal of which the reader knows the name. Character assessments abound: Goldsmith does not shrink from attributing to animals qualities such as courage, fidelity, or tenderness where deemed appropriate, nor from identifying the turpitudes of cowardice and cruelty.

Acknowledging the French naturalist Buffon as his guide, Goldsmith nevertheless claims that his own Natural History offers

> a work to the public, of a kind, which has never been attempted in ours, or any other modern language, that I know of. The ancients, indeed, and Pliny in particular, have anticipated me in the present manner of treating Natural History.[4]

What Goldsmith hopes to do, he tells us, is 'allure' his reader — as he had been allured by Pliny:

> The delight which I found in reading Pliny, first inspired me with a work of this nature. Having a taste rather classical than scientific, and having but little employed myself in turning over the dry labours of modern system-makers, my earliest intention was to translate this agreeable writer, and by the help of commentary to make my work as amusing as I could [...]. Upon the appearance, however, of Mr Buffon's work, I dropped my former plan, and adopted the present, being convinced by his manner, that

---

[3] Oliver Goldsmith, *An History of the Earth and Animated Nature* (London, 1819; first published 1774), p. vii.

[4] Ibid, p. viii.

the best imitation of the ancients was to write from our own feelings, and to imitate Nature.[5]

Goldsmith had reason to acknowledge the work of *Mr* Buffon — otherwise known as George Louis Le Clerc, Comte de Buffon — for Buffon's *Histoire naturelle* was pioneering, accessible, and immensely popular. The publication of its successive parts extended over fifty-five years, between 1749 and 1804, though only the history of quadrupeds had been completed when Goldsmith decided to produce his *History of the Earth*. Buffon's work was criticized (by Goldsmith and others) for its lack of method. Nevertheless, it was translated into several languages, including English, and — according to the eleventh edition of the *Encyclopaedia Britannica* — is considered to have 'effected much good in its time by generally diffusing a taste for the study of nature'.

Sadly, Goldsmith did not live to witness the popularity of his own work, which was first published in 1774, the year of his death. Several handsomely-illustrated editions had appeared by the time Maggie (and Mary Ann Evans) were nine years old, and many more by the time George Eliot was writing *The Mill on the Floss*. Though highly derivative, fanciful, and often misleading, *Animated Nature* is beguiling: the reason for its appeal to Maggie is apparent as soon as it is perused. Along with *The History of the Devil* and *Pilgrim's Progress*, it would have nourished her imagination. It would also have both stimulated her intellect, and added greatly to the store of knowledge she so craved to extend.

Just as worth stressing is the significance of Goldsmith's work — buttressed as it was by Buffon's work — to Maggie's, and George Eliot's, literate contemporaries. Although assuredly not read by anyone *but* Maggie at Dorlcote (it presumably found its way into the house among the job lots purchased by Mr Tulliver), both the abbreviated title used by Maggie, and the work itself, would have been familiar to many, or possibly most, of the novel's first readers, to whose own education Goldsmith's increasingly scientifically discredited natural history may well have contributed. Maggie's recommendation of it to Luke would therefore have touched sympathetic chords of recognition in the 1860s — the influence of Darwin, George Henry Lewes and others notwithstanding. Together with Buffon's volumes, and works such as the Reverend W. Bingley's *Animal Biography, or Popular Zoology* (1803; 4th edition 1813), *An History of the Earth and Animated*

---

[5] Ibid, p. viii.

Nature was, in the late 1820s — the period in which the first part of the novel is set — a fair representation of what constituted popular natural history.

In deciding to follow the manner of the ancients, Goldsmith wisely rejected the 'numerous fables' adopted by them. However, Pliny's *Natural History* of AD 77 is much cited by Goldsmith, and clearly provided a sort of model for him, though Pliny is even more fanciful than his eighteenth-century successor. Particularly relevant are the Roman's eighth, ninth, and tenth books, which describe, respectively, 'The Nature of the Terrestrial Animals', 'The Natural History of Fishes', and 'The Natural History of Birds'. Also to be found in Pliny is a definition of the word 'garum', which lends itself as the name of the place where we have already seen Tom tormenting the fat toad.

The Latin name acknowledges the long-ago presence in the locality of the Roman legions who 'turned their backs' (I, 178) on the spot where St Ogg's took root. It is also, according to Pliny (and the Oxford English Dictionary refers for its definition to Pliny), the name of a sauce; a liquid

> of a very exquisite nature [...]: it is prepared from the intestines of fish and various parts which would otherwise be thrown away, macerated in salt; so that it is, in fact, the result of their putrefaction.[6]

This ancient Roman (originally Greek) recipe was considered also to have medicinal properties, and bequeathed itself to Renaissance Britain as a decoction for the treatment of certain ailments afflicting horses, into whose *left* nostrils it was apparently poured.[7]

From wherever George Eliot drew her inspiration for the name Garum, it is the parish's legacy from its pre-parochial Roman past. Although that past is as forgotten by the parishioners as the 'Saxon hero-king' and the 'dreadful heathen Dane'[8] (I, 179), whose shadows still rise and walk, it cannot be expunged from the evolution of the fictive place, but remains part of its spirit. Though obscured by time, the unDodsonian, epicurean connotations of the name have their correlative in the manifestly unexotic Pullets' divertingly

---

[6] *The Natural History of Pliny*, trans. by John Bostock and H. T. Riley, 6 vols (London, 1855-57), Book XXXI, Ch. 43.

[7] If horses 'have any frets or galles on the pastornes, ye shall playster thereon the paste of Barly meale, and open the impostume if there by any, and heale it with tentes of lynt, and such oyntments as afore is mentioned, with a pynt and a half of Garum, which I take to be saltfishe water with a pound of oile olive mixed together, and put into his left nostril, and put thereunto the whites of three or foure egges', Leonard Mascall, *The Government of Horses* (London, 1587), pp. 122-3.

[8] The 'Saxon hero-king' is Alfred the Great (849-99); the 'dreadful heathen Dane' is King Sweyn 'Forkbeard' (d. 1014), who conquered England in 1013.

exotic menagerie. At Garum Firs, there was a peacock that would display his tail.

> All the farmyard life was wonderful [...] — bantams, speckled and top-knotted; Friesland hens, with their feathers all turned the wrong way; Guinea-fowls that flew and screamed and dropped their pretty-spotted feathers; pouter pigeons and a tame magpie; nay, a goat, and a wonderful brindled dog, as large as a lion. Then there were white railings and white gates all about, and glittering weathercocks of various design, and garden-walks paved with pebbles in beautiful patterns — nothing was quite common at Garum Firs: and Tom thought that the unusual size of the toads there was simply due to the general unusualness which characterised uncle Pullet's possessions as a gentleman farmer. Toads who paid rent were naturally leaner. (I, 132)

It is impossible to believe that that last conceit belongs in any way to Tom: rent-paying toads inhabit the same imaginary realm as socially shocked or embarrassed spiders. But that aside, the point about the peacock, the Friesland hens, the lion-sized dog and so on is that, while they are wonderful to behold, no reassuringly domestic or native characteristics are associated with them. Their habitat is distinctly not the children's habitat, and the white railings, white gates, and pebble-paved walks that define their setting all help to establish the sense of a foreign environment where the children are not at their ease. In other words, the Garum Firs garden is not part of that childhood Eden from which Maggie and Tom are to be expelled in consequence of their father's lost law-suit. Therefore, when Tom transgresses by leaving the garden, his disobedience to aunt Pullet is not to a God-like authority, as has been argued.[9] He is not venturing from a representative Garden of Creation into the forbidden wilderness. It is the countryside *beyond* the contrived, 'prim' (I, 152) garden that constitutes the childhood Eden — where the pond with the indigenous pike that Tom wishes to see lies about a field's length away. This is why Tom's choice of Lucy for a companion, and his cruel exclusion of Maggie, are so momentous. It is Maggie who is his natural and rightful consort in this realm; but by his decree, she is usurped by Lucy. This usurpation is to be painfully reversed in Book Sixth, when Maggie displaces Lucy as Stephen's consort in her cousin's authorially-designated Paradise.

The celebrated pike that lurks in the pond to which Tom is drawn is 'a highly interesting monster; he was said to be so very old, so very large, and to

---

[9] Indicating that Tom and Lucy 'walk to the forbidden end of the garden' rather than beyond it, U. C. Knoepflmacher says that 'God in this child-world is any adult, even one as severely limited in authority and understanding as Mrs Tulliver's favorite sister', *George Eliot's Early Novels* (Berkeley: University of California Press, 1968), pp. 185-6.

have such a remarkable appetite' (I, 153).[10] Though he remains invisible, he has considerable significance and I shall return to him.   What Tom spots instead of the pike, and invites Lucy to behold, is a water-snake, which inevitably Maggie yearns to see too. No longer content merely to ignore her, however, Tom actually orders her off. Already transformed by jealousy into 'a small Medusa with her snakes cropped' (I, 150), it is now that Maggie performs the vindictive act of pushing little pink-and-white Lucy into the cow-trodden mud, and is afterwards uncharacteristically unrepentant. The damage to Lucy is limited to bewilderment and discomfort; as an allusion to Aristotle's *Poetics* makes clear, the act itself is not the stuff of tragedy. But the passions at war in Maggie are *potentially* the stuff of tragedy: they are intimations of the epic struggle her by then different passions are to undergo in the Paradise setting of 'The Great Temptation', when 'a cruel selfishness seemed to be getting possession of her' (II, 302). It is to continue in 'The Final Rescue' as the struggle of a character whom George Eliot herself described as 'essentially noble but liable to great error'.[11]

Three years before beginning work on the *Mill*, George Eliot applied the profound interest in natural history she shared with George Henry Lewes to her important *Westminster Review* essay on Riehl, 'The Natural History of German Life'. Ideas expressed in this essay are explored in the novel. Central to both Riehl and George Eliot is the sense of a 'vital connexion with the past' — a connection which, George Eliot asserts, 'is much more vividly felt on the Continent than in England'.[12] What she sought to do in the *Mill* was to make that 'vital connexion with the past' as vividly felt as it is on the Continent, and to do that she had to make the past in which the novel is set — the past of her own childhood and youth — vividly present; vividly alive.

---

[10] This description endorses Goldsmith's character of the pike, which is, he claims, the most 'voracious' of all freshwater fish; 'our poets [...] have called it the tyrant of the watery plain' (op. cit., p. 604). Goldsmith's unacknowledged authority is almost certainly Izaac Walton, whose 'Observations of the Luce or Pike with Directions how to fish for him' begins, 'The mighty *Luce* or *Pike* is taken to be the Tyrant [...] of the fresh waters', and goes on to inform the reader that this 'longest lived of any fresh water fish' has a 'bold, greedy, devouring disposition', *The Compleat Angler* (London, 2nd edition, 1655), p. 193. The age of George Eliot's pike clearly mattered to her since she had originally identified it several times as a 'jack'-pike and then deleted each 'jack' in the manuscript, overlooking one. A jack-pike is a young or small pike.

[11] *Letters*, III, 318.

[12] George Eliot, 'The Natural History of German Life', reprinted in *George Eliot's Selected Critical Writings*, ed. by Rosemary Ashton (Oxford: Oxford University Press, 1992), p. 283.

She had to animate the natural history that, as Rosemary Ashton observes, 'so thoroughly informs the writing of *The Mill on the Floss* that it contributes to both the comedy and the tragedy of the book'.[13]

'In the cultivated world', it is suggested in the article on Riehl,

each individual has his style of speaking and writing. But among the peasantry it is the race, the district, the province, that has its style; [...]. This provincial style of the peasant is [...] a remnant of history to which he clings with the utmost tenacity.[14]

Among the cases that are described is that of the Wends, a Slavonic race who live 'either scattered among the German population or in separate parishes',[15] but in their villages they retain all the customs indicative of their agricultural origins. They have, for example, 'traditional modes of treating their domestic animals. Each cow has its own name, generally chosen carefully, so as to express the special qualities of the animal'.[16] This sympathetic generic custom of acknowledging and respecting the individualizing qualities of herd animals is one that George Eliot adapts for the *Mill*. Including the three dogs — Maggie's and Tom's Yap, Bob Jakin's Mumps, and Lucy's Minny, all of whose 'special qualities' and susceptibilities are observed and interiorized — the animals in the novel, domestic and otherwise, are used analogically or associatively as a means of helping to individualize the members of the Oggian race.

St Ogg's as a social organism, and most of the novel's principal human individuals, are compared or identified — sometimes, by other characters, mistakenly — with other species or particular beasts, or are yoked, as it were, to them. The book teems with instances of characters presented as more helplessly themselves through animal simile, metaphor, or fable. The often-noted representative of the inflexible (by nature) Mr Stelling, for example, is Mr Broderip's beaver, who poignantly constructs his dam as earnestly 'up three pair of stairs in London, as if he had been laying his foundation in a stream or lake in Upper Canada' (I, 213). Mrs Glegg, whose store of garments is geologically stratified, and whose table-linen is all contemptible 'Big checks and live things, like stags and foxes' (II, 292), has a mentally active husband who

---

[13] Rosemary Ashton, *The Mill on the Floss: A Natural History*, Twayne's Masterwork Studies No. 54 (Boston: Twayne, 1990), p. 35.

[14] George Eliot, *Selected Critical Writings*, p. 268.

[15] Ibid, p. 268.

[16] Ibid, p. 269.

surprised himself by his discoveries in natural history, finding that his piece of garden-ground contained wonderful caterpillars, slugs, and insects, which, so far as he had heard, had never before attracted human observation. (I, 185-6)

In fact, Mr Glegg is rather one of those 'industrious men of business [...], who made their fortunes slowly, almost as the tracking of the fox belongs to the harrier — it constituted them a "race"' (I, 187). And then there is Mrs Tulliver, who variously and tellingly evokes an amiable but ineducable gold-fish, a protective sheep, and a water-fowl, but is pre-eminently associated with the chickens in her yard (which she is quite ready to kill when they '*wants killing*' as on p. 13) — until she is herself metamorphosed into a cackling, fluttering hen taking disastrously to stratagem. Her sister-in-law is also associated with chickens which, though depicted as silly or even hysterical in themselves, are in her case indicative of maternal protectiveness — as we see when her brother arrives to demand the return of the money he has lent her husband, and four of her children (having in the manuscript merely 'clustered themselves round their mother') run out 'like chickens whose mother has been suddenly in eclipse behind the hencoop' (I, 120).

One of the most-discussed, most overt correlations in the novel with natural history occurs in the first chapter — 'A Variation of Protestantism Unknown to Bossuet' — of Book Fourth, 'The Valley of Humiliation'. The chapter opens with the effect produced by the sight of the 'dismal remnants of commonplace houses' (II, 3) that stud the banks of the Rhône — an effect that is contrasted with that of 'natural fitness' (II, 4) produced by the sublime spectacle of the castles of the Rhine. This effect is romantically enhanced in our imaginations by the narrator's reflection that these castles were built by robber-barons who, if they 'were somewhat grim and drunken ogres', nevertheless 'had a certain grandeur of the wild beast in them — they were forest boars with tusks, tearing and rending, not the ordinary domestic grunter' (II, 4).

The transformation from fairy-tale ogre to magnificent, emblematic beast, channels the reader's imagination towards a thrilling, 'grand historic vision of humanity', a vision that is vibrant with colour and 'glancing steel and floating banners': an heroic vision of a time 'of living, religious art and religious enthusiasm' (II, 4). The contrast between the chivalric vision sprung by the image of the Rhine boars, and the traces along the Rhône of obscure ant- or beaver-like human vitality, prepares us for the association of the sordid concerns of those Rhône-dwellers with the 'oppressive narrowness' (II, 6) of the 'emmet-like' (II, 6) Dodsons and Tullivers, whose lives are 'irradiated by no sublime principles, no romantic visions, no active, self-renouncing faith' (II, 5) or distinctive creed.

While Tom experiences his share of the suffering 'which belongs to every historical advance of mankind' (II, 6), it is Maggie's accidentally-illuminated striving — her intellectual and spiritual need to emerge from the oppression and confinement — that achieves a sort of grandeur. Although her world is manifestly not Riehl's 'cultivated world', her 'style' distinguishes itself from that of her race or clan both through self-cultivation, and because her evolved and still evolving intelligence yet recognizes and honours the 'connexion with the past' that to both Riehl and George Eliot was so vital. In finally conceding to the claims of that connection, Maggie of course renounces much; but the renunciation accords with what she has struggled to define and to articulate. It ratifies the nobility with which her author hoped she had invested her, and relates her story — her troublous life — to the 'grand historic', chivalric vision associated with the Rhine castles and the heraldic boars — which recur as 'the cherished emblems of a noble family once the seigniors' (II, 256) of St Ogg's' old hall.

The relationship between the heroic vision and Maggie's story is further sustained by Maggie's own longing for some chivalry. As a child, when she was alarmed by 'visions of robbers and fierce animals haunting every hollow' (II, 48) of the Red Deeps, her eyes — 'full of unsatisfied intelligence, and unsatisfied, beseeching affection' (I, 278) — had reminded Philip 'of the stories about princesses being turned into animals' (I, 278); but it is the Shetland pony, Skye terrier, rough puppy, or captive bear — the creatures with which she has variously been compared, or (in the case of the bear) has compared herself — who is to be transformed by Lucy, and by delicious offerings to her needy intelligence and affections, into a princess. 'Lucy is like a fairy godmother: she has turned me from a drudge into a princess in no time' (II, 227), she tells Philip in 'The Great Temptation' when he re-enters her life. Unfortunately, Philip is not destined to serve the princess. It is Stephen who, having initially beguiled her with his account of 'Buckland's wonderful geological story' (II, 176) of Creation, seductively proffers the steadying hand, the supporting arm, the solicitous concern, the footstool, the protecting cloak; ultimately all that he can bestow, including reputation. In necessarily adapted terms, he fulfils the chivalric code; but, paradoxically, he cannot fulfil it in honour. Maggie must retrieve herself and seek refuge at the home of Bob Jakin, who evolves from the boy who was 'not sensitive on the point of honour — not a chivalrous character' (I, 76) into the most truly chivalrous man in the book.

Although Maggie's childhood expressiveness approximates sometimes to the unrestrained or impulsive behaviour of a young animal, it is a mark of the distinction conferred on her by her author that no particular creature or class of creature qualifies as emblematically hers. In the dream-revisitation of the novel's opening chapter, 'that queer white cur with the brown ear' (I, 6) — whose antics crucially animate the scene — is presented as the playfellow of the little, unidentified figure in the beaver bonnet who is rapt in the movement of the unresting mill-wheel. But though the highly-individualized Yap appears here to be Maggie's familiar, he is Tom's too: he belongs to both children while remaining essentially himself.

At school, Tom misses Yap in terms of the dog's readiness to obey, and takes special notice of him only as a way of snubbing Maggie, who is never seen similarly to appropriate the dog, but thinks of him tenderly when she is away, and he is dying from a lump in his throat, while she wishes to protect Tom from the upsetting knowledge. In fact, Maggie has no relationship with any pet animal in the novel who is not also the adjunct of somebody else, though the relationships she does have — with Bob's sagacious, confidential, Dickensian Mumps, for example, and with Lucy's little King Charles spaniel, Minny, whom she comforts in Lucy's absence — are all revealing. Minny himself has the sagacity to mistrust Stephen, and hides when Stephen's 'full-toned bass' (II, 157) thunders out a version of the Old Testament, prelapsarian alternative to natural history: Raphael's aria from Haydn's *Creation*, the aria which describes God's creation of the beasts, and impersonates them.

Maggie's sensitive awareness of animals is one of her defining qualities, and is authorially acknowledged on the last day of Maggie's allotted life, when, with the first dawn light, she begins to row on the flood towards the river and St Ogg's and 'could soon see the poor dumb beasts crowding piteously on a mound where they had taken refuge' (II, 395). In the legend of St Ogg, the Blessed Virgin had proclaimed after Ogg's act of mercy that his boat would 'save the lives both of men and beasts' (I, 180). Tom's sensitive awareness of animals is equally indicative, but of a different sort. Unable to grasp the relation in Latin between cases and terminations, or 'to recognize a chance genitive or dative' (I, 214), he 'had never found any difficulty in discerning a pointer from a setter' (I, 215) or predicting 'with accuracy what number of horses were cantering behind him' (I, 215). It is an added poignancy, then, that his imagination fails to be quickened by the fact that Latin was once a living language spoken by people 'who bought and sold sheep and oxen' (I, 217), while the 'mysterious sentences' (I, 228) in the Latin Grammar present themselves to Maggie as material for the naturalist; for 'like strange horns of beasts, and leaves of unknown plants — brought from some far-off region, [they give] boundless scope to her imagination' (I, 228). They also suggest boundless educability. Tom, on the other hand, is not even prompted to discover what the sentences he has to commit to memory mean.

These sentences in fact take elementary classifications from natural history to demonstrate the rules for the genders of nouns. If instead of calling Maggie a donkey for reading the English key given in the Grammar, Tom had himself consulted it, in his stumbling rendition he would perhaps not have offered the Latin for Oyster (Ostrea) and Whale (Cetus) as names of birds, or even, in the case of the oyster again, as the name of a wild beast; but George Eliot's choice of this section of the Grammar to illustrate the nature both of Tom's sufferings at school, and of Maggie's frustrated potential, enables her through Maggie's vivifying imagination to make what is dead to Tom alive to the reader.

Neither classicist nor naturalist, Tom nevertheless impresses Maggie with his knowledge of wildlife; yet even this is inferior to the equally blood-thirsty Bob's singularly unWordsworthian, guilt-free natural learning, while his inability to draw live creatures (though he is quite satisfied with his houses and chimneys) is, as Philip[17] (who can draw them) intimates, a mark of his failure to look well at things. His association with horses prevails throughout the novel, but his sense of them arises not from studying them, but from their place in the field and their enhancement of his self-image. Although in his second half-year at school his vision seems widened by the learned Philip's rich fund of stories from Greek history and poetry (including the *Iliad* and Sophocles' *Philoctetes*), and from Sir Walter Scott, Tom responds only to fighting stories that flatter his idea of himself. Despite the splendour of Hector's horses in the *Iliad*, however, and even greater wondrousness of Achilles' horses,[18] Homeric battles are rejected in favour of the immediacy of the local drilling master's 'episodes of warlike narrative' (I, 266) about the Duke of Wellington. After all,

> there were no cannon in the *Iliad*, and besides, Tom had felt some disgust on learning that Hector and Achilles might possibly never have existed. But the Duke of Wellington was really alive, and Bony had not been long dead [...]. (I, 266)

and Mr Poulter's credentials as an old Peninsular soldier ensure that his 'reminiscences [...] were removed from all suspicion of being mythical' (I, 266). Nevertheless, it turns out to be the mythical Philoctetes with the 'very

---

[17] Philip's name is Greek and means 'lover of horses' ('phil-hippoi'). I am grateful to Lesley Gordon for pointing this out to me.

[18] Achilles' Xanthus and Balius (foaled by Podarge, the storm-filly; sired by the Western Gale) are an immortal pair, but the valiant trace-horse, Pedasus, is mortal, and is killed in battle.

bad wound in his foot' (I, 285) whom this 'excellent bovine lad' (I, 275) is actually to resemble (though, in his own opinion, he is himself the more heroic of the two) when, impersonating the living Wellington for Maggie's terrified edification, he accidentally inflicts a sword-wound on his own foot.

Of Philip's stories, Tom's favourites self-revealingly include those about Scott's Hal of the Wynd[19] and Robert Bruce 'because they laid about them with heavy strokes' (I, 258). And

> when Robert Bruce, on the black pony, rose in his stirrups, and, lifting his good battle-axe, cracked at once the helmet and the skull of the too hasty knight at Bannockburn, then Tom felt all the exaltation of sympathy, and if he had had a cocoa-nut at hand, he would have cracked it at once with the poker.[20] (I, 259)

The intense physicality of Tom's sympathy with the actions of the Scottish king begs for mounted expression on the battlefield; but though the outlet of physical engagement and the glory of physical conquest are withheld from Tom, his actual fight demands its own pedestrian form of heroism. While Maggie's enforced powerlessness confines her life-struggles to her own soul, 'Tom was engaged in a dustier, noisier warfare, grappling with more substantial obstacles, and gaining more definite conquests. So it has been since the days of Hecuba, and of Hector, Tamer of horses' (II, 64). Granted the man's privilege of action, Tom's battlefield is bathetically only the figurative battlefield of the commercial world; his weapons those of pride, abstinence, and self-denial. Despite his boyhood enthusiasm for Scott's heroes, and his dismissal of the *Iliad*, it is the narrator's association of him with Hector (he 'would have liked to be a Tamer of horses'; II, 66) that points to a course no less thwarted than Maggie's, and a destiny no less tragic; for it is Hector's fate to die by Achilles' lance, his soul 'bewailing its lot and the youth and manhood that it left'.[20] It is a hideous irony that the corpse of this horse-tamer should be ignominiously and barbarically fastened to Achilles' chariot, and sped, head dragging, through the dust. Afterwards, though,

---

[19] Henry Gow, or Smith, the artisan hero of Scott's *Fair Maid of Perth* (1828), is also known as Henry or Harry or Hal of the Wynd. His character is developed from that of Henry Wynd, the *Gow Chrom* or bandy-legged smith whose fearless exploits with the broad-sword are described by Scott in *Tales of a Grandfather* (1827), Ch. 17.

[20] George Eliot (and Philip) closely follow Scott's account of the incident: 'But as [the knight] passed, King Robert rose up in his stirrups, and struck Sir Henry [de Bohun] on the head with his battle-axe so terrible a blow, that it broke to pieces his iron helmet as if it had been a nutshell, and hurled him from the saddle. He was dead before he reached the ground' (*Tales of a Grandfather*, Ch. 10). The king then refers to his 'good battle-axe'. Interestingly, Philip suppresses the information (which might have been unpalatable to Tom) that Bruce, having not expected to fight, is at this point 'poorly mounted' on a 'little' pony.

Hector's body is relinquished to the Trojans, who lamentingly consign it to the pyre before building their hero's barrow over his honoured bones. The last words of the *Iliad* translate as 'Such were the funeral rites of Hector, tamer of horses'.[21]

It is Maggie who is clearly the heroine of *The Mill on the Floss*, and Maggie who, in the novel's Conclusion — its formal parting from its readers — represents for the two men who visit her tomb 'their keenest joy and keenest sorrow' (II, 402). But her brother shares that tomb, and its epitaph, in Dorlcote churchyard, where the father also lies. There can be no Homeric ceremony, but in uniting Tom with his sister in death, George Eliot honours her would-be Tamer of horses with the rites that are his due.

Tom's conscious ambition is to resemble the zoologically named, decidedly English Sir John Crake,[22] the master of the harriers. He intends to own many dogs and horses; to make a figure on a fine hunter, as his father once had; to be 'master of everything' (I, 205). He wishes that he could, 'be brought up to his father's business, which he had always thought extremely pleasant, for it was nothing but riding about, giving orders, and going to market (I, 205-6).

Tom's dual perspective — of himself and of his father (or himself as his father) — demonstrates an established kinship between the malely domineering and the boyishly impressionable; for if the youth of today is unawed by our wisdom, the narrator has suggested, Greek boys probably thought even Aristotle 'extremely queer' (I, 138). 'It is only when you have mastered a restive horse, or thrashed a drayman, [...] that these shy juniors feel you to be a truly admirable and enviable character' (I, 138).

Mr Tulliver is not inherently violent: he has never thrashed a drayman. But after his illness we learn of his beating his mill-boy — having already beaten his horse, which 'scene had left a lasting terror in Maggie's mind' (II, 20). The shockingness of this incident is intensified by the reader's immediate recollection of the miller's past relationship with his horse. Right up to the moment when, 'still predominating in his imagination' (I, 309), he discovers that the mortgage on his property has been transferred to Wakem, we observe Mr Tulliver, oscillating between decisiveness and indecisiveness, communicate all the nuances of his emotions to or through his psychologically indispensable horse. Thus we see him riding to Basset to demand the return of his money, determined not to dismount from his horse when his sister Gritty appears: 'If a man means to be hard, let him keep in his saddle and speak from

---

21 *The Iliad*, trans. by E. V. Rieu (Harmondsworth: Penguin Books, repr. 1972), p. 406.

22 A crake is a Eurasian rail (the corncrake, for example, which has a harsh, rattle-like cry).

that height, above the level of pleading eyes, and with the command of a distant horizon' (I, 119).

But Mr Tulliver's determination to be hard is indicative of his tendency to be soft, and the softening effect on him of his sister's maternal protectiveness towards her daughters, and towards their claim on their brothers' love, expresses itself in the little stroke he gives his horse's flank. Equally, anger with himself at this relaxation from severity is converted into angry reprimand of the 'innocent' (I, 122) beast. Nevertheless, he has been sufficiently disarmed to feel 'that he should be more likely to show a due spirit of resolve if his sister were not present' (I, 123) during his interview with her husband. Consequently, he descends from his saddle and the vantage position he had previously determined on, and faces his brother-in-law — who has 'the depressed, unexpectant air of a machine horse' (I, 124) — on the poor farmer's poor ground. Surrounded by the evidence of failure, Mr Tulliver succeeds in inflating his irritation sufficiently to carry through his resolve, but the conditions and manner in which the result is achieved deny it moral conviction, and the reader is not surprised when, once outside the yard-gate, Mr Tulliver's unextinguished kindliness re-establishes itself. Remounted, he is able to give force to his graceless 'good-bye' to Gritty by 'turning his horse's head, and riding away' (I, 126), but, channelled through his love for his daughter, the claims of love for his sister re-assert themselves as a

> sudden thought. He checked his horse, and made it stand still in the same spot for two or three minutes, during which he turned his head from side to side in a melancholy way, as if he were looking at some painful object on more sides than one. Evidently, after his fit of promptitude, Mr Tulliver was relapsing into the sense that this is a puzzling world. He turned his horse, and rode slowly back, giving vent to the climax of feeling which had determined this movement by saying aloud, as he struck his horse, 'Poor little wench! she'll have nobody but Tom, belike, when I'm gone.' (I, 126)

With his demand for his money rescinded, the miller rides back long the rutted lanes 'with the sense of a danger escaped' (I, 127).

Mr Tulliver is in fact incapable of escaping the dictates of his own nature. 'There are certain animals to which a tenacity of position is a law of life', we are told at the beginning of 'The Downfall':

> they can never flourish again, after a single wrench: and there are certain human beings to whom predominance is a law of life — they can only sustain humiliation so long as they can refuse to believe in it, and, in their own conception, predominate still. (I, 308-9)

And Mr Tulliver is still predominating in his imagination when that fatal 'single wrench' comes; but the fact that he is outdoors, an established equestrian figure when he receives the news about his property, is an instance of George Eliot's fine dramatic judgement. The welded image of man and beast to which she has accustomed us is sundered, and the image of the unmounted grey horse 'snuffing uneasily' (I, 311) about his insensible master both describes, and intensifies the sense of, that master's downfall.

After Mr Tulliver's slow recovery — which is compared to 'a living creature making its way from under a great snowdrift, that slides and slides again' (I, 381) — the miller images himself as a yoked horse, whose harness will 'gall' him as he draws along 'the old road' (I, 415); and indeed, during his four years of gloom and deprivation, he is seen riding along 'with his head hanging down, casting brief, unwilling looks on those who [force] themselves on his notice' (II, 137). But after his honour-restoring meeting with his creditors, when he is filled with 'the potent wine of triumphant joy' (II, 138), he rides still slowly, but 'with up-lifted head and free glances, along the principal street' (II, 138). His equestrian stance proclaims that he has achieved enough for the man; but it is not enough for Vengeance. And so, when he meets the haughty, hated Wakem on his fine, black horse, there follows the famous confrontation, with Mr Tulliver 'spurring his horse and raising his whip' (II, 139) in grim heroic parody, causing Wakem's horse to rear and throw his rider. It is with the ignominious, crazed flogging of his defenceless enemy that the dismounted, confused Tulliver fulfils the destiny his unforgiving temperament has determined; and it is Mr Wakem, unable to remount his own high horse, who rides Mr Tulliver's low beast out of the novel.

Part of the pathos of Mr Tulliver's revenge-driven decline is that the hatred is not mutual. Lawyer Wakem merely regards the 'unsuccessful plaintiff' as a 'pitiable, furious bull entangled in the meshes of a net' (I, 395) while to Tulliver, all lawyers — along with rats and weevils — 'were created by Old Harry' (I, 17) in the first place. Wakem therefore simply fulfils a designated role in the miller's earlier view of the law as 'a sort of cock-fight' (I, 241) or 'cockpit' (I, 395) in which, since 'Wakem had already had his comb cut for once in his life' (I, 16), Lawyer Gore could cut it again on behalf of Mr Tulliver. Unfortunately, this time it is Lawyer Gore who has his comb cut.

It is intrinsic to the tragic compound of personal failing and uncontrollable circumstance that shapes Mr Tulliver's life that he should be deeply mistaken concerning Mr Wakem, though his conviction in Book Second concerning the lawyer — that he is '(metaphorically speaking) at the bottom of Pivart's irrigation' (I, 244), and that Wakem and Pivart are 'as thick as mud' (I, 246) with each other — reveals an intuitive understanding of Wakem's nature that poor Mr Tulliver is himself incapable of fathoming: for the lawyer is no game-cock, but — analogically and anthropomorphically — a lurking, opportunistic pike. And so,

> To suppose that Wakem had the same sort of inveterate hatred towards Tulliver, that Tulliver had towards him, would be like supposing that a pike and a roach can look at each other from a similar point of view. The roach necessarily abhors the mode in which the pike gets his living, and the pike is likely to think nothing further even of the most indignant roach than that he is excellent good eating; it could only be when the roach choked him that the pike could entertain a strong personal animosity. (I, 394)

But Mr Wakem is a pike of epicurean discernment who (unlike some of his kind)[23] can recognize what would choke him. Therefore he will have no transactions with Tom Tulliver, he tells Philip in 'The Great Temptation'. 'If you like to swallow him for his sister's sake, you may; but I've no sauce [or garum?] that will make him go down' (II, 254).

The dispositional association of lawyer and pike refers Mr Wakem to that celebrated 'highly interesting monster' with the 'remarkable appetite' who reputedly lurks in the pond in the childhood Eden beyond the confines of Garum Firs, but which Tom — who would dearly have loved to land 'a big pike' (I, 256) — is unable even to see. Mr Wakem is not exactly a monster, but in that he is so calamitously the focus of Mr Tulliver's living vindictiveness and bequeathed vengefulness, he is central to the novel's action, and fulfils his narrative function according to the identification which determines his classification within the imaginatively-adapted scheme that informs it. As we have seen, that system draws on a culturally boundless

---

[23] Goldsmith asserts that the pike 'will attack every fish less than itself; and it is sometimes seen choked, by attempting to swallow such as are too large a morsel [...]. Gesner [Conrad Gesner (1516-65); Swiss naturalist] tells us of a mule that stooped to drink in the water, when a famished pike, that was near, seized it by the nose, nor was it disengaged till the beast flung it on the shore' (*op. cit.*, p. 604). Although Goldsmith acknowledges Gesner, his direct source appears still to be Walton (see n. 10 above), who — also citing Gesner — tells essentially the same story (see Walton, pp. 195-6). The only significant discrepancy between Goldsmith's generalized pike and Walton's is that, though Walton's will indeed 'devoure a fish of his owne kind, that shall be bigger then [*sic*] his belly or throat will receive', it is not, like Goldsmith's, 'choked', but will swallow part of its prey, 'and let the other part remain in his mouth till the swallowed part be digested, and then swallow that other part that was in his mouth, and so put it over by degrees [...]' (pp. 196-7). Walton had also heard of a woman bitten by a pike 'in *Killingworth* Pond, not far from Coventry' (p. 196). A. F. Adams of Coventry informs me that Killingworth is the former name of Kenilworth and that the 'pond' was probably one of the ponds of the Abbey fed by Inchford Brook. Since (as Mr Adams confirms) George Eliot knew her local legends, the apocryphal Kenilworth pike quite possibly suggested the Garum monster.

range of allusions that substantiate George Eliot's presentation of character, and illuminate her vision of tendencies and relations. Despite her narrator's often-cited lament to 'the greatest ancient', Aristotle, for his inferred dictum 'that we can so seldom declare what a thing is, except by saying it is something else' (I, 216), the unfolding of the vision depends on her sustained and comprehensive use of animal analogy and animal metaphor, a use that in turn draws on close and (usually) sympathetic observation of the creatures that engender it, and which are themselves intrinsic to the larger social and natural organism.   In its manner of embracing Riehl, acknowledging Goldsmith and — by extention — those such as Buffon, and especially Pliny, who anticipated or 'guided' him, *The Mill on the Floss* claims a retrospective place in the natural history of Natural History.

Chapter Eleven

From Reality to Fiction: Benefits and Hazards in Continental Education

Linda K. Robertson

The significance of a sound education which is appropriate to the needs of the individual is an important but too often overlooked theme in the writings of George Eliot. In her fiction, essays, and letters, Eliot repeatedly points out ways in which people are influenced by their educational experiences or the lack of such experiences. As part of this process, she not only examines various sorts of schooling in England but also looks northward to Scotland and across the Channel to the Continent.

Eliot's concern with the type of instruction available ranges from the real-life decision of where to send the sons of George Henry Lewes for further education to the 'both narrow and promiscuous' schooling experienced by the fictional Celia and Dorothea Brooke and even to Tertius Lydgate's medical training. An examination of the full range of Eliot's writings ties together her interest in the role of educational issues, as they were seen in contemporary public policy debates and parliamentary commissions, and her reflection of these issues in the lives of fictional characters. Many of Eliot's acquaintances, including the more memorable examples of Coventry ribbon manufacturer Charles Bray, Herbert Spencer (and others Eliot met at John Chapman's establishment in London), Barbara Bodichon and Emily Davies were concerned with educational theory, educational reform, or the establishing of new educational institutions. Of course, a variety of investigations, debates, schemes for improvement, and legislation addressed the state of education in England throughout the period covered in Eliot's writing.

For example, after the Reform Bill of 1832 there was renewed interest in educational questions, prompting the *Report of the Parliamentary Committee on the State of Education* in 1834. In 1839, the Committee of Council for Education was established, and Dr James Kay (later Kay-Shuttleworth) was appointed secretary. The parliamentary commissions investigating Oxford and Cambridge in 1852, the Newcastle Commission (which produced the *Report of the Commissioners Appointed to Inquire into the State of Popular Education in England*) in 1861, the Clarendon Commission (which produced the *Report of Her Majesty's Commissioners Appointed to Inquire into the Revenues and Management of Certain Colleges and Schools, and the Studies Pursued and Instruction Given Therein*) in 1864, and the Taunton Commission or Schools Inquiry Commission in 1868 issued landmark reports on the status of the entire range of schooling available. Other analyses were produced by a variety of organizations, most notably the Manchester Statistical Society. The inquiries and debates also resulted in direct intervention to change existing conditions. Major legislation during this period includes the Revised Code of 1862 and the Elementary Education Act of 1870.

Concern about educational theory and practice was not limited to what was going on in England, Wales, and Scotland. American and, particularly, Continental educators and schools were the focus of numerous investigations. Kay-Shuttleworth reported on his travels to Switzerland, Holland, and Germany in his *Memorandum on Popular Education*.[1] The Earl of Clarendon made inquiries about schools on a trip in Prussia taken while he was heading the parliamentary inquiry into the public schools. As part of the Newcastle Commission investigation into popular education, Eliot's friend the Reverend Mark Pattison was appointed to investigate schools in Germany, and Matthew Arnold was assigned to investigate education in France; Arnold also included Switzerland and Holland in his inquiries.

Eliot wrote to George Smith in 1868 recommending that he talk with Dr Perry whose 'long experience as an educator and his close acquaintance with German life have given him rare advantages for the observation of German schools, of which it is especially desirable for us English to get some accurate knowledge just now'.[2] German universities were developing an international reputation for research and scholarship, and critics charged that these endeavors had been dangerously neglected by the English institutions. In fact, it was not until the 1873 Devonshire Commission report that an official document asserted that research was a primary duty of a university.[3]

---

[1] James Kay-Shuttleworth, *Memorandum on Popular Education* (London: Rigway, 1868; rpr. New York: Augustus M. Kelley, 1969), p. 25.

[2] *The George Eliot Letters*, ed. by Gordon S. Haight, 9 vols (New Haven: Yale University Press, 1954-1978), VIII, 417. Further references to the *Letters* are given in the text.

[3] *The Modern University*, ed. by Margaret Clapp (Hamden: Archon, 1986), p. 48.

In mid-century, a number of infant schools began to incorporate ideas from the German educator Friedrich Froebel's work on the kindergarten. Andrew Bell, remembered for his contribution to the monitorial system in schools, is among a number of English visitors to Swiss educator Johann Heinrich Pestalozzi. The Hofwyl School, attended by the sons of George Henry Lewes, was established by Philip Emanuel von Fellenberg, a former student of Pestalozzi.

In 1856 Eliot and Lewes were trying to choose a school which would be appropriate for the Lewes boys. The Hofwyl School proved to be very satisfactory, but Eliot wrote in an 1856 letter to Charles Bray, 'The risk of placing children with entire strangers is terrible' (*Letters*, II, 235). Charles and Thornton Lewes arrived at the school in 1856 and remained until 1860; Herbert arrived in 1857 and did not leave until 1863. Some of the reasons that Eliot was pleased with Hofwyl are reflected in her letter to Sara Hennell reporting a visit Lewes made to his older sons after they had been at the school for a year. Eliot states that the boys 'can speak German quite well, and, what is better, their dispositions seem to be under a favourable influence. They are happy and ruddy, and picking up all sorts of practical knowledge as well as school learning' (*Letters*, II, 383). Sara Hennell had originally given Eliot and Lewes a prospectus on the school, and they later recommended it to others.

Founded by Fellenberg in 1804, Hofwyl not only was less costly than an English public school but offered a broader curriculum and a quite different philosophy of education. At its peak, the institution included numerous operations: a Model Farm, an Experimental Farm, two workshops for developing and perfecting 'Rural Instruments' (otherwise known as farm equipment), a School of Industry for poor boys (ages five to twenty-one), a school for poor girls, an academy for middle class boys, and a Normal School consisting of summer institutes for schoolmasters.[4] The school for girls and some branches in other locations were rather short-lived, but the rural or agricultural training school (with the necessary farms and shops) and the school for middle class boys continued for many years. The influential educator Johann Jakob Wehrli took over management of the rural school in 1808, and Dr Eduard Müller directed the academy from 1855.

Sample study schedules for individual students in 1842 include strong emphasis on German (the language of most instruction) and such subjects as

---

[4] F. A. Ismar, *Emanuel Fellenberg's Institution at Hofwyl, in Switzerland: Two Lectures Delivered in Georgetown, DC* (Georgetown, DC: Columbian Gazette Office, 1831).

English, writing, drawing, gymnastics, fencing, and carpentry for new students. More advanced students added geography, mathematics, natural history, French, religion, music, and singing. Still more advanced students might add Latin, Greek, German literature, and physics. Fellenberg's system emphasized a course of study designed for the individual student, not the placement of students into a pre-designed curriculum.[5] To facilitate customized study plans and to enhance cohesiveness among the students, no more than a few new students were admitted at one time, and students did not go away for holidays. Parents could, however, come for brief visits of a few days at infrequent intervals, and there were even hotel accommodations on the school property. Walking trips were arranged for the boys to provide a summer break in routine, and the pupils were strongly encouraged to write letters to their families.

The attention given to students' individual abilities is illustrated in an 1864 letter from the headmaster, Dr Müller, to the father of a pupil named Willie Muller. Mr Muller had expressed concern about his son's intellectual abilities and his future occupation. Müller responds:

> He is not nor will he ever be much in the way of *book*learning or *school*learning, but he is far from being a fool, and has plenty of practical good sense about him [...]. Let him go on quietly at school, learning as much useful knowledge as he can, and when the time comes for him to leave, then [...] consult with him what he would wish to undertake and what he is likely to be fit for.[6]

This attitude contrasts strongly with that of such teachers as Mr Stelling in *The Mill on the Floss*, who have a very rigid idea of curriculum and of appropriate student achievement.

Hofwyl had an international clientele, and thus it had an international influence and reputation. Furthermore, its influence has continued to the present. For example, in 1856 George Columbus Dent named a rice plantation in Georgia after the school where he received his education.[7] Today, Hofwyl-Broadfield Plantation is a state historic site, which is particularly popular with Swiss tourists. The Hofwyl school property became

---

[5] Mrs L. M. B. Barwell, *Letters from Hofwyl by a Parent, on the Educational Institutions of De Fellenberg* (London: Longman, Brown, Green, and Longmans, 1842), pp. 124-5.

[6] Maria Henrietta Burdon Muller, *Letters Received* (Letters from Mrs Muller's son Willie, recounting his school life at Hofwyl College near Bern). Library of the Bostom Athenæum.

I am grateful to the Library of the Boston Athenæum and its director, Rodney Armstrong, for permission to quote from these unpublished letters.

[7] Victoria Reeves Gunn, *Hofwyl Plantation* (Atlanta: State of Georgia/Department of Natural Resources, Office of Planning and Research: Historic Research Section, 1976), p. 72.

the location of the canton's normal school in 1884, and today it is still the site of a teachers' college.

In contrast to the philosophy and curriculum at Hofwyl in the nineteenth century, parents who wanted to find an English school which taught modern languages and encouraged practical skills found their search difficult, particularly before the last quarter of the century. Even a public school with a good reputation provided what Eliot considers to be a distressingly parochial education. In comments to Harriet Beecher Stowe on the reception of the 'Jewish element' in *Daniel Deronda*, Eliot writes:

> I find men educated at Rugby supposing that Christ spoke Greek. To my feeling, this deadness to the history which has prepared half our world for us, this inability to find interest in any form of life that is not clad in the same coat-tails and flounces as our own lies very close to the worst kind of irreligion. The best that can be said of it is, that it is a sign of the intellectual narrowness — in plain English, the stupidity, which is still the average mark of our culture. (*Letters*, VI, 302)

This 'intellectual narrowness', limitation in both information and attitude, is the basis for many of her criticisms of schools. Eliot's main example of education at an endowed grammar school is the experience of Daniel Deronda. Sir Hugo Mallinger sends Deronda to a tutor and then to Eton as part of his plan for providing the boy with the education of an English gentleman. Later, Sir Hugo comments on the breadth of his ward's education:

> 'I'm glad you have done some good reading outside your classics, and have got a grip of French and German. The truth is, unless a man can get the prestige and income of a Don and write donnish books, it's hardly worth while for him to make a Greek and Latin machine of himself and be able to spin you out pages of the Greek dramatists at any verse you'll give him as a cue. That's all very fine, but in practical life, nobody does give you the cue for pages of Greek.'[8]

The 1864 Clarendon Commission report strongly recommended further steps to broaden the studies in 'modern' subjects at the public schools; and since *Daniel Deronda*, Eliot's only relatively contemporary novel, was not published until 1876, some reform in public school curriculum had taken place by the time it was written.

The difficulty with curriculum was not always the imposition of a classical education at the price of practical training. The problem could work the other way around, as illustrated by the case of Latimer in 'The Lifted Veil'. Latimer's elder brother was sent to Eton and Cambridge 'for the sake of

---

[8] George Eliot, *Daniel Deronda*, ed. by Graham Handley (Oxford: Clarendon Press, 1984), Ch. 16, p. 161. Further references to this edition are given in the text.

making connections'.[9] His father, supported by Mr Leatherall's phrenological interpretation, then decides that a scientific education would be best for Latimer:

> [...] it was presently clear that private tutors, natural history, science, and the modern languages, were the appliances by which the defects of my organization were to be remedied. I was very stupid about machines, so I was to be greatly occupied with them [...]. I read Plutarch, Shakespere, and Don Quixote by the sly [...]. (7)

This inappropriate scheme continued until Latimer was sent to Geneva to continue his studies when he was sixteen.

One alternative to the prevailing 'narrowness,' as illustrated by the case of Latimer, was the practice of sending children and young people elsewhere for their schooling. Eliot's fictional examples range from the Brooke girls to young adults enrolled in universities or pursuing other kinds of studies. For some, Scotland was a compromise embodying many of the advantages of a Continental education closer to home. The best case is probably that of Christie Garth in *Middlemarch* who enjoys his study of English literature at the University of Glasgow. This ambitious eldest child of the Garths is described with great pride by his mother: 'He has paid his expenses for the last year by giving lessons, carrying on hard study at the same time. He hopes soon to get a private tutorship and go abroad'.[10] In regard to cost, social class, and subject matter, it is to Christie's advantage to attend a Scottish university.

Eliot brings both Scottish and Continental influence into her presentation of professional education. Tertius Lydgate is a new sort of physician-hero, as Patrick J. McCarthy notes in 'Lydgate, "The New, Young Surgeon" of *Middlemarch*'.[11] Unlike most previous medical practitioners appearing as major characters in novels, his professional role is emphasized and is an essential part of the plot. Lydgate's medical training forms the basis for his diagnostic methods and his theories of treatment. First apprenticed to a country practitioner, he later studied in London, Edinburgh, and Paris. While he was in Paris, Lydgate's interest in research was influenced by Marie François Xavier Bichat, the French anatomist and physiologist who did ground-breaking work in tissue classification. The budding researcher studied

---

[9] George Eliot, *The Lifted Veil* (New York: Virago/Penguin, 1985), p. 6. Further references to this edition are given in the text.

[10] George Eliot, *Middlemarch*, ed. by David Carroll (Oxford: Clarendon Press, 1986), Ch. 57, pp. 558-9. Further references to this edition are given in the text.

[11] Patrick J. McCarthy, 'Lydgate, "The New Young Surgeon" of Middlemarch', *Studies in English Literature*, 10 (1970), 805-16.

under René Théophile Hyacinthe Laennec, who invented the stethoscope (*c.* 1819), and he uses a stethoscope as a diagnostic tool.

Lydgate is quite rightly appalled at the present state of medical practice, and he offers his analysis of the cause of the problem and its solution:

> '[W]ith our present medical rules and education, one must be satisfied now and then to meet with a fair practitioner. As to all the higher questions which determine the starting-point of a diagnosis — as to the philosophy of medical evidence — any glimmering of these can only come from a scientific culture of which country practitioners have usually no more notion than the man in the moon.' (Ch. 13, 123)

Naturally, the arrival in Middlemarch of a youthful new practitioner who is not shy about voicing his theories and has very different ideas about how a medical practice should be run is upsetting to the established medical professionals.

The question of what specialized education should be required in England was further complicated by men who had received part or all of their professional training elsewhere. According to Gordon S. Haight, biographer of Eliot and of John Chapman, 'In the eighteenth century a degree at St Andrew's could be procured *in absentia* for £10 [...]. In 1857 [...] the fee had risen to about £25'.[12] This Scottish institution had only one professor of medicine and no hospital or laboratory. Nevertheless, 'it granted as many as 605 degrees in 1862' (94). Haight states that 'by hook or crook [Chapman] managed to compress the whole of his medical education into nineteen months' (95). In fact, he was also continuing his publishing business at this same time. As a Fellow of the Royal College of Physicians, he claimed to cure such diverse problems as diarrhœa, epilepsy, paralysis, diabetes, and even cholera through the use of strategically placed spinal ice bags (114).

A different sort of limited knowledge is illustrated by the Reverend Edward Casaubon. Dorothea Brooke sees the narrowness of her own learning, but she is totally misled (or actually misleads herself, because Casaubon launches no campaign to deceive her) about this 'intellectual' who seems to share her most precious interests. The shallowness and the contradictory forces within Casaubon are highlighted, not reduced, when he and Dorothea return home after an extended wedding trip (which he spent mostly in Roman libraries). As his second cousin Will Ladislaw points out, he is also handicapped by his prejudice against German scholars and his resulting ignorance of their studies. Nineteenth-century critics of the English universities showed that they were falling behind German institutions in original research, and Casaubon

---

[12] Gordon S. Haight, *George Eliot and John Chapman* (New Haven: Yale University Press, 1940), p. 93. Further page references to this work are given in the text.

likewise fails to take advantage of German contributions to his field. Ladislaw tells Dorothea, '[...] it is a pity that [Casaubon's labor] should be thrown away, as so much English scholarship is, for want of knowing what is being done by the rest of the world. If Mr Casaubon read German he would save himself a great deal of trouble' (Ch. 21, 201-2).

Casaubon is annoyed with the apparent frivolity of young Ladislaw, who insisted on studying at Heidelberg instead of an English university, pursues an interest in art while he travels abroad, and seems to have no desire for what Casaubon considers a conventional occupation. Ladislaw does, of course, develop a successful career in politics, eventually ending up in Parliament.

Like Ladislaw, Daniel Deronda finds non-traditional, self-guided study to be a key to his changing aspirations. Deronda's Continental travel and independent study are a better preparation for him to understand the ideas of Mordecai Cohen and of his own grandfather in regard to Jewish heritage than is his experience at Cambridge. After an unsatisfying attempt to read law, Deronda is without a goal in life when he meets Mordecai. Soon, he begins to study Hebrew and starts to accept Mordecai's hopes for the future. Deronda tells Gwendolen Harleth,

> 'I am going to the East to become better acquainted with the condition of my race in various countries there [...] The idea that I am possessed with is that of restoring a political existence to my people, making them a nation again, giving them a national centre, such as the English have, though they too are scattered over the face of the globe. That is a task which presents itself to me as a duty [...].' (Ch. 49, 747)

Deronda hopes to apply what he learns in working toward a specific goal, even though that goal may not be reached in his lifetime.

The question of women's education is one of Eliot's major concerns. Throughout her novels, Eliot reminds the reader of the deplorable state of education for women and the effects that poor education has upon the individual. Patricia Beer says of *Middlemarch*, 'Nowhere in the nineteenth-century novel do we get a more chilling picture of the education provided for young women'.[13] Dorothea and Celia Brooke were reared and educated 'on plans at once narrow and promiscuous, first in an English family and afterwards in a Swiss family at Lausanne' because this was the best scheme their scatterbrained uncle could think of for their care and schooling (Ch. 1, 8). Dorothea tells Mr Brooke that she cannot understand the relationship between nature and art and does not appreciate seeing pictures which others

---

[13] Patricia Beer, *Reader, I Married Him: A Study of the Women Characters of Jane Austen, Charlotte Brontë, Elizabeth Gaskell and George Eliot* (London: Macmillan, 1974), p. 181.

praise. Her uncle blames her lack of interest in art on 'a bad style of teaching [...] else this is just the thing for girls — sketching, fine art and so on' (Ch. 9, 78). He cannot comprehend her enthusiasm for drawing plans for cottages and feels that her interest is highly inappropriate for a young lady. To what extent Dorothea's interests can be attributed to her Continental education cannot be determined, particularly since Celia's tastes are very conventional and a number of Dorothea's ideas spring from her religious fervor. However, Mr Brooke may be more than usually correct in his assumptions about the non-traditional nature of what she was taught. Nevertheless, the shortcomings of her education are one of the key ideas in the novel.

Eliot places much of the blame for Dorothea's infatuation with Casaubon on her schooling. Eliot states: 'For to Dorothea, after that toy-box history of the world adapted to young ladies which had made the chief part of her education, Mr Casaubon's talk about his great book was full of new vistas [...]' (Ch. 10, 84). To a considerable extent, it is the contrast between the ideas which Casaubon says he is researching and the 'shallows of ladies'-school literature' to which she has been limited that attracts Dorothea (Ch. 3, 24).

Several of Eliot's other women are criticized by men because of their lack of education or intelligence. For example, when Felix Holt first meets Esther Lyon, who teaches French and has been reading Byron, he decides that she is shallow and silly. There is considerable truth in his condemnation of Esther's superficial pursuits and artificially refined tastes. However, she is also a victim of her education, largely in a French Protestant school.

Another kind of teaching, customized to the student but not offered in a school setting, is illustrated by the case of Lady Cheverel in 'Mr Gilfil's Love Story', who studies music with no intention of pursuing a career. During her travels in Italy, she engages a maestro for singing lessons whenever she plans to stay long in a particular city. When it becomes obvious that her ward Caterina Sarti has considerable musical talent, Lady Cheverel gives the girl lessons and eventually engages an Italian singing master for her.

Whether the subject is male or female, Eliot shows that education on the Continent, either formal schooling or independent study, has the potential to broaden a character's understanding and to help the individual go beyond stereotypes. However, this is only potential. Esther Lyon does not move past shallowness in her studies, and Casaubon allows his prejudices to limit his opportunities. On the other hand, Will Ladislaw and Daniel Deronda gain useful information and breadth of vision in their own lives, as well as pointing out the importance of understanding more about what is going on across the Channel.

In her use of Continental education, as in her development of other issues regarding education, Eliot presents the reader with a variety of fictional characters and individual situations. She does not prescribe curriculum or institutional policy changes; she does not demand new teacher-training standards; and she does not advocate the widespread development of Hofwyl clones. Instead, she points out problems and possibilities; and, above all, she advocates an ongoing fight against 'intellectual narrowness' (*Letters,* VI, 302).

Chapter Twelve

Renaissance and Risorgimento in
Romola

Tom Winnifrith

In one of the most sympathetic and perceptive contemporary reviews of *Romola*, R. H. Hutton described the Renaissance as that era which has so many points of resemblance with the present.[1] George Eliot was pleased with the review and expressed herself satisfied that Hutton had divined her intentions.[2] Other readers, both contemporary and modern, have been less pleased with the weight of Renaissance scholarship, to which George Eliot's notebooks and correspondence bear eloquent testimony. The correspondence has been edited in a masterly fashion; the fact that the notebooks in the British Library and the Beinecke Library at Yale are still unpublished is perhaps an indication that George Eliot's learning is a trifle formidable. The 'dried jokes', 'the light Florentine buzz', 'two pages of cram'[3] are damning indictments from a generation, more serious than our own, more anxious to learn, and less likely to dismiss historical novels as neither good history or good novels. There were, it is true, great Victorians who admired *Romola* especially when they read the novel as a whole rather than in monthly parts, and the verdict of these immense bigwigs, as Eliot rather touchingly calls them, should be borne in mind when considering the reputation of *Romola*.[4] Contemporary critics of course pined for the world of *Adam Bede*, another novel set in the past, but a recognizable past. Modern critics look to the careful structure of *Middlemarch*, also set in the past, a past as remote now in 1995 as the Renaissance was to Victorian readers, but one that Eliot recreates

---

[1] Cited in *George Eliot: The Critical Heritage*, ed. by David Carroll (London: Routledge & Kegan Paul, 1971), p. 200.

[2] Gordon S. Haight, *The George Eliot Letters*, 9 vols (New Haven and London: Yale University Press, 1954-78), IV, 96-7.

[3] *Critical Heritage*, pp. 197, 199, 208.

[4] *Letters*, IV, 75.

firmly but unobtrusively. In *Romola*, however, the dried husks of Florentine history are perpetually getting in the way of the reader eager to explore the universal themes of love and heroism, temptation and corruption, which Romola, Tito and to a lesser extent Savonarola, Bardo and Baldassarre represent.

Modern defenders of *Romola* have seized upon the universal myths to which the symbols in the novel point, correctly noting the keen interest Lewes and Eliot displayed in myths, just emerging from the contempt of Casaubon-like scholars.[5] In a way this approach is similar to that of Hutton who saw resemblances between the Renaissance and the Victorian era, and dissimilar from Leslie Stephen and the reviewer in *The Westminster Review* who regretted that Romola was not a modern Englishwoman. For the purpose of this paper, however, it is not the general affinities between people of all ages, but the particular links between the Renaissance and the nineteenth century which will be considered.

Hutton seizes upon the conflict between liberal culture and the more passionate form of Christian faith as the central issue of the Renaissance and of *Romola*, where the two central symbols are the crucifix and the triptych, presented to Romola by her brother and her husband. The Victorian Age was, at any rate by modern standards, passionately interested in religion, but liberal culture, even when defined and explained by Hutton, is harder to relate to Victorian concerns.   Hutton talks of the discoveries of Columbus and Copernicus and the way in which the new learning cleared away the petty rubbish of Romanist superstition and resolved the mighty simplicities of the great age of Greece. Columbus, appropriately for a novel which begins in 1492, is mentioned in the Proem, but thereafter plays no part in a Florence which can hardly have taken much notice of his explorations. Scientific discoveries, which play little part in *Romola*, must have been felt to be important by Eliot since Lewes's main work during this period was in the area of science,[6] but though Copernicus made his discoveries in Northern Italy, he did not make them until well after the main action of *Romola* and even after the Epilogue. The rediscovery of classical learning plays a large part in *Romola*, but not a very satisfactory one. Bardo, Tito and Baldassarre are, or have been, good scholars, but are less good men, and proper scholars like Poliziano are mentioned briefly and without a great deal of respect for their

---

[5] Felicia Bonaparte, *The Triptych and the Cross: The Central Myths of George Eliot's Poetic Imagination* (New York: New York University Press, 1979).

[6] Rosemary Ashton, *G. H. Lewes: A Life* (Oxford: Oxford University Press, 1991), pp. 212-5.

achievements. Curiously, the Victorian age did see a rebirth of classical scholarship with careful textual emendations becoming the business of classical scholars in a way not all that different from the work of the great Renaissance humanists.[7] It is unlikely, however, that either Eliot or Lewes, who dabbled in classical translation, but who had very little formal classical education, would have been unduly interested in or sympathetic to pedantic classical scholars;[8] much more evident in Eliot's work is a more interesting and more modern appreciation of classical literature as a vehicle of timeless truth, and something of this attitude does come out in *Romola*, although it is more Renaissance than Victorian.

Other features of Renaissance life which play a large part in *Romola*, but which do not seem to have immediately obvious counterparts in the Victorian era, are art and politics. Wisely, Eliot did not allow some of the really great figures of the Renaissance to obtrude on her canvas. We hear of Leonardo da Vinci and Michelangelo, but Piero di Cosimo, an important figure of the second rank, is the only artist to play a major role.[9] Eliot was interested in contemporary painting as we learn from her description of Naumann in *Middlemarch* and her correspondence with Leighton. Few would find it easy to equate Victorian achievements in art with those of the Renaissance, although large canvases and classical subjects are a feature of Victorian painting. In her famous reference to Dutch painting in *Adam Bede*,[10] Eliot does seem to be saying that her earlier books are realistic pictures of humble life. In *Romola* and subsequent works she was attempting a grander theme of which both Renaissance artists and inferior Victorian imitators would have approved.

In politics Eliot mentions the young Machiavelli, but the main political manipulator is of course Tito Melema, quite prepared to take any side that suited him. It is difficult for those of us not involved in the intricacies of Florentine politics of the Renaissance to distinguish the various parties in *Romola* which fought for mastery. The Medici lose power to an aristocratic

---

[7] J. Sandys, *A History of Classical Scholarship* (Cambridge: Cambridge University Press, 1903).

[8] Bonaparte, pp. 34-71, shows that Lewes and Eliot were widely read in the Classics, but the very width of their reading reveals their antipathy to pedantry and the narrow textual and grammatical grind. In naming Casaubon after a famous textual scholar, Isaac Casaubon, Eliot is probably showing the same antipathy.

[9] Hugh Witemeyer, *George Eliot and the Visual Arts* (New Haven: and London: Yale University Press, 1979).

[10] *Adam Bede*, Ch. 17.

faction, proud of Florentine independence, which is in turn crushed by a democratic revolution favoured by Savonarola which accuses Bernardo and other leaders of favouring the Medici. After the failure of Savonarola to produce a miracle the mob turns on him, and, after the book has ended, eventually the Medici are invited back. In the background are the mysteriously ineffective Charles VIII of France, whose march into Italy promises much and achieves little, and the sinister figure of the Pope stirring up trouble against Savonarola. This crude summary of the complex politics of *Romola* bears some resemblance to Italian history in Eliot's time, and it is surprising that more attempts have not been made to link the two.[11] Anyone who has read Eliot's British Museum notebook with its careful notes on Florentine history stretching well back into the time of Dante,[12] would be unwilling to accuse her of trying to fit the past into the mould of the present. It is much more likely that *Romola* is a perhaps rather detached answer to those who saw an easy answer to Italy's nineteenth-century problem. *Romola* was written shortly after the stirring days of 1859 and 1860; after the earlier humiliations of 1848 Italy, apart from Rome and Venice, had in these years become united. As in *Romola* there was in the movement for Italian independence both a conservative and a revolutionary element, the former led by the great statesman Cavour working by diplomacy and constitutional means, the latter prompted by Mazzini and Garibaldi advocating violent measures to attack the Austrians and occupy Rome.

Eliot refers very little to contemporary Italy. Writing on 18 May 1860 to Blackwood she declares that Lewes's health is more important to her than Garibaldi, and that selfishly she cares more for the doings of Giotto and Brunelleschi than for those of Count Cavour. 'On a first journey to the greatest centres of art, one must be excused for letting one's public spirit go to sleep a little.'[13] By the time of Eliot's next visit in 1861 Italy had been united and Cavour had died, but one would find it hard to know about this from her correspondence. She refused in 1865 to contribute to a subscription to Mazzini on the grounds of his association with, and advocacy of, armed insurrection.[14]

---

[11] Joan Bennett, *George Eliot: Her Mind and Art* (Cambridge: Cambridge University Press, 1948) links *Romola* with English religious doubt and controversy in the nineteenth century.

[12] Additional Manuscript no. 40768.

[13] *Letters*, III, 294.

[14] *Letters*, IV, 199-200.

We do not form a particularly favourable impression of Eliot from these remarks and from the absence of many other allusions to contemporary Italy in Eliot's correspondence. She seems at first sight rather like a typical tourist, annoyed with the naughty foreigners for letting their silly revolutions get in the way of her husband's health or of her sightseeing. But Eliot was not one to allow her public spirit to go to sleep for long, and it is possible to see *Romola* as her answer to the intrigues and factions, high revolutionary ideals and low political cunning which dominated Florentine politics in 1492 and 1861. All the plots and counterplots of *Romola* lead in the end to nothing, and bring good men like Bernardo as well as bad men like Tito to their deaths. The survivors are Romola and Piero di Cosimo, carrying out their tasks of caring for other human beings and creating immortal works of art, preferring timeless moral and aesthetic virtues to ephemeral political gains.

Savonarola, it would seem, is a character who at some point eschews eternal glory for temporary advantage, and pays the penalty. In describing his downfall Eliot, always sympathetic to sinners like Arthur Donnithorne, her sympathy even in a curious way extending to Tito Melema, faces the difficulty that she does not really believe in Savonarola's dour but sincere puritanism, even though it is the lapse from this sincerity that brings about his fall from grace. Savonarola is an odd subject for any writer, since he neither conjures up the artistic glories of the Renaissance, nor, since he is so much earlier than Luther, does he bring to mind the problems of the Reformation, problems much in the minds of the Victorian public, suspicious of Catholic revival before and after Newman's conversion in 1845.

In dealing with religion we may feel that Eliot has forsaken an objective portrait of the Renaissance in order to impose her own views. Eliot was once deeply sympathetic to the Evangelical religion, a religion which with its emphasis on purity of conduct and absolute right and wrong, is not unlike that of Savonarola. She, however, rejected the tenets of this religion, denying absolutely the supernatural element in Christianity, while subscribing to most of the moral commands of the New Testament. Many Victorians probably felt the same way, although not honest or intelligent enough to state their position so clearly. Others turned less abruptly from the Low Church, fashionable in George Eliot's childhood, to the High Church, more fashionable in the middle of the century, or more abruptly from conventional religion to outright atheism.[15] Eliot's position at any rate in the period when

---

[15] D. Newsome, *The Parting of Friends* (London: Murray, 1966) and Owen Chadwick, *The Victorian Church* (London: Black, 1966) give many examples. Perhaps the best is A. J.

she wrote her novel is fairly consistent. Put very crudely the lesson of *Romola* would seem to be that neither the religion of the heroine's brother Dino and Savonarola, as represented by the crucifix, nor the paganism of Tito and Bardo, represented by the painting of Bacchus and Ariadne, is satisfactory. Instead Romola painfully works her way through a new baptism in the village struck by the plague to a new religion based upon benevolence towards humanity, conspicuously lacking in Bardo's arid humanism, Tito's specious opportunism and even Savonarola's and Dino's asceticism.

In balancing the cross against the triptych, whether consciously or unconsciously, Eliot tends to favour the cross. Dino and Tito both abandon their fathers, but Tito's treachery, magnified by his later treachery to Dino's and Romola's father, is clearly far more selfish and sinful than Dino's decision to enter the church. Tito is of course a clear pagan; in stressing the paganism of Bardo and his hostility towards Dino, Eliot would seem to be taking a few liberties with the Renaissance, since there is little evidence of open hostility to religion among the early Humanists. Savonarola's hardheartedness towards Bernardo, his cowardice in refusing to face the ordeal by fire, and even such ridiculous bouts of puritanism as the Pyramid of Vanities are seen as aberrations from a high ideal, examples perhaps of attacks on religion in politics rather than on religion itself.

The reviewer of *Romola* in *The Westminster Review* was less keen to find resemblances between the Victorian age and the Renaissance than Hutton was.[16] In a rather pompous passage, whose meaning is obscured by Victorian prudery, the reviewer suggests that Romola has the character of a modern Englishwoman rather than an Italian lady of four centuries since, and that the long and elaborate disquisition on the relation between the sexes as a moral question is set forth by George Eliot too much in the colours of the nineteenth century. One assumes that the writer of this review thought that fidelity to the marriage tie was a peculiarly nineteenth-century phenomenon. In fifteenth century Italy Tito, it is suggested, would have had Romola poisoned or stabbed; no evidence is put forward for this claim. Romola would have presumably put up with Tito's infidelities, or in modern fashion comforted herself with another lover; the vast change in sexual morals within the last hundred years does of course cast doubt on Eliot's claim in her Proem that human nature changes very little in the same way as mountains and rivers change very little. But neither Eliot nor her reviewer could anticipate our own

---

Froude, an early acquaintance of Lewes, who was a friend of Newman, but wrote *Nemesis of Faith* (1849).

[16] Cited in Carroll, *The Critical Heritage*, pp. 213-20.

permissive age, and in making Romola join the long line of Eliot's nineteenth-century heroines, either collapsing through the deception of treacherous men or able to ennoble themselves in spite of this deception, Eliot was probably drawing attention to the sad fact that men have exploited women through the ages in very much the same way.

She may also have been obliquely criticising the philosophy of Comte which saw gradual progress in human history. Comte's hostility to Christianity made him unpopular in the nineteenth century, and his optimism makes him unfashionable now, but he and his Positivist followers are important for students of Victorian attitudes to the Renaissance. Eliot's attitude to Comte is difficult to ascertain. Her friends, the Congreves, ardent Positivists, with whom Eliot remained friends for the whole of her writing career, stated that she accepted the general view of Humanity but never the details of the system,[17] and *Romola* would seem to bear this out, since in the novel the heroine eventually finds fulfilment in serving her fellow men and women, but without any sense that this is a profound triumph. In 1859 we find Lewes reading Comte at the same time as Congreve's lectures on the Roman Empire in the West.[18] In July 1861 Eliot mentioned reading Comte's account of the Middle Ages. She defended Comte against some cheap sneers by Fitzjames Stephen in the *Cornhill*, saying that fewer studies were more full of luminous ideas and that she was thankful to learn from it.

A postscript in the same letter adds that she thought Positivism one-sided.[19] In a later letter to Frederic Harrison, another Positivist, who quarrelled with Congreve, Eliot said she could not write a Positivist novel, as a novel with a dogmatic purpose would not be a novel, and she expressly denied that *Romola* was a novel with this purpose.[20] *Romola* could have been a Positivist novel if Eliot had been more hostile to the aspects of Christianity which Comte regarded as ultimately selfish. It is true that Dino leaves his father and is of not much use to his sister, although by an ironic coincidence it is he who could have enlightened her about Tito's character. It is true that Savonarola forces Romola back into a loveless union with Tito and later abandons Bernardo to his fate, but it is difficult to equate his or Dino's self-

---

[17] *Letters*, I, 242.

[18] *Letters*, III, 101.

[19] *Letters*, III, 438.

[20] *Letters*, IV, 300-1. This criticism of Positivism is not quoted by either T. R. Wright, 'George Eliot and Positivism', *Modern Language Review*, 76 (1981), 257-72, or J. B. Bullen, 'George Eliot's *Romola* as a Positivist Allegory', *Review of English Studies*, 261 (1975), 425-35.

righteousness with complete selfishness. Bardo accuses Dino of abandoning all rules of human duty, but his conduct towards his son and daughter is hardly altruistic or admirable.

On the other hand Romola does eventually learn that personal abnegation in religion is less satisfying than the religion of humanity in the same way that Dorothea Brooke in *Middlemarch* learns that the life of St Theresa does not consist of sacrificing herself to sterility with Casaubon. Looking after Tessa's children and marriage to Ladislaw are not very adequate final achievements, and perhaps this is really what Eliot is trying to say both about the Victorian age and the Renaissance. Both were eras when it was felt that a great many new discoveries must lead to a general improvement in the lot of man, but many promising beginnings led to disillusion and confusion. New religious movements like Protestantism, Evangelicalism, Tractarianism or Positivism suggested that they had all the answers, and new scientific discoveries promised exciting panaceas, but Romola ends up in a happier state than Lydgate who has sold his soul to Mammon and Rosamond, and dies early at fifty.

The pessimistic conclusion of the Proem to *Romola* should be noted, as it gives a clue to Eliot's attitude to the Renaissance and her own age. Eliot imagines the spirit of a Florentine who had died in 1492 looking down at the Florence of 1862 and wondering what has happened to the city which looks so similar to the city of the Medici, and is a reminder that we still resemble the men of the past more than we differ from them. He sees minor points of difference and wonders parochially and anachronistically whether the voting with the black and white beans is still going on, and whether Lorenzo de' Medici ever got over his illness. Our Spirit is a man of the fifteenth century, a mixture of pagan and Christian, of belief and unbelief, of Epicurean levity and Fetishistic dread, and, though sceptical that a Pope Angelico would ever purify the Church from scandal, he wonders how Savonarola, whom he admires, has succeeded. A visit to the well-remembered buildings will, the Spirit thinks, solve all these problems, but Eliot dissuades him. Political, economic and scholarly problems are not longer the same; what has endured are the great walls, the great churches, the same chants, the little children and the longing for peace and righteousness, 'For the Papa Angelico is not come yet'.[21]

The people who believe in Pope Angelico's coming are of course simple peasants, still steeped in the miracles of the Middle Ages; examples, if we

---

[21] *Romola*, ed. by Andrew Brown (Oxford: Clarendon Press, 1991), p. 9.

like, of the religious age of man, to be succeeded according to the Positivists by the metaphysical age, heralded by the Renaissance, and then by the Positivist age, ushered in by the scientific discoveries of the nineteenth century. But none of these ages had brought in the reign of peace and justice for which all had hoped. Indeed idealists, full of optimism for improvement, like Lydgate and Dorothea and Savonarola, suffer more from the disappointment of their hopes than those who face reality with calm acceptance like Mary Garth and Romola at the end of the novel.

It would seem that Eliot's attitude towards the Renaissance differed from that of the Positivists in that the latter thought it the dawn of a new age, similar but inferior to their own new dawn, whereas Eliot more realistically saw both her age and the end of the nineteenth century as full of false dawns. The spirit is advised not to look too closely at the present condition of Florence, and indeed in culture, trade, even in politics the city must have degenerated sadly since the brave days of the Renaissance. So much for the new era to be ushered in by the religion of humanity. The discomforts of nineteenth century travel over the Alps must have helped Lewes and Eliot form rather a jaundiced impression of contemporary Italy, especially if they were used to greater luxuries in England and Germany, but this trivial cause is not the only reason why both in the Proem and in her letters and journals Eliot appears to speak slightingly of modern Florence and Florentines.[22]

The idea that human beings, so far from progressing, can in unfavourable political circumstances actually degenerate is highlighted by the fact that Tito Melema is a Greek. He is a curiously rootless figure, born in the Greek-speaking part of Southern Italy, but travelling widely in the mainland of Greece. Most educated Victorians like their modern successors knew very little about mediaeval Greece, but regarded its history as a sad decline from the glorious days of Pericles and Sophocles. Conscientiously we find Eliot trying to find books about mediaeval Greece to fill in the gaps in her knowledge, but these books are only likely to have reinforced the impression, perhaps best summed up in Byron's 'Childe Harold', that the story of Greece in post-classical times was one of a depressing decline in culture and morality.[23] Only recently has modern scholarship tried to reverse this picture and been able to paint the achievements of Byzantine Greece as something different from and not necessarily inferior to the glory of classical Greece. Most Victorians like Congreve dismissed Byzantium as a sad afterthought,

---

[22] Gordon S. Haight, *George Eliot: A Biography* (Oxford: Clarendon Press, 1968), pp. 340-8.

[23] Bonaparte, pp. 69-70.

and were like Nello in thinking that, since the old Furies went to sleep, your Christian Greek is of so easy a conscience that he would make a stepping-stone of his father's corpse.[24]

Tito appears as the degenerate representative of these descendants of the classical Greeks, and as is natural in a novel about the Renaissance, there are plenty of allusions to Classical Greece to drive the point home. It would have been hard to make the same point about a decline from the high standards of the past in a book about French Canada, which Harrison improbably suggested as the proper setting for a Positivist novel, a suggestion which Eliot wearily and courteously refused.[25] Finding information about French Canada would have been a difficult task, and Harrison's tactlessness ignored two other features which made the Renaissance peculiarly suitable in Eliot's eyes for placing the modified form of the Religion of Humanity that she was preaching. These are the small size of Florence in the Renaissance and the feeling that the beginning of the fifteenth century was a time of very important changes.

In the 1860s Florentines were being asked to accept, and for the most part were accepting, the need to abandon their parochial loyalties in favour of a common Italian cause. The creation of a large nation had its disadvantages. It is a feature of Romola's Florence that everybody seems to know everyone else. Tito's anxiety to escape from Florence and the way in which he keeps coming across Baldassarre are reflections of the fact that in a closed community it is much harder to escape the consequences of crime than it is in, for example, a modern metropolis. As Eliot says in the Proem, the politics of a Florentine who died in 1492 had

> the passionate intensity and the detailed practical interest, which could only belong to a narrow sense of corporate action; only to the members of a community shut in close by the hills and by the walls of six miles circuit, where men knew each other as they passed in the street, set their eyes every day on the memorials of their commonwealth, and were conscious of having not simply the right to vote, but the chance of being voted for.[26]

It was different in the Florence of 1861. Curiously, in deploring the growth of the city state, Eliot is echoing, probably unconsciously, the words of Caccaguida in Dante's *Paradiso*, mourning the fact that, in between his lifetime in the twelfth century and the time of Dante, Florence had grown in

---

[24] *Romola* , p. 37.

[25] *Letters*, IV, pp. 284-9.

[26] *Romola*, p. 37.

size and prosperity to such an extent that nobody knew anybody else.[27] The change from a city state to a national state was a feature of the Renaissance and oddly enough of the Risorgimento when Italy ceased to be what Metternich had called it in 1847, 'a geographical expression'. It is true that Eliot, as we have shown, seemed curiously uninterested in these political forms of national identity. On the other hand one of the demands of the Italian State was that Rome should be its capital, and Eliot did make the name of her heroine Romola, apparently a deliberate attempt[28] to associate with an inhabitant of Florence, a different city, uniquely a city that spoke for the whole world, urbi et orbi, combining the classical and Christian heritage.

But for some in the 1860s Rome was mainly a political issue. In 1848 Mazzini and Garibaldi had set up the short-lived Roman republic. This had been crushed by the French, and it was not until the French defeat by Prussia that Rome finally became the capital of Italy.

Lewes had known Mazzini before he had met Eliot, when he and Thornton Hunt had befriended various radical thinkers, and we find the young Thornton Lewes praising Garibaldi. But Eliot was not impressed by Mazzini, by the bloodshed he had caused and for which he continued to plot. She also spoke disparagingly of Garibaldi, whose heroic feats had included defeats as well as victories, and who, in 1862 after the death of Cavour, had been crushed at Aspromonte by his former Piedmontese allies. The Risorgimento like *Romola* is a story of the fading of youthful enthusiasms, shifting political alliances and heroic figures whose heroism does not quite succeed.[29]

It is not all pessimism however. One of the authors that Eliot read during the composition of Romola was Gibbon.[30] Gibbon would have approved of the portrait of Tito, a degenerate Greek, but might have been less enthusiastic about Eliot's surprising sympathy with religion. The final chapters of *The Decline and Fall of The Roman Empire* are however devoted not to the Greek

---

[27] See Bonaparte, pp. 26-7, for Eliot's reading of Dante during the composition of *Romola*. David Carroll, in *George Eliot and the Conflict of Interpretations* (Cambridge: Cambridge University Press, 1992), p. 323, suggests that the spirit from the shades summoned in the Proem is based on Caccaguida, although Caccaguida is, unlike the spirit, more knowledgeable about the present and more gloomy.

[28] *Letters*, V, 174.

[29] References to Mazzini and Garibaldi may be found in *Letters*, IV, 199; III, 294, and Ashton, pp. 54, 86, 93, 107.

[30] Bonaparte, p. 213 seems to suggest that Eliot had read *The Decline and Fall of the Roman Empire*, although the Yale MS 1 entries, as she notes on p. 43, seem to suggest that in preparing for *Romola* Eliot was principally concerned with Gibbon in a more optimistic mood on the revival of learning.

Byzantine Empire, but to Rome. *Romola* is in some sense an answer to Gibbon's melancholy reflection, incorporating as it does some degree of nineteenth-century optimism, expanding the narrow vision of the English enlightenment with a vaguer but more European ideal.

Gibbon approaches Rome as a battered desert of broken monuments, although in a brisk paragraph he does allow some degree of artistic regeneration in the fifteenth and sixteenth centuries. Eliot read Ruskin conscientiously, and Frederic Leighton, a keen student of the Renaissance, dutifully illustrated *Romola* for her, but we must feel that Victorian painting is sadly lacking in inspiration. Art is however very important in *Romola*, even though she ignores the major artists and concentrates instead on the relatively minor figure of Piero di Cosimo, seen by some as the key character in the novel.[31]

Leonardo da Vinci, whose pupil Piero was, first saw man rather than God as the centre of his art. Michelangelo, the pupil of Ghirlandajo, makes his towering achievements a testimony to God's power. The fact that Michelangelo was born later and lived longer than Leonardo is an interesting contradiction of the Positivist thesis that history in general, and the Renaissance in particular, saw a general moving away from religion.

For obvious reasons Eliot did not select either of these figures to play a part in her story; their artistic achievements would have got in the way, and their particular slant towards Man or God would have disturbed the delicate balance between religion and humanity which *Romola* tries to strike. Nor is there any mention of Raphael, so frequently alluded to in the other novels, whose painting the Sistine Madonna became something of a cult among Positivists.

Instead we have at the beginning of the novel Piero di Cosimo's imaginary painting of the three masks, the satyr, the stoic and the sorrowing Magdalen, and at the end of the novel a portrait painted in words by Eliot herself of *Romola*, Monna Bregida and Tito's other family decorating the altar. Both portraits are clearly open to several interpretations, but fit into the pessimistic and realistic view of the Renaissance which I have been putting forward in this paper.[32] Tito, whose quick superficial mind makes the wrong

---

[31] Witemeyer, pp. 56-60, points out that, because so little was known of Piero, Eliot could mould him to her needs in the novel.

[32] Many naturally associate the Magdalen with Romola herself in her religious mood. For different interpretations of the mask, as well as Witemeyer see W. J. Sullivan, 'The Sketch of the Three Masks in *Romola*', *Victorian Newsletter*, 41 (1972), 9-13; 'Piero di Cosimo and the

interpretation of the three masks, sees the little child in whose lap they rest as the Golden Age that needs neither worship nor philosophy. He seems to ignore the satyr here, although not in his second likening of the child to the philosophy of Epicurus. We naturally associate Tito with the satyr, linked as he is to other symbols of paganism like the portrait of Bacchus and Ariadne, whereas Bardo is associated with the Stoic, and Savonarola and Romola in her religious phase are associated with the Magdalen. All three masks distort the potential happiness of the Renaissance, where the exclusive adoption of selfish excess, rigid pedantry and ascetic religion leads to misery and death. One of the features of Piero di Cosimo's workshop is its untidiness; this is not just a reflection of the conventional disorganization of the artist, and a genuine piece of biography, but a tribute to the need in art and in life to include everything, and not to exclude, as do the wearers of the masks, anything that is not congenial to a particular philosophy.

Romola in spite of its pedantic faithfulness to detail, about which Henry James was so rude, is a work designed to show that life and art do not conform to strict rules. Savonarola and Bardo and the Positivists and the extreme Italian revolutionaries tended to be hostile to anything that did not fit in with their views. Their tenacity is more admirable than the pliable philosophy of Tito Melema, who is ruled entirely by self-interest and political expediency. But ultimately it is wrong. Instead hope lies in human kindness and the unconventional but basically happy portrait of Romola looking after Tito's family at the end of the novel. This portrait, a kind of antithesis to the Sistine Madonna, has not received much critical attention. There are not any very strict or sure rules about looking after one's husband's illegitimate children. But we are sure Romola is doing the right thing.

Higher Primitivism in George Eliot's Art', *Nineteenth Century Fiction*, 26 (1972), 390-405 and Barbara Hardy, *The Novels of George Eliot* (London: Athlone Press, 1963), p. 176.

Chapter Thirteen

Greek Scholarship and Renaissance Florence in George Eliot's *Romola*

Lesley Gordon

It is well-known that George Eliot researched intensively for *Romola*, covering many aspects of Renaissance Florentine life. One of these aspects was the revival of the study of classical Greek, which, with the rediscovery of many ancient texts, was integral to the progress of the Renaissance in Italy. In the notebooks the novelist kept during the course of her research there are numerous references to fourteenth and fifteenth-century scholars and scholarship; in addition, the ancient texts themselves were by no means new to her. Already familiar with Latin, she had begun to learn Greek after her removal to Coventry in 1841, her teacher being the Reverend Thomas Sheepshanks, the headmaster of Coventry Grammar School. She seems to have been a good pupil, for the Reverend Sheepshanks told his grand-daughter that 'he was astonished by her power of application and retentive memory'.[1] By the time she came to work on *Romola*, she had become familiar with many of the major Greek writers, either in Greek or English. She had read the *Iliad* and the *Odyssey,* most of Xenophon, several plays of Sophocles and of Aeschylus, as well as some Euripides, Theocritus, Menander, Plutarch, Plato and Aristotle. She was to go on in the ensuing years to read more. The enthusiasm she felt for the Greek world is clear: 'I rush on the slightest pretext to Sophocles' she wrote in 1857;[2] in 1858, she found *Philoctetes* 'one of the finest dramas in the world' (*Letters,* VIII, 201); in 1862, she called Aristotle 'that greatest of ancients' (*Letters,* IV, 4); in 1870, Lewes found it hard to 'seduce Polly away from her beloved

---

[1] Lawrence and Elisabeth Hanson, *Marian Evans and George Eliot* (London: Geoffrey Cumberledge [O.U.P.], 1952), p. 331.

[2] *The George Eliot Letters*, ed. by Gordon S. Haight, 9 vols (New Haven and London: Yale University Press, 1954-1978), II, 319. Further references to the *Letters* are given in the text.

Theocritus' (*Letters*, VIII, 481); and, according to her friend the classical scholar Benjamin Jowett, Homer gave her relief from sorrow when, after Lewes's death, 'feeling that she must do something for herself, she read through, in the Greek, the *Iliad* and the *Odyssey*, because that most completely separated her from useless and painful thoughts'.[3] The preference she seems to have had for Greek over Latin was common in nineteenth-century Britain.

The nineteenth-century 'renaissance' in Greek studies in Britain was prefigured in a much more vigorous form by the fifteenth century Italian Renaissance. To the Victorian age, the texts themselves were not new, but the century in which *Romola* opens was, in the West, the great era of the rediscovery and dissemination of the language and literature of ancient Greece. To a degree, of Latin too; but, while this language and some of its literature had been transmitted through the centuries, albeit, at times, precariously, the break between the old Roman West and the Greek world of Byzantium meant that, in Europe, Greek had almost been lost. But in the East, in Constantinople, Greek studies were well-established and, with the Crusaders' conquest of that city in 1204, Greek learning very gradually began to make its way west, a process which continued in later years through the diplomatic missions sent to appeal for help against the attacking Turks. A member of one of those missions, Manuel Chrysoloras, gave in Florence the first ever series of lectures on Greek in Italy, and the year, 1397, has as a consequence been called 'a date of fundamental importance in the cultural history of Europe'.[4] In the fourteenth and fifteenth centuries, too, the attacks of the Turks on the Byzantine Empire caused a gradual migration of scholarly Greeks to Italy, bringing with them precious manuscripts; and the eventual fall of Constantinople in 1453, with the ensuing further dispersal of scholars, was considered to be, as *Romola*'s Tito Melema puts it, 'the gain of the whole civilized world'.[5] Further, not only did Eastern scholars move west, but humanists from the west travelled east in search of ancient manuscripts, large numbers of which were brought back to Italy and found their way into scholarly libraries.

---

[3] Evelyn Abbott and Lewis Campbell, *The Life and Letters of Benjamin Jowett*, 2nd edn, 2 vols (London: John Murray, 1897), II, 280.

[4] D. Reynolds and N. G. Wilson, *Scribes and Scholars: a Guide to the Transmission of Greek and Latin Literature*, 3rd edn (Oxford: Clarendon Press, 1991), p. 147.

[5] *Romola*, ed. by Andrew Sanders (Harmondsworth: Penguin Books, 1980), Ch. 32, p. 353. My subsequent references to George Eliot's novels give the chapter numbers, together with the page numbers of the Penguin edition.

By the date at which *Romola* opens, 1492, a knowledge of Greek culture was well-established in Italy, and the leading city in Greek studies, not only in Italy, but in Europe, was Florence. Traditionally known as 'a second Athens', described in the novel as 'the scholarly city' (Ch. 26, 302), and called by George Eliot herself 'this Italian Athens' (*Letters*, III, 300), the city and its inhabitants provide a classical, and, more particularly, a Greek, ambience not to be found in such a manner anywhere else in her fiction.[6] In order to give historical accuracy to the scholarly background, a number of the Byzantine refugees and other learned men of the Renaissance are mentioned by name. They include Manuel and Giovanni Crisoloras, Joannes Argiropoulos, the Athenian Demetrius Chalcondyles (or, as he is called by the Florentines in the novel, Demetrio Calcondila), as well as Italian humanists such as Giovanni Aurispa, Cristoforo Landino, and Angelo Poliziano, known as Politian, tutor of Lorenzo de' Medici. In addition, almost a whole chapter (Ch. 7) is devoted to narrating the true story of 'A Learned Squabble' between Politian and Bartolommeo Scala, the Secretary of the Florentine Republic. The verisimilitude attempted through the allusions to genuine scholars is supported by the technique of using further learned men and women as prototypes for some of the fictional characters. Of this group, it is likely that Romola and Tito are based on the learned Alessandra Scala and her Greek husband Michael Tarchaniota Marullus (d. 1500), usually known as Marullo. George Eliot made extensive notes about the latter in particular, and had in her library a copy of his poems.[7] Like Tito, he was a widely travelled pagan Greek, accomplished in classical learning, who married a beautiful Florentine; even his death by drowning is echoed in that of his fictional counterpart. The connection between historical and fictional character is established through Nello's remark that Tito's command of Italian is 'better even than that of the accomplished Marullo, who may be said to have married the Italic Muse in more senses than one, since he has married our learned and lovely Alessandra Scala' (Ch. 3, 74); and it is confirmed in Nello's further comment to Tito that 'You are of the same mind as Michele Marullo, [...] when he [...] talks of the

---

[6] For a full survey of George Eliot's application of Greek literature to her novels, see my 'Concepts from Classical Greek Literature in the Novels of George Eliot' (doctoral thesis, University of Newcastle upon Tyne, 1989).

[7] Gennaro Anthony Santangelo, 'The Background of George Eliot's *Romola*' (doctoral dissertation, University of North Carolina, 1962), pp. 263-5, refers to the novelist's interest in Marullo and points out that Alessandra Scala married a Greek. Felicia Bonaparte, *The Triptych and the Cross: the Central Myths of George Eliot's Poetic Imagination* (Brighton: Harvester Press, 1979), pp. 70-71, discusses the pagan Marullo as a 'gloss' on Tito.

gods awaking from their long sleep and making the woods and streams vital once more' (Ch. 3, 77-8). The 'learned and lovely' Florentine lady who married Marullo should be recalled when Romola appears. She also is beautiful and has been brought up by Bardo on the pagan classics, as Alessandra was by her father, Bartolommeo. Her teacher of Greek was, like Alessandra's, Demetrius Chalcondyles (Ch. 5, 100). A parallel with Romola is further suggested by several allusions to Alessandra in the novel, especially when Bartolommeo Scala, waiting for Tito's visit, is presented as sitting with 'his beautiful daughter Alessandra and her husband, the Greek soldier-poet Marullo' (Ch. 7, 123), and when Bardo compares the Scala marriage to that of Tito and Romola (Ch. 12, 182).

Bardo too has a real-life counterpart in Niccolò Niccoli (1364-1437), about whom George Eliot took notes in the course of her research for Romola. A scholar who had little interest in the wool trade which he had inherited, Niccolò spent his time and his fortune building up a large library of books and antiquities, which on his death became the core of a library open to the public. Just so did Bardo forsake trade in order to concentrate on scholarship and collecting, and he too wished his library to be a memorial to him. Further, they both devoted themselves to the minutiae of scholarship, and both, too, in the end had little to show for their labours.[8] The identity with Niccolò is established in the first chapter in which Bardo appears when the old man remarks:

> If even Florence only is to remember me, it can but be on the same ground that it will remember Niccolò Niccoli — because I forsook the vulgar pursuit of wealth in commerce that I might devote myself to collecting the precious remains of art and wisdom, and leave them, after the example of the munificent Romans, for an everlasting possession to my fellow-citizens. (Ch. 5, 99)

He goes on to find that his own library, though smaller, is choicer than that of Niccolò (Ch. 5, 101-2).

Still more historical accuracy is achieved by allusions to the invention of printing from movable type, a process which was first introduced into Italy in 1465 and accelerated the spread of classical texts in the Renaissance. Though Latin texts proliferated early, the output of Greek books in Italy was initially very low until, in 1494, Aldus Manutius set up his press in Venice with the primary intention of printing Greek (though he did also print Latin). In the

---

[8] Andrew Brown, in the Clarendon editon of *Romola* (Oxford: Clarendon Press, 1993), p. 613 (note to p. 53), refers to the similarities between Bardo and Niccolò. George Eliot's notes about Niccolò are in 'Florentine Notes' (British Library Additional MSS 40, 768) and 'Quarry for *Romola*' (Princeton University Library).

ensuing years up to his death in 1515, he became responsible for the first printing of much of the corpus of classical Greek literature. In particular, between 1502 and 1504, he produced first editions of Sophocles, Euripides, Herodotus, Thucydides and Demosthenes. But this was in Venice; Florence, whether or not George Eliot realized it, was not, in numerical terms, a great centre of printing, producing in the fifteenth century only about a fifth of the quantity of books produced in Venice. Yet amongst these there were some fine achievements, such as editions of Apollonius Rhodius, Euripides, Callimachus, the Greek Anthology and especially Homer, which appeared in 1488 and was the first printing of Homer in Greek in Italy.[9] It is described in the 'Proem' of *Romola* as 'that fine Homer which was among the early glories of the Florentine press' (47) and is the same 'fine Florentine Homer' (Ch. 39, 424) which is used to test Baldassarre in the Rucellai Gardens. It was edited by Demetrius Chalchondyles, who is named in the novel as Romola's Greek tutor.

The historical fact that this new invention was not welcomed by all is expressed through Bardo, in his fears that the more general availability of texts would 'make learning a base and vulgar thing' and that any lack of textual safeguards in the printing process would lead to the spreading of bad texts and so 'flood the world with grammatical falsities and inexplicable anomalies' (Ch. 5, 96). It was certainly the case that the editions produced by the early printers were not always accurate, since their copy-texts, often Renaissance copies of earlier manuscripts, contained the errors which are to be expected in manuscripts several stages removed from the original. It is Bardo, too, who, early in the novel (Ch. 5, 102), is made to name Aldus Manutius (or, in its Italian form, Aldo Manuzio) when he remarks that he has refused the latter's request that he might borrow his annotated manuscripts. Though Aldus's first book (an edition of Musaeus) was not printed till 1494-5, his preparation for the setting up of his press had taken some years, and could indeed have encompassed a search for suitable copy-texts as early as 1492, the date of Bardo's comment. Yet despite George Eliot's research and her care for detail, she can be detected in an error in making Nello refer to the 'correct editions' of the Cennini press (Ch. 4, 86) and in placing Tito in employment as a corrector of their Greek sheets. Though a genuine historical printing house, of which the founder Bernardo Cennini did indeed, as the narrator says, cast his own types in Florence (Ch. 4, 86), only one book of

---

[9] George Eliot refers to the Aldine Press in 'Quarry for *Romola*' and to the achievements of the Florentine presses in 'Florentine Notes'.

theirs is known.   This was a commentary on Virgil, Servius Maurus Honoratus's *Commentarius in Vergilium* (1471-2), which was the first book to be printed in Florence and not a Greek one.

George Eliot had noted that, in Renaissance Florence, 'no-one was held deep even in Latin literature who did not know Greek',[10] and the special enthusiasm the Renaissance humanists felt for Greek over Latin is presented in the novel first of all through the numerous allusions in the dialogue to Greek literature and myth, many of which also have a significance (which it is not the purpose of this paper to discuss) far beyond the 'local colour' they provide.[11]   To quote only a few of many, Nello describes Tito as a young Bacchus or Apollo, Tito wants to write a Theocritan idyll for Tessa, and Bardo refers to scholarship as honey from Hymettus (Ch. 4, 87; Ch. 10, 158; Ch. 5, 102).   More importantly, this same enthusiasm is expressed through the way in which certain characters are assessed by themselves and by others through their attachment to the Greek world.   One of these characters is Bardo, whose commitment is entirely to Greece.   He has given a 'fervid study [...] to the Greek tongue' (Ch. 5, 97), he admires 'the supreme Greek intellect' (Ch. 5, 101), he thinks that Greek is a 'nobler language' than Latin (Ch. 6, 114), and he finds Latin literature 'derivative' (Ch. 6, 106).   It is a predilection recognized by Romola when she humours him by saying that in his knowledge of the ancient language he is more fortunate than Petrarch (Ch. 5, 97), who, historically, was unsuccessful in his attempts to learn any more than elementary Greek.   Another such character is Baldassarre, who assesses his faculties through the recovery and ensuing further loss of his ability to read not Latin but Greek, and who is tested in the Rucellai Gardens by means of a Homer.   Further, it is a knowledge of Greek in particular which establishes Tito in Florence and wins him special favour with Bardo.

George Eliot's statement in 1869 that 'the ardent Scholar has always been a character of peculiar interest to me' (*Letters*, V, 30) should also be recalled when considering her delineation of Renaissance humanism, especially in relation to her attitude to classical learning as expressed in her other novels. She finds pedantry sterile, whether presented ironically through Mr Stelling of *The Mill on the Floss* in his intention to 'invent several new readings' for a Greek play (Bk 2, 1, 204), or pathetically through Casaubon.   Yet the 'ardent Scholar' Bardo, who, it should be remembered, has lived through the era of

---

[10] In 'Florentine Notes'.

[11] A full discussion of the Greek allusions in *Romola* is to be found in Chapter 7 of my thesis. See also my article, 'Tito, Dionysus and Apollo: an Examination of Tito Melema in *Romola*', *The George Eliot Review*, 25 (1994), 34-38.

the rediscovery of much of the canon of classical Greek literature, and who names as his teachers of Greek some of the greatest scholars of the age (Ch. 5, 97), is by no means entirely depicted in terms of what one critic has called 'sterile pedantry', nor is he, as another has said, 'a sterile Renaissance scholar who loses all sense of perspective because of a study that has no fruitful issue'.[12]   Bardo is esteemed for his learning by the volatile Nello, who addresses him 'in a more measured and more respectful tone than was usual with him' (Ch. 6, 105); he had in his youth been considered able to debate with the leading scholar Thomas of Sarzana (Ch. 5, 98), later Pope Nicholas V and the founder of the Vatican Library; he is named 'a worthy scholar' by Bartolommeo Scala (Ch. 7, 129); and a compliment has been paid to him by the great printer Aldus Manutius, long famed for his own scholarship and the accuracy of his texts (though that has more recently been disputed),[13] who has asked him for the use of his annotated manuscripts (Ch. 5, 102).   Attention should also be paid to the language used in relation to Bardo.   He had a youthful 'fire' which, it is clear, now irradiates his scholarship, into which, Bernardo, though without understanding, acknowledges, he has 'put his heart' (Ch. 31, 347), and Bardo himself speaks of his 'fervid study' of Greek (Ch. 5, 97) and admits to his preference for 'the far-stretching, lasting light' of 'the great dead' over the 'spectres' of the living (Ch. 5, 96).   His library too is not entirely oppressive.   The first description of the room represents it as being 'long', 'spacious' and 'in scrupulous order'; a feminine torso, though indeed a torso, is 'beautiful'; a statue, though 'headless' and 'wielding a bladeless sword', has 'an uplifted muscular arm'; and an infant's limbs, though made of 'cold marble' and 'severed from the trunk', are 'rounded' and 'dimpled', inviting a kiss (Ch. 5, 93).   Further, while the colours are 'chiefly pale or sombre', there is relief to the darkness in the 'gleams of brightness' which will reach the room, even if they only come through 'narrow' windows when the sun is high (Ch. 5, 93).   An allusion to Teiresias, the great blind seer of classical antiquity, also defines Bardo the first time he appears in the novel. As the reader is reminded by the passage recounting Teiresias's story which Romola reads to her father, he was blinded by Minerva (or, in Greek myth, Athene), in her anger at his having seen her naked; yet, though blind, he forever carried in his mind's eye the image of the naked goddess (Ch. 5, 94) and has further compensation in Athene's gift to him of prophecy and a long

---

[12] Virgil A. Peterson, 'Romola: a Victorian Quest for Values', PhilP, 16 (1967), 52; Santangelo, p. 152.

[13] See Martin Lowry, The World of Aldus Manutius: Business and Scholarship in Renaissance Venice (Oxford: Blackwell, 1979).

life. Account of the full myth has not been taken by those who argue that Teiresias's physical blindness is a metaphor for Bardo's inner deficiencies,[14] for, in fact, both the seer's outward blindness and his inward compensation form a metaphor for Bardo's situation. To the latter, what Romola, humouring him, calls the 'inward blindness' of Petrarch's ignorance of Greek is far worse than any 'outward blindness', and, in addition, as he himself puts it, he 'carries within him' an image, that of the 'fruits' of his Greek learning (Ch. 5, 97). These fruits, a suitable gift, it could be said, from Athene, goddess of wisdom, are sustained by another image, the memory of the location of the books in his library (Ch. 5, 95), and by a further 'light', that of 'those far-off younger days which still shone in his memory' (Ch. 5, 92). He also shares with Teiresias a long life, as well as his gift of prophecy in the sense that he suspects that his work will be forgotten.

Not only Bardo, but also Baldassarre, receives light and warmth from learning when, his faculties restored, 'the light was come again' (Ch. 38, 405), and when the power the ancient Greeks themselves thought resided in their alphabet is reflected in the way in which the Greek letters of the chapter title in Pausanias, understood once more, have a 'magical' ability (Ch. 38, 402, 405) to give him a 'glow of conscious power' (Ch. 38, 405). George Eliot was delighted by the comments of her contemporary Richard Holt Hutton in his recognition of 'the subtle skill with which the dominant influence of this scholarship over the imagination of the elder generation of that time — the generation that saw the first revival of learning — is delineated in the picture of Bardo and Baldassarre'. These two, Hutton pointed out, felt for their scholarship 'a passion' and gained from it 'a sense of large *human* power'.[15] This, the novelist said in 1863, was exactly what she was trying to express through these two characters: 'You have seized with a fulness which I had hardly hoped that my book could suggest, what it was my effort to express in the presentation of Bardo and Baldassarre' (*Letters*, IV, 97). The vitality of the humanists indeed finds expression in the novel.

---

[14] See Bonaparte, p. 49; Joseph Wiesenfarth, *George Eliot's Mythmaking* (Heidelberg: Carl Winter, 1977), p. 153, n. 16.

[15] See Hutton's review of *Romola*, first published in the *Spectator*, 18 July 1863, and reprinted by John Holmstrom and Laurence Lerner, *George Eliot and her Readers: a Selection of Contemporary Reviews* (London: Bodley Head, 1966) and David Carroll's *George Eliot: the Critical Heritage* (London: Routledge & Kegan Paul, 1971). Mathilde Partlett, 'George Eliot and Humanism', *SP*, 27 (1930), p. 26, misreads Hutton and George Eliot's appreciation of his remarks in saying that he concluded that the novelist was attacking humanism through the characters of Bardo and Baldassarre.

Romola, therefore, describes and sympathises with the Renaissance classical scholars' enthusiasm for their studies. After all, that which the narrator describes as 'that laborious erudition, at once minute and copious, which was the chief intellectual task of the age' (Ch. 12, 171-2) is precisely what George Eliot herself had undertaken in her research for the novel. Nevertheless, she does not endorse scholarship as a complete way of life. Bardo's failing is not his devotion to scholarship as such, but the fact that he shuts himself away from all else, expressed through the negative aspects of his library: colourlessness, darkness and broken statues. Opposition to the scholarly way of life is also expressed through the attitudes of some of the other characters. Monna Brigida speaks of 'those mouldy ancients' (Ch. 12, 175) and Bernardo, though acknowledging his friend's enthusiasm, feels that the 'fiery spirit' Bardo displayed in his youth has been dissipated among 'shadows' (Ch. 31, 347). As Richard Holt Hutton also pointed out, the younger generation, too, fails to find in scholarship that which so attracts their elders. Dino rejects the pagan classics in favour of ascetic monasticism; Romola finds only oppression in her father's cherished library, the contents, for her, being 'lifeless', the statues 'mutilated' and the bronzes and clays 'obsolete' (Ch. 5, 98), and refers little to the literature in which she has been brought up; even Nello, whose talk is full of classical allusions, so much so as to make Tito remark upon it at their first meeting (Ch. 3, 74), and who, according to Bardo, has the potential to be a scholar, rejects the life of learning for modern literature and the conversation of his shop (Ch. 6, 108-9); and there is the particularly interesting case of Tito. Though there is no suggestion that he does not have genuine scholarly accomplishments, he displays no commitment to learning for its own sake; instead, it is a means of self-advancement rather than, as with Bardo, an end in itself. George Eliot therefore represents two attitudes towards a scholarly life. There is the passion for the new learning for its own sake of Bardo and Baldassarre; but, for the others, scholarship in itself is not enough. For them, if it cannot be turned to the purpose of personal, social or political advancement, it must be rejected.

The word 'sterile', to which allusion was made above, does however apply to Bardo's work in the sense that it is unpublished and, as a result, doomed to be forgotten. In this connection, it will be worth looking for a moment at a comparable case in George Eliot's fiction, that of Casaubon in *Middlemarch*.

The two characters are alike, in the sense that scholarly activity gives meaning to their lives, to the exclusion of all else. Both, too, fail to publish during their lifetimes, and the posthumous memorials for which they leave instructions never come to fruition. However, there are crucial differences. Bardo is a respected scholar who, in the age of Renaissance humanism, has been working on newly-discovered texts, and there is no suggestion that his research is not in itself worthwhile. Further, though he restricts himself physically to his library, his intellectual horizons in his chosen field are wide, in that he is as much aware of the work of others, as others, Aldus Manutius for example, are aware of his. He is also, like Maggie Tulliver and Dorothea Brooke, partly a victim of circumstance. He laments that blindness has hindered his research (Ch. 5, 97); that his son, who, he feels, should have been his helper, had left him for the cloister (Ch. 5, 99); that the death of Lorenzo de' Medici has compromised the future security of his library (Ch. 5, 99-100), and that his fear that other scholars would take the credit for his work has prevented him lending his annotated manuscripts and making public his translations (Ch. 5, 95, 102). Casaubon, on the other hand, though he has social contacts, works in mental isolation. As a result, and especially because of his lack of German, he is unaware of recent discoveries and his theories are obsolete. Many of his difficulties, too, lie within himself, in that he lacks the real enthusiasm so evident in Bardo and, as was said of his namesake, the sixteenth century scholar Isaac Casaubon (1559-1614), he is 'destitute of poetic feeling' and without sympathy for the 'human and naturalistic elements' of the classics.[16] The language and imagery used in relation to the two characters aid the distinction. It has already been shown that, though to some, especially to Romola, Bardo's library is a place of darkness and oppression, to Bardo himself it represents light and warmth; but Casaubon, surrounded by 'Tartarean shades' (Ch. 10, 112) and wandering through 'anterooms and winding passages which seemed to lead nowhither' (Ch. 20, 228), is 'indifferent to the sunlight' (Ch. 20, 230). There are different reasons too for the similar fates of their hoped-for memorials. The *Key to All Mythologies* is consigned by Dorothea to oblivion because she feels unable to undertake what she recognizes to be a worthless task; but the oblivion which also overtakes Bardo's library, which he had intended would survive him and carry his name (Ch. 5, 101-2), is for the contrary reason. It is the very value of the books and antiquities that enables Tito to sell them, so dispersing the collections and depriving Bardo of the posthumous fame he craves. In the end, however, there is pathos in both Casaubon and in Bardo. In the former, it results from his recognition of the inadequacies within himself and in his

---

[16] See Mark Pattison, *Isaac Casaubon 1559-1614*, 2nd edn (Oxford: Clarendon Press, 1892), pp. 197, 441.

life's work; in the latter, it is from his realization that, though his work is indeed worthwhile and his library a choice one, he is in danger of being forgotten by posterity. Unlike Teiresias, neither will speak from the tomb.

Bardo's humanism also makes him 'one of the few frank pagans of his time' (Ch. 15, 209); as a result, he represents one side of an irreconcilable conflict between paganism and Christianity, which, as has long been recognized, is central to the novel. The impossibility of their reconciliation is depicted through Romola, caught as she is between the two. Her 'clashing deities' of 'mad joy' and 'wailing' (Ch. 17, 238) are symbolized by her husband's placing of her brother's crucifix behind the images of Bacchus and Ariadne. Yet it is noticeable that, just as scholarship is not in itself devalued, opposition to Christianity is not so much directed at the faith itself as at its expression in the extremes of asceticism, sado-masochism and fanaticism. In the end, however, the historical fact of what Richard Holt Hutton, in that same review, called 'the conflict between liberal culture and the more passionate form of Christian faith in that strange era', is not resolved by the adoption of one or other extreme, but through Romola's rejection of both for sympathy for the trials of humanity.

In *Romola*, therefore, George Eliot depicts, in its setting of fifteenth-century Florence, the effect the discovery of the Greek classics had on the scholars of the time. The enthusiasm humanists felt for their work is recognized and valued, and the reader is made aware that the new scholarship, criticized only in its extremes, had a vitality which was not communicated to the succeeding generation. Further, in the conflict between classical and Christian cultures, the reader is asked to look beyond both when the novel ends in the triumph of neither but in that of care for humanity.

Chapter Fourteen

'Too intensely French for my taste': Victor Hugo as Read by George Eliot and George Henry Lewes

Shoshana Milgram Knapp

Over a period of nearly forty years, George Henry Lewes and George Eliot assessed and appreciated Victor Hugo, whose variety of career and life experiences — as playwright, novelist, poet, polemicist, and intermittent exile — resembled their own. George Henry Lewes's early reviews, in 1840, paid passionate tribute to Hugo's dramas; George Eliot's final book, in 1879, made multiple allusions to Hugo's novels. Their judgements of his work, however, were ambivalent: George Henry Lewes came to see Hugo as superficially impressive, but emotionally shallow, and George Eliot singled out for praise in Hugo's poetry the least Hugolian aspects she could find. This essay examines their direct references to Hugo's work — in published reviews, in letters, in journals, and in fiction — and it will lead, in the end, to the speculation that George Eliot's reading of Hugo's *The Man Who Laughs* (1869) may be partially responsible for her departure, in *Daniel Deronda*, from the aesthetic of 'natural history' expressed in her essays and early fiction.[1]

---

[1] Morris Greenhut and Edgar W. Hirshberg have examined Lewes's articles on Hugo as indications of his critical practice: Morris Greenhut, 'George Henry Lewes as Critic of the Novel', *Studies in Philology*, 45 (1948), 491-511; and 'G. H. Lewes's Criticism of the Drama', *PMLA*, 64 (1949), 350-68; Edgar W. Hirshberg, *George Henry Lewes* (New York: Twayne, 1970). My account here focuses more closely on the passages and techniques Lewes finds worthy of comment. To my knowledge, there has been no study of George Eliot's reading of Hugo.

The Forties

Lewes, at twenty-three, displayed early enthusiasm for Hugo's plays. At a time when contemporary reviewers attacked Hugo's plays as morally depraved, Lewes hailed Hugo as the finest French *Romantic* playwright, as Racine was the finest French *Classical* playwright. In a long review article in the *Westminster Review*, 1840, he singled out for praise the characterization of the heroine of Hugo's *Marion de Lorme* (who purchases her lover's life with the loan of her body) and compares her favourably to Shakespeare's Isabella in *Measure for Measure*, who rejects a similar arrangement. Shakespeare's Isabella, Lewes maintains, is by design 'a clap-trap heroine, talking a good deal about her virtue' who is nonetheless 'at heart but a cold and selfish creature'.[2] Hugo's Marion, in Lewes's view, is noble, devoted, and utterly undefiled by her physical infidelity. 'To suppose a woman less chaste because she has been violated, is as reasonable as to suppose a man murdered on the highway for his gold, is a *particeps criminis* [...]. The play is full of poetry and passion, and like all *true* things, is a noble tribute to the majesty of Virtue' (323). Lewes thus defended — morally and aesthetically — the very play that had been attacked as evil, gross, licentious.

A few years later, however, Lewes wrote, in the *British and Foreign Review* (1844), that whereas Racine was a 'dramatist' and 'truly national', Hugo was a mere 'playwright', 'as pernicious as he is paradoxical', with 'anti-national' dramatic form, emotions and characters lacking in realism, and language 'by turns admirable and ludicrous'.[3] He explicitly contrasted Hugo's colourful brilliancy with the 'more peaceable but refined and lasting pleasure' of Racine and writers who 'preserve the logic of passion in the truth of character'. In the *Foreign Review* (1845-6), Lewes attacked Hugo both as an individual artist and as a representative of the Romantic school, which he continued to attack as unhealthy, a 'noisy, tawdry, lifeless thing.'[4] The change was in Lewes's sensibility, not in the appearance of new texts.

Yet traces of his earlier enthusiasm persisted. In spite of his recorded opinions of the French romantics, his own play *The Noble Heart* (1849)

---

[2] George Henry Lewes, 'The French Drama: Racine and Victor Hugo', *Westminster Review*, 34 (1840), 287-324 (322).

[3] George Henry Lewes, 'The State of Criticism in France', *British and Foreign Review*, 16 (1844), 327-62 (360-1).

[4] George Henry Lewes, 'The New Classic Drama in France', *Foreign Quarterly Review*, 36 (1845-6), 32-7.

included a tirade that, in William Archer's view, is 'unmistakably borrowed from the picture-scene in Hernani'.[5]

The Fifties

Lewes remained officially hostile. He attacked *Ruy Blas* as 'unreal from first to last', 'long and tiresome', with 'a want of life', 'no heart, no reality, no pulse of life. Nothing but antitheses and tirades'.[6] The antithesis, moreover, 'is not a vice of language merely, it is equally a vice of conception', given that it replaces logical structure, sympathetic characterizations, and realistic situations.

Within a few months of this review of *Ruy Blas*, Marian Evans became his regular theatre companion; within a few years, he shared with her his name, his views, and presumably his books. As part of an extensive *Belles Lettres* piece in the *Westminster Review* (1856), she produced her only review of Hugo, one that acknowledged his ability while also voicing reservations Lewes had expressed.[7]

George Eliot apparently did not look forward to reading and reviewing Hugo's poetry for the *Westminster Review*. She wrote to Charles Bray, from a zoological trip to Ilfracombe, that Spencer's yachting expedition to Hugo's home in exile on the island of Guernsey was likely to be 'pleasanter [...] than making acquaintance with Victor Hugo's two volumes of "Contemplations" which the Fates have unfortunately introduced *me* to'.[8] She apparently felt that Hugo in person might present a lesser ordeal than two volumes of his verse.

In consideration of the reader who might feel likewise, she suggests, in her review, that a reader 'who distrusts his own power of persevering through two rather stout volumes of French poetry' should turn straightaway to Hugo's poems about his daughter Leopoldine (who had died thirteen years earlier in a boating accident shortly after her marriage), 'simple, tender verses' characterized by 'real affection and real sorrow,' allowing the reader to 'share

---

[5] William Archer, 'George Henry Lewes and the Stage', *Fortnightly Review,* n.s. 69 [o.s. 65] (1 January 1896), 216-30.

[6] George Henry Lewes, 'Ruy Blas', *Leader* (27 March 1852), p. 306.

[7] George Eliot, 'Belles Lettres and Art', *Westminster Review,* 66 (July 1856), 257-78 [Review of 'Les Contemplations' by Hugo, 262-4].

[8] *The George Eliot Letters,* ed. by Gordon S. Haight, 9 vols (New Haven: Yale University Press, 1954-78), II, 253. Further references to the *Letters* will be given in the text.

in this exquisite expression of his grief' (262). George Eliot comments that she prefers such poems to the 'loftier strains' of discourses regarding God, the universe, the angels, and the tomb, 'but readers who prefer him in that loftier vein will find plenty of poems to their taste in these two volumes of "Contemplations" ' (264). She fulfilled her duty to Hugo by commending Hugo's tenderness rather than his full-blast grandeur and by quoting at length instead of analyzing in depth. She quotes, at similar length, from the poetic work *Gabriel*, by Bessie Rayner Parkes, a friend of several years who has never been acclaimed as a poet. Lewes was later to review, with humour and ambivalence, Hugo's collection *Les Chansons des rues et des bois*. Her enthusiasm for Hugo's poetry appears guarded, selective, and muted.

The Sixties

A similarly mixed response can be seen in Lewes's response to Hugo's *Les Misérables*, which was published in parts beginning in 1862. Lewes offered to write a review for *Blackwood's*:

> If no one has anticipated me I should like to write a paper on Victor Hugo's new Romance. I must tell you that although admitting his power—nay genius—he is too intensely French for my taste; and the article would show up his *tinsel* and antithesis without remorse. (*Letters*, IV, 27)

Lewes wanted to acknowledge genius while exposing empty glitter.

This review, published as 'Victor Hugo's Last Romance', shows what Lewes valued in Hugo, and what he found intolerable.[9] The review, moreover, shows the editorial judgement of John Blackwood, who explained to Lewes that Hugo's sexual content was too intensely French to quote even for the purposes of attack. Blackwood wrote to Lewes:

> The passages you quote from Victor Hugo in the beginning of the paper gave me such a turn against him that I felt indisposed for any review of him. Claude Frollo's *complaissance* to the charms of Esmeralda [in *Notre-Dame de Paris*, Hugo's previous novel] is so supremely disgusting that I think I would at all events suppress it. The paper is a good one but I do not much fancy it as Victor Hugo's theories inspire me with a stronger feeling of disgust than you express. (*Letters*, IV, 47-8)

---

[9] George Henry Lewes, 'Victor Hugo's Last Romance', *Blackwood's*, 92 (August 1862), 172-82. [Review of 'Fantine', the first part of *Les Misérables*, along with an assessment of Hugo's earlier work].

In the review as published, Lewes complies with Blackwood's advice. After quoting a brief passage from the Waterloo section of *Les Misérables*, Lewes comments that

> we think every Englishman will understand what we mean when we remark that the writer who could account for the fall of Napoleon by saying '*Il gênait Dieu*' [He annoyed God] must be one so intrepid in silly bombast, so willing to sacrifice every consideration to paltry "effect", that he could never be fondly cherished in this country. (173)

Too silly, too bombastic, too French. Lewes refers also to a passage 'more supremely disgraceful'; that is, the scene Blackwood had asked him to suppress; it is rendered here as

> a speech we dare not soil our pages by repeating, but to which we refer any reader who may suppose we are using language too strong for the occasion. We know nothing equal to it in blasphemous bad taste – in irreverent silliness.

Hugo's priest expresses the belief that God Himself would have preferred Esmeralda to Virgin Mary, would have chosen to be born of her. When Lewes says that Hugo is too intensely French for his taste, he means 'taste' in the sense of judgement and decorum (good taste vs bad taste), rather than merely preference or inclination.

Observe that Lewes has introduced, in what is ostensibly a review of an 1862 novel, a novel of 1831; he also cites the plays of the thirties. Lewes has gone back not only to Hugo's early career, but to his own, as if to deny again his article of 1840 and his early admiration for Hugo's writing.

Lewes attacks Hugo for blasphemy, silliness, the 'galimatias of turgid rhetoric'. He maintains, moreover, that Hugo commits errors of construction, presents superficial portrayals, depends too much on crude antitheses, and is guilty of radical insincerity ('it fails because it is not true'). One can almost hear him saying: Well, can't you see how inferior Hugo is to a writer who tells the truth and appeals to our sympathies?

> It is the besetting sin of most French writers to be incapable of trusting to the truth; and Victor Hugo is eminently French. They appeal to our sympathies on grounds which make it impossible for us to respond.

Why, asks Lewes, cannot Hugo be satisfied simply to portray Fantine as pitiable?

> We could not think of a mother's agony hurrying her into sin, without feeling deeply moved. But Victor Hugo is not contented with the simple story. He makes Fantine degraded as well as wretched; he intensifies her prostitution by every art of his powerful style; and having painted a brawling, flaunting street-walker, he audaciously calls upon us to accept her as a model of chastity and purity! Instead of appealing to

our pity for the woman and the mother, he insults our understanding by demanding our belief in her modesty. (179)

On the positive side, Lewes admires Jean Valjean's mental battle with his conscience: 'Few things finer in fiction can be named than the exhibition of the struggle in Jean's mind, and the final triumph of his better principles' (181). And Lewes admits that others, especially the French, may be less offended by the irreverence, less disgusted by references to sexual passion, and more impressed with the prose style. Lewes's verdict is that it is very good of its kind, but that it is a very bad kind.

Lewes did not review the remaining volumes of *Les Misérables*, but he did read them and discuss them with George Eliot (*Letters*, IV, 59-60), who was researching *Romola* and too busy to read them herself at that time. She wrote to François D'Albert Durade, a friend of many years, that critics had overlooked in Hugo a flaw of construction that in other writers would have drawn attack (*Letters*, IV, 59-60).

Lewes's objections to Hugo remained strong, and he voiced them again in a review of a collection of poems, three years after his review of *Les Misérables*. In his review of *Les Chansons des rues et des bois*, in the *Fortnightly Review* (1865), Lewes announces his project as justifying 'my own slight estimation of them, and the slight interest they are likely to excite out of France'.[10] While admitting that Hugo has 'extraordinary powers of language, and an immense fertility in novel expressions', he finds the poet indefensible before the 'court of International Criticism', whose judges are 'Imagination, Philosophy, and Common Sense' (183). Lewes's basic technique is to submit Hugo's metaphors to literal scrutiny:

Sur ces deux bouches, il semble| Que le ciel met son frisson
[On these two mouths, heaven seems to have set its shiver]

'What the shiver of the sky may be, and how it appeared on the lips of two lovers, is by no means clear' (184). Lewes decries 'the absolute impossibility of making any definite image' from Hugo's metaphors, and condemns the poems as 'demonstrably absurd, tasteless, and incorrect', with 'the great radical faults of vagueness and incongruity' — hence 'the cant of literature, not the experience of life' (189-90).

---

[10] George Henry Lewes, 'Victor Hugo's Latest Poems', *Fortnightly Review*, 3 (December 1865), 181-90 (182).

The following year, Lewes reviewed *Les Travailleurs de la mer* and its authorized English translation *The Toilers of the Sea*. This article contains Lewes's standard tributes to Hugo ('high aims and splendid talents', 'greatest of modern French poets', 'gorgeous enormity') and his standard objections (implausible plotting, unsympathetic characterizations, impossible metaphors).[11] Do not be impressed by verbal fireworks, he warns the reader.

> If the reader who has been delighted with the *brio* of one of Victor Hugo's descriptions, and astounded at its wealth of images, will only think of the thing described, and ask himself whether it has become more vivid to him – whether through these images he has learned to see it with a keener and a nobler vision, or finds himself in any way enriched, he will be able to estimate aright the value of this prodigal rhetoric. (46)

The reviews written by both Lewes and George Eliot share a discomfort with excess, colour, passion, the extraordinary. George Eliot praises Hugo's 'simple, tender verses' about his daughter, which she prefers to his 'loftier vein'. Given that Hugo is known more by that lofty vein, she is implicitly attacking Hugo at his most characteristically Hugolian. In his own reviews, Lewes makes a similar attack more explicitly.

Hugo is undeniably great and brilliantly talented, Lewes maintains, but he is not a great artist: he does nothing to enlarge our sympathies, and he does not lead us to see and feel with him. Lewes repeatedly reproaches Hugo for falling short of the aesthetic ideal of sympathy and sincerity. 'A great poet would have irradiated these scenes with the light of passion; would have had his own nature stirred to its depth, and found there the expressions to stir our hearts, but Victor Hugo finds nothing, absolutely nothing' ('Victor Hugo's Last Romance', 175). Hugo 'is so deficient in the cardinal qualities of Vision and Sincerity [...] that he excites little of the loving admiration which is so willingly given to poets who touch and teach' ('Victor Hugo's Latest Poems', 190). 'I never feel myself looking with his eyes' ('Victor Hugo's New Novel', 31). Hugo does not, in other words, measure up to George Eliot, who valued 'this rare, precious quality of truthfulness' (*Adam Bede*, Ch. 17) and who wrote to Charles Bray: 'If Art does not enlarge men's sympathies, it does nothing morally' (*Letters*, III, 110-11). Victor Hugo is not of the same ilk or in the same league.

George Eliot's reading of *The Man Who Laughs*, however, marks a sharp change in attitude.

---

[11] George Henry Lewes, 'Victor Hugo's New Novel', *Fortnightly Review,* 5 (15 May 1866), 30-46.

1869-1872

Hugo's *L'Homme qui rit* [The Man Who Laughs] was published in 1869. George Eliot apparently read this novel not only with care, but soon after it was published. Swinburne's review of the novel appeared in the *Fortnightly Review* number of 1 July 1869,[12] a number to which she refers in the Folger *Middlemarch* Notebook.[13] It seems likely that she read Swinburne's review before or during the time she recorded in her journal her own reading of the novel (3 July 1869).

In his review of *The Man Who Laughs*, Swinburne claimed greatness for the book because it 'deals greatly with great emotions' (74). Do not, he warned, judge it according to the standards of realism. 'It is a book to be rightly read, not by the lamplight of realism, but by the sunlight of his imagination reflected upon ours [...].' The beauty it has, and the meaning, are ideal; and it cannot be impaired by any want of realism. It cannot even be considered, generically, a novel. 'It is not, whatever it may seem, a novel or a study, historical or social. What touches on life or manner we see to be accidental byplay as soon as we see what the book is indeed; the story of the battle of a human spirit, first with Fate, then with the old three subordinate enemies: the World, the Flesh, and the Devil' (74).

The Man Who Laughs was indeed far from realism. Gwynplaine, the kidnapped son of the exiled Lord Clancharlie, has a permanent laugh engraved on his face by the *comprachicos* who steal him, and then abandon him, as a child, on the isthmus of Portland, in England. As he walks through a snowstorm, he rescues a blind baby girl (almost frozen in the arms of her dead mother) and carries her to safety: the caravan of Ursus, a solitary, melancholy man who shelters them and names the baby girl 'Dea'. Fifteen years later, they have become travelling actors, presenting an allegorical play, *Chaos Vanquished*, in which Dea's song rescues Gwynplaine, whose identity has remained unknown. Dea and Gwynplaine are in love, serenely and purely.

---

[12] Algernon Charles Swinburne, 'Victor Hugo: "L'Homme qui rit" ', *Fortnightly Review*, n.s. 6 [o.s. 12] (1 July 1869), 73- 81.

[13] *George Eliot's 'Middlemarch' Notebooks: A Transcription*, ed. with an introduction by John Clark Pratt and Victor A. Neufeldt (Berkeley, CA: University of California Press, 1979), p. 112.

Josiane, a duchess who is physically chaste and morally perverse, sees the performance, and, attracted by Gwynplaine's physical deformity, writes to him and invites him to become her lover. He is tempted to reply, but resists. When his identity is discovered, he is taken away, without explanation, to the home of Lord Clancharlie, i.e. his own home. There he finds Josiane, more than half-nude, in a secluded room; she assumes he has arrived in response to her note, and she begs him to degrade her. He is on the point of yielding. But Barkilphedro, an envious courtier who resents Josiane, has hatched a plot. Just as Gwynplaine is about to embrace Josiane, she receives a note from Queen Anne, informing her that Gwynplaine is not only a lord, but her future husband. She immediately loses interest, and disappears from the narrative.

Gwynplaine addresses the House of Lords, attempting to speak the revolutionary thoughts he has harboured in his secret heart. Masked by his face, he tries to unmask his society. The response is laughter. Finally recognizing that his identity as Lord Clancharlie is as corrupt as Josiane, he searches for the caravan. Ursus and Dea, not knowing that he is alive, are on board a vessel, about to sail. When he appears, Dea dies of joy, and Gwynplaine drowns himself, to achieve eternal union with her.

Swinburne praised the novel; he was almost alone among the British and French readers of his time and, indeed, later times. The grotesque elements — the face carved with a laugh, the nude duchess proclaiming that 'Woman is clay, aspiring to become mire', the peculiar names (Barkilphedro, Gwynplaine, Lord Dirry-Moir), the errors regarding British history — were overwhelming and distracting. Read properly, the novel is a symbolic fantasy of the Promethean spirit, in which Hugo translates history and all human affairs into the battle between matter and spirit, embodied in a story of suspenseful adventure. The usual objections Lewes raised to Hugo's novels are clearly irrelevant: anyone can see that this plot lacks realism. This book, as Swinburne points out, is something entirely different.

George Eliot may have consented to take this novel on its own terms and to acknowledge its powerful interest, although it is a work of a very different order from her own. She not only read *The Man Who Laughs*, quoting from it in *Middlemarch*, but also returned to one of Hugo's earlier novels, *Les Misérables*, copying extracts from it into one of her *Middlemarch* notebooks.[14] The connection between her reading of Hugo and *Daniel Deronda*, although less explicit, is perhaps more significant. I shall begin

---

[14] Victor Hugo, *Les Misérables*, trans. by C. E. Wilbour, rev. by Lee Fahnestock and Norman MacAfee (New York: NAL, 1987); *Les Misérables* [French] ed. by M. F. Guyard, 2 vols (Paris: Garnier, 1963). References are to these editions.

with the known — the references to Hugo in a *Middlemarch* notebook and in *Middlemarch* itself — and proceed to the unknown: possible parallels between Hugo and *Daniel Deronda*.

Early in the Folger *Middlemarch* notebook (19-20) George Eliot copied three French quotations, identified as such, from Hugo's *L'Homme qui rit*.

The first:

> L'inconvénient des mots, c'est d'avoir plus de contour que les idées. Toutes les idées se mêlent par les bords; les mots, non. Un certain côté diffus de l'âme leur échappe toujours. L'expression a des frontières, la pensée n'en a pas. [15]

In English:

> The inconvenience of words is that they are more marked in form than ideas. All ideas have indistinct boundary lines, words have not. A certain diffused phase of the soul ever escapes words. Expression has its frontiers, thought has none.[16]

Although the immediate context is the battle in Gwynplaine's soul between the divine love of Dea and the carnal temptation of Josiane, Hugo appears to be speaking more generally of what he takes to be the transcendent inexpressibility of some phases of consciousness. Although it would be over-reaching to attribute the treatment of the deficiencies of language in *Middlemarch* entirely to the quoted passage from *The Man Who Laughs*, Hugo's evocation of the limitations of language appears to be echoed in George Eliot's novel.

Caleb Garth's 'talent did not lie in finding phrases',[17] he has 'a sense that words were scantier than thoughts' (280); he borrows from the Bible: 'In his difficulty of finding speech for his thought, he caught, as it were, snatches of diction which he associated with various points of view or states of mind [...] ' (284). Dorothea's and Rosamond's mutual rescue is not characterized by articulate eloquence; on the contrary, Dorothea pauses 'in speechless agitation' and Rosamond can find 'no words' (Ch. 85, 550).   Most dramatically, Dorothea and Will are 'full of thoughts which neither of them could begin to utter' (Ch. 83, 559). 'Dorothea's heart was full of something

---

[15] Part II, Book 3, Ch. 8.   Victor Hugo, *L'Homme qui rit*, 2 vols (New York: Nelson, 1960), II, 65.

[16] *The Man Who Laughs*, trans. by Joseph Blamires, rev. by Patricia Le Chevalier (Milpitas, CA: Atlantean Press, 1991), p. 344.

[17] *Middlemarch*, Norton Critical Edition, ed. by Bert G. Hornback (New York: Norton, 1977), Ch. 14, p. 277.   Further references to this edition are given in the text.

that she wanted to say, and yet the words were too difficult. She was wholly possessed by them; at the moment debate was mute within her. And it was very hard that she could not say what she wanted to say' (560). Later on, when Celia asks Dorothea to 'tell' her 'how it all came about', Dorothea refuses: 'No, dear, you would have to feel with me, else you would never know' (Ch. 84, 567). A certain diffused phase of the soul, as Hugo asserted, ever escapes words in *Middlemarch* as well as in *The Man Who Laughs*.

The following chapter of *The Man Who Laughs*, 'Abyssus Abyssum Vocat', portrays the love idyl of Gwynplaine and Dea; it is the source for the second and third passages George Eliot copied in the Folger notebook (20). She quotes:

> Le coeur se sature d'amour comme d'un sel divin qui le conserve; de là l'incorruptible adhérence de ceux qui se sont aimés dès l'aube de la vie, et la fraîcheur des vieilles amours prolongées. Il existe un embaumement d'amour. C'est de Daphnis et Chloë que sont faits Philémon et Baucis. Cette vieillesse là, *ressemblance du soir avec l'aurore* [emphasis added by George Eliot].

In English:

> The heart saturates itself with love as with a divine salt that preserves it, and from this arises the incorruptible constancy of those who have loved each other from the dawn of their lives, and the affection which keeps its freshness in old age. There is such a thing as the embalmment of the heart. It is of Daphnis and Chloe that Philemon and Baucis are made. The old age of which we speak, evening resembling morning [...]. (348)

George Eliot incorporated this passage in French, without the underlining and with a small spelling alteration ('prolongés' for 'prolongées'), as the epigraph for Chapter 86 of *Middlemarch*, in which Mary and Fred, who have loved each other since they were children, become engaged.

The third passage George Eliot copied, a page later in Hugo's novel (II, 72), appears immediately following the second in the Folger notebook:

> En amour, rien n'est tel qu'une habitude. [...] La réapparition de l'astre est une habitude de l'univers.

The elided phrase is 'Toute la vie s'y concentre.' In English:

> In love there is nothing like habit. [The whole of life is concentrated in it.] The reappearance of the stars is the custom of the universe. (349)

This quotation, along with the one used as the epigraph to Chapter 86, is reflected, I believe, in additional references to the relationship of Mary and Fred. As Mary explains to Farebrother: 'I have too strong a feeling for Fred to give him up for any one else. [...] It has taken such deep root in me — my gratitude to him for always loving me best, and minding so much if I hurt myself, from the time when we were very little. I cannot imagine any new feeling coming to make that weaker' (Ch. 52, 359). She is, in fact, able at least to *imagine* a new feeling ('It was impossible to help fleeting visions of another kind — new dignities and an acknowledged value of which she had often felt the absence', Ch. 57, 400), but she resolves not to yield to temptation: 'And we can set a watch over our affections and our constancy as we can over other treasures.' Gwynplaine, too, wished to guard his affection for Dea from the threat of his passionate attraction to Josiane; George Eliot sets up a parallel situation, but allows Mary to pass the test Gwynplaine all but fails.

The novel's final image of Mary and Fred literalizes the epigraph, almost as if George Eliot wanted to teach Hugo how to improve his literary art. Instead of simply alluding to Daphnis and Chloe, Philemon and Baucis, she draws the picture. From the Finale (575):

> On inquiry it might possibly be found that Fred and Mary still inhabit Stone Court – that the creeping plants still cast the foam of their blossoms over the fine stone-wall into the field where the walnut-trees stand in stately row – and that on sunny days the two lovers who were first engaged with the umbrella-ring may be seen in white-haired placidity at the open window from which Mary Garth, in the days of old Peter Featherstone, had often been ordered to look out for Mr Lydgate.

George Eliot's interest in Hugo appears to have led her to return to one of his earlier novels. The Folger *Middlemarch* notebook contains not only three quotations from the Hugo novel she had just read, but also, on p.116, two shortened quotations from 'Cosette', the second part of *Les Misérables*.

The first excerpt reads: ' "Nous avons un devoir; travailler à l'âme humaine &c &c : – Écheniller Dieu." Victor Hugo, Les Misérables' (62). The full passage, which appears in Part II, Book VII, Chapter 5 ('La Priére'), reads as follows:

> Nous avons un devoir: travailler à l'âme humaine, défendre le mystère contre le miracle, adorer l'incompréhensible et rejeter l'absurde, n'admettre, en fait d'inexplicable, que le nécessaire, assainir la croyance, ôter les superstitions de dessus la religion: écheniller Dieu. (I, 618-9)

In English:

> We have a duty to perform, to cultivate the human soul, to defend mystery against miracle, to adore the incomprehensible and reject the absurd; to admit nothing that is inexplicable except what is necessary, to purify faith and obliterate superstition from the face of religion, to remove the vermin from the garden of God. (517-8)

The second brief excerpt, 'Trimalcion législateur', comes from the same section, Ch. 7 ('Précautions à prendre dans le blâme'). The full citation in French reads:

> L'histoire et la philosophie ont d'éternels devoirs qui sont en même temps des devoirs simples; combattre Caïphe évêque, Dracon juge, Trimalcion législateur, Tibère empereur; cela est clair, direct et limpide et n'offre aucune obscurité. Mais le droit de vivre à part, même avec ses inconvénients et ses abus, veut être constaté et ménagé. (I, 621)

In English:

> History and philosophy have eternal duties, which are at the same time simple duties – to oppose Caiaphas [under whom Christ was condemned to death] as bishop, Draco [Athenian law-maker who made the judicial code stricter] as judge, Trimalcio [vulgar, gluttonous character from Petronius's *Satyricon*] as legislator, Tiberius [Roman ruler, AD 14-37] as emperor. This is clear, direct, and limpid and presents no obscurity. But the right to live apart, even with its inconveniences and abuses, must be verified and dealt with carefully. (520)

Both passages come from a digression within a digression. After a long history of the convent of the Petit-Picpus, at which Jean Valjean and Cosette have sought shelter, Hugo moves into what even he calls a 'Parenthesis' on convents in general. The presence of these two passages in George Eliot's notebook shows not only that she was interested in Hugo's criticism of religious institutions and his concern for protecting religion itself from the mysticism and fanaticism of its adherents, but that she read closely passages many readers managed to skip.

What relevance do these passages have to *Middlemarch*? She may have intended to explain at greater length Farebrother's 'lax' religious views (Ch. 18, 127), which are inconsistent with Bulstrode's 'spiritual religion' (Ch. 17, 121), and, given his interest in natural history, are presumably non-mystical. Or she could have copied the passage because the emphasis on rationality resonated with Lydgate's ambition for 'enlarging the scientific, rational basis of his profession' (Ch. 15, 101), helping 'to define man's thought more accurately after the true order' (102), and 'combining and constructing with the clearest eye for probabilities and the fullest obedience to knowledge' (Ch. 16, 113).

Whatever the specific relevance of the quoted passages, it is surprising to see evidence of her interest in a writer she and Lewes had previously disparaged. This interest, moreover, may have contributed to additional parallels between Hugo's novels and *Middlemarch*. Bulstrode's predicament — a shameful past catching up with a man who has reinvented himself — is Jean Valjean's. In his review, Lewes had singled out this section of *Les*

Misérables for rare praise, acknowledging 'the power of the situation' of Valjean's 'irresistibly affecting' struggle.

> For many years Jean has devoted all his energies to escape the infamy of his former life, to hide from all eyes the fact that he had passed such a life, and to prepare himself, by Christian love and humility, for the life to come. In both he has succeeded. [...] Can he now consent to destroy this hardly-won reputation? (181)

Bulstrode, after attempting to use Christianity to conceal and shield, is similarly confronted by the self he left behind him.

> With memory set smarting like a reopened wound, a man's past is not simply a dead history, an outworn preparation of the present; it is not a repented error shaken loose from the life: it is a still quivering part of himself, bringing shudders and bitter flavours and the tingling of a merited shame. (Ch. 61, 425)

The similarity of situation highlights the contrast in the resolution.

Lydgate's perception of his marital disappointment may draw on an instructive contrast to the idyl of Gwynplaine and Dea in *The Man Who Laughs*. 'They sufficed to each other. They imagined nothing beyond each other. To speak to each other was a delight, to approach was beatitude; by force of reciprocal intuition they became united in the same reverie, and thought the same thoughts' (Part 2, Book 2, Ch. 5, 268). Their life, in poverty or prosperity, is described as 'Eden', 'Paradise', 'the ideal'. Lydgate's conception of happiness in poverty, which he formulates when it is too late for him to achieve it, is reminiscent of Hugo's portrait: 'He was beginning now to imagine how two creatures who loved each other, and had a stock of thoughts in common, might laugh over their shabby furniture, and their calculations how far they could afford butter and eggs. But the glimpse of that poetry seemed as far off from him as the carelessness of the golden age [...]'. (Ch. 69, 484).

A final connection between Hugo and *Middlemarch* is very practical, and may have had its source in George Eliot's new interest in Hugo. Seeing George Eliot copy Hugo into her *Middlemarch* notebook may have reminded Lewes of the publication history of *Les Misérables* (five volumes, published separately, in 1862). In 1871 Lewes suggested the same system — publishing a long work in several volumes, months apart — to Blackwood for *Middlemarch* (*Letters*, V, 145-6).

1874-1876

It has often been noted that *Daniel Deronda* is unique among George Eliot's novels: the only one with a setting in contemporary England, the only one with an opening *followed* by the characters' backgrounds and immediate past histories, the only one with an ending that entails significant uncertainty about the main characters' course of action. *Daniel Deronda* is also distinctive in other ways: The combination of coincidence and symbolism that allows heritage to become an option for the dispossessed hero to accept or reject; the presence of a woman who is playfully perverse, energetically witty, and radiantly attractive; the intense focus on moments of colorful drama and on extraordinary lots.[18]   The latter elements may have been affected in part by *The Man Who Laughs*.

Daniel Deronda, to be sure, is not entirely or imitatively derived from Hugo.   The inspirations for the Jewish element and the opening gambling sequence of *Daniel Deronda* are well-known, and have nothing to do with George Eliot's reading of Hugo.   The Jewish element, however, does not depend on an heir ignorant of his parentage.   Nor does Gwendolen's gambling require a woman of such 'iridescence' and perversity.   The portrayals of both main characters, conveyed by means of a narrative pulse that encompasses shock, reversals, and improbabilities, are reminiscent of Hugo's 'loftier vein' and of what Swinburne called 'a book to be rightly read not by the lamplight of realism; but by the sunlight of his imagination reflected upon ours'.

Hugo's Gwynplaine both inherits and chooses his destiny.   The walls of Ursus's caravan contain hand-written inscriptions of the laws of the peerage and a list of peers, the last of whom is Gwynplaine's father.   Consider the amazing coincidence: Gwynplaine, disfigured and dispossessed, has walked through a snowstorm to a house on wheels, on whose walls is written his personal history.   When he later learns his true identity, he realizes that he already knows it.

> Gwynplaine knew all the words pronounced by Barkilphedro. They were written in the last lines of the two scrolls which lined the van in which his childhood had been passed,

---

[18] Many critics have dealt with the departure of *Daniel Deronda* from George Eliot's earlier fiction. See especially: Gillian Beer, *George Eliot* (Bloomington: Indiana University Press, 1986), pp. 214-8; David Carroll, *George Eliot and the Conflict of Interpretations: A Reading of the Novels* (Cambridge: Cambridge University Press, 1992), pp. 273-315; Peter Dale, 'Symbolic Representation and the Means of Revolution in *Daniel Deronda*', *Victorian Newsletter*, 59 (1981), 25-30.

and from so often letting his eyes wander over them mechanically, he knew them by heart. On reaching, a forsaken orphan, the traveling caravan at Weymouth, he had found the inventory of the inheritance which awaited him; and in the morning, when the poor little boy awoke, the first thing spelt by his careless and unconscious eyes was his own title and its possessions. It was a strange detail added to all his other surprises, that, during fifteen years, earning his bread day by day, picking up farthings, and living on crumbs, he should have traveled with the inventory of his fortune placarded over his misery. (Part 2, Book 5, Ch. 4, 426)

Daniel, dispossessed and ignorant of his origins, finds he is drawn to Jewish culture, in a way far more developed than Fedalma's sudden awareness of her destiny in *The Spanish Gypsy*. At a time when he is searching for a role and a life purpose, he meets Mirah, then Mordecai — just the people he needs to prepare him to accept his inheritance when he encounters it. He accepts Mordecai's manuscript (the counterpart of the scrolls that line Ursus's caravan), and he accepts his family heritage. As he explains when he claims his grandfather's box, 'I have lately, before I had any true suspicion of my parentage, been led to study everything belonging to their history with more interest than any other subject. It turns out that I have been making myself ready to understand my grandfather a little' (Ch. 60, 690).

Hugo's Gwynplaine, long before he knows he has been born to leadership, has meditated on misery and the possibility of serving as saviour.

> His spirit was enwrapt in the contemplation of every succeeding apparition of widespread misery [...]. There was never a suffering, not an anger, not a shame, not a despair, of which Gwynplaine did not see the wrinkle [...]. Gwynplaine felt above him the thoughtless trampling of the powerful, the rich, the magnificent, the great, the elect of chance. Below he saw the pale faces of the disinherited [...] [and] felt the vague oppression of a keen, universal suffering [...]. Absurd notions crossed his brain. Because formerly he had succored an infant, he felt a ridiculous desire to succor the whole world. (Part 2, Book 2, Ch. 10, 291-3)

Daniel too has meditated on rescue and redemption. He has 'a subdued fervour of sympathy, an activity of imagination on behalf of others [...] a hatred of all injury [...] a meditative interest in learning how human miseries are wrought',[19] 'a passion for people who are pelted' (Ch. 59, 785), and a tendency to love 'too well the losing causes of the world' (Ch. 32, 413). Although Felix Holt and Lydgate desired to do good, neither envisioned himself as savior in the way that Daniel and Gwynplaine do.

---

[19] *Daniel Deronda*, ed. by Barbara Hardy (Harmondsworth: Penguin Books, 1967), Ch. 16, pp. 218-9. Further references are to this edition.

When Gwynplaine and Daniel come into their inheritances, they imagine themselves acting along these lines on a larger scale. Gwynplaine, upon accepting his title, pictures himself entering the House of Lords: 'I shall appear as a torch-bearer, to show them truth; and as a sword-bearer, to show them justice' (Part 2, Book 5, Ch. 5, 435). And so he does, diagnosing evil and prophesying 'the ascent of mankind' (Part 2, Book 8, Ch. 7, 558). Daniel ultimately accepts Mordecai's mission. Daniel's ambition, at the end, is that of 'restoring a political existence to my people, making them a nation again, giving them a national centre [...]. At the least, I may awaken a movement in other minds, such as has been awakened in my own' (Ch. 69, 875).

Gwynplaine and Daniel encounter, and are loved by, two women of opposite temperaments: Josiane-Gwendolen and Dea-Mirah. Barbara Hardy, in her introduction to the Penguin *Daniel Deronda*. has called attention to the vitality in Gwendolen, to the 'play of her personality' (25). Gwendolen's nervous energy, which George Eliot calls 'iridescence', resembles the radical and colourful wilfulness of Hugo's Josiane; both characters are described as goddesses, nereids, Dianas and duchesses (Josiane by legal title, Gwendolen by the resemblance Hans sees between her and the Van Dyke portrait).

Both are characterized by perversity. As long as Josiane views a prospective romance with Gwynplaine as transgressive, she pursues him. The instant she learns that he is in fact a lord, and the husband chosen for her by the queen, she asks him to leave.

Gwendolen, similarly, enjoys violating expectations. 'Gwendolen rather valued herself on her superior freedom in laughing where others might only see matter for seriousness' (Ch. 7, 109). She tells Rex: 'I am not fond of what is likely; it is always dull. I do what is unlikely' (Ch. 7, 100). She wants, everywhere and always, to do as she likes, and often defines what she likes and what others do not.

One aspect of Gwendolen's appearance, moreover, has parallels with Josiane's. The novel opens with Daniel's revealing questions: 'Was she beautiful or not beautiful? and what was the secret of form or expression which gave the dynamic quality to her glance? Was the good or evil genius dominant in those beams?' (Ch. 1, 37). Perhaps the notion that eyes can emit a good or evil genius owes something to Hugo's symbolic description of Josiane's eyes. 'One of her eyes was blue and the other black. Her pupils were made for love and hate, for happiness and misery. Night and day were mingled in her look' (Part 2, Book 1, Ch. 3, 199). Although George Eliot did not go so far as to give Gwendolen eyes of different colors, she suggests the presence in Gwendolen of dramatically contrary qualities.

Although Gynplaine is drawn to Josiane, his true partner is Dea, as Mirah is Daniel's appropriate wife. Mirah, like Dea, is an angelic singer, rescued by a man who perseveres in 'blessed protectiveness' (Ch. 70, 879). The woman is pure, the relationship chaste. As Dea feels threatened by Josiane on the day she appears among the spectators, so Mirah expresses jealousy of Gwendolen (Ch. 61, 794). Dea is blind; Mirah is described as 'listening with a blind look in her lovely eyes' (Ch. 37, 523). In both novels, temporary fascination is contrasted with abiding love.

Beyond these parallels in the nature and situations of the chief characters, *Daniel Deronda* may reflect George Eliot's reading of Hugo in its blatant departure from the 'ordinary' and the 'truthful' she had praised in her reviews and her early fiction. We see this not only in Mordecai's idealism and Gwendolen's sensitivity, in Daniel's ambition and his mother's talent, but in the heightened passion of the rhetoric. Consider, for example, Mordecai's prophecy, which recalls Hugo's description of the indistinctness of ideas, a passage that George Eliot had copied into her *Middlemarch* notebook.

> 'It will be seen – it will be declared,' said Mordecai, triumphantly. 'The world grows, and its frame is knit together by the growing soul; dim, dim at first, then clearer and more clear, the consciousness discerns remote stirrings. As thoughts move within us darkly, and shake us before they are fully discerned – so events – so beings: they are knit with us in the growth of the world. You have risen within me like a thought not fully spelled: my soul is shaken before the words are all there. The end will come – it will come.' (Ch. 40, 559)

This speech of Mordecai's could have been written by Hugo, as could Mordecai's final words, a possible parallel with *Les Misérables*. Mordecai's death scene — surely not an obvious way to conclude *Daniel Deronda* — resembles a trimmed recapitulation of Jean Valjean's death scene. A weary, benevolent man, at close of day, sits in his chair, with a young married couple holding his hands, his 'eyes full of some restful meaning', asserting that 'Death is coming to me as the divine kiss which is both parting and reunion — which takes me from your bodily eyes and gives me full presence in your soul' (Ch. 70, 882). Jean Valjean is similarly seated in his chair, with the 'light of the unknown world already visible in his eyes' (Part 5, Book 9, Ch. 5, 1460), accompanied by Marius and Cosette. Both novels, moreover, end with four lines of verse conveying nobility of spirit and the tranquil acceptance of death.

Although *Daniel Deronda* does not quote directly from Hugo, his impact may be 'as thoughts move within us darkly'. Later comments by George

Henry Lewes and George Eliot indicate respect for Hugo, untempered by the reservations expressed in their published reviews.

1877-1879

Writing to Barbara Bodichon in 1877, Lewes recommends Hugo's *L'Histoire d'un crime*, a romantic pseudo-historical account of Louis-Napoleon's 1852 coup d'état. Although Lewes admits, 'I haven't read it' (*Letters,* VI, 429), one can assume the recommendation was intended to be genuine, not ironic. Some of the other books on the list are acclaimed enthusiastically ('*Very* good', 'eloquent and interesting'), and Lewes seemed to express a similiar, if anticipatory, enthusiasm for *L'Histoire d'un crime*; it appears that Hugo's standing, in Lewes's estimation at this point, was sufficient to justify a recommendation for even an unread book.

George Eliot's final allusions to Hugo reflect similar approval and interest. In her final book, *Impressions of Theophrasus Such* (1879), George Eliot mentions Hugo's novel *Notre-Dame de Paris* (1831) in 'The Too Ready Writer' (Ch. 14).   The reference is favourable.   Pepin, the writer under analysis, apparently sees Hugo as one of the 'illustrious but overrated' authors of historical romances, whose errors he does not intend to repeat in his own 'grand scale' works.   But Pepin's views are not endorsed by George Eliot. Given George Eliot's own theory and practice in historical fiction, she is on the side of the 'overrated' Hugo whom Pepin rejects.

In Chapter 8, 'The Watch-Dog of Knowledge', she alludes to *The Man Who Laughs* by using the term 'comprachico' to describe an act of facial mutilation.   'The word Comprachicos was created by Hugo; [...].   The compound word itself (which means child-buyers) does not include the element of facial deformity.'[20] Hugo invented the term and extended its meaning; George Eliot borrows Hugo's word and Hugo's meaning.   Only readers of *The Man Who Laughs* would understand her meaning; it thus fits into the collection of what Nancy Henry has called the 'erudite joke,' the 'test to her readers measuring their knowledge of "high" culture'.[21]

George Eliot died in 1880, Hugo in 1885. I know, incidentally, of no indication Hugo read George Eliot.   His English, as he admitted to

---

[20] John Boynton Kaiser, 'The Comprachicos', *Journal of the American Institute of Criminal Law and Criminology*, 4 (July 1913), 247-64 (249).

[21] George Eliot, *Impressions of Theophrasus Such,* ed. and introd. by Nancy Henry (Iowa City, Iowa: University of Iowa Press, 1994), p. xxix.

Swinburne, was weak, and he was, in any event, more likely to borrow from himself than from any other writer. Gwynplaine's snowstorm rescue of the baby Dea owes more to Jean Valjean's forest rescue of Cosette than it does to Silas and Eppie. The response in the other direction, however, is strong and continual. Lewes reviewed Hugo's plays, poetry, and novels over a span of twenty-six years; George Eliot reviewed the poetry, made notes on two novels, cited Hugo at least three times in her books; Lewes criticized Hugo for lack of the specific virtues that were distinctly characteristic of George Eliot; *Daniel Deronda* contains suggestive Hugolian parallels.

I shall close with what appears to be a joke on George Eliot's part. At one point in *Daniel Deronda*, she mocks the antitheses and sudden reversals of French romantic drama, as described by Lewes:

> [T]o know Grandcourt was to doubt what he would do in any particular case. It might happen that he would behave with an apparent magnanimity, like the hero of a modern French drama, whose sudden start into moral splendour after much lying and meanness, leaves you little confidence as to any part of his career that may follow the fall of the curtain. Indeed, what attitude would have been more honourable for a final scene than that of declining to seek an heiress for her money, and determining to marry the attractive girl who had none? (Ch. 25, 326)

This is, of course, what Grandcourt does, but this novel shows his true motivations, as well as what happens after the play is over. The French romantic hero is an extremely bad bet. In another passage, she points out that romantic actions are not always accompanied by romantic panache.

> Hardly any man could be more good-natured [...]; indeed in his kindliness, especially to women, he did actions which others would have called romantic; but he never took a romantic view of them, and in general smiled at the introduction of motives on a grand scale, or of reasons that lay very far off. This was the point of strongest difference between him and Deronda [...]. (Ch. 32, 418)

The actual romantic, in other words, does not appear to be so. Nonetheless, romantic is as romantic does. The character's name, of course, is Sir Hugo.

Chapter Fifteen

George Eliot, Balzac and Proust

John Rignall

On 9 May 1880, while on her honeymoon in France with Johnnie Cross, George Eliot writes to Eleanor Cross from Paris describing the couple's crossing to Calais and their stop in Amiens:

> Then the next morning we had a millenial cabin on the deck of the Calais-Douvre and floated over the strait as easily as the saints float upward to heaven (in the pictures). At Amiens we were very comfortably housed at the Hotel du Rhin and paid two enraptured visits, evening and morning, to the Cathedral. I was delighted with Johnnie's delight in it. And we read our dear old Cantos of the Inferno we were reading a year ago, declining afterward on 'Eugénie Grandet'. The nice woman who waited on us made herself very memorable to me by her sketch of her own life. She went to England when she was nineteen as a lady's maid — had been much 'ennuyée de sa mère' — detested 'les plaisirs,' liked only her regular everyday work and 'la paix.' [1]

This passage presents a web of suggestive connections. The couple's delight in the Cathedral, one of the architectural masterpieces of mediaeval Christianity, is followed by a reading of familiar Cantos from the great epic poem of that same culture; and then, as a decline or a coming down to earth, they turn to a secular representation of the nineteenth-century provincial France they are visiting. It is as if Balzac's novel is the appropriate reading for their comfortable lodging in the Amiens hotel, just as Dante's poem is the appropriate reading for their experience of the Cathedral. Indeed, the woman who waits on them presents one of those 'scenes of provincial life' that Balzac is wont to describe, a life which, in its quiet regularity and absence of pleasure, bears a passing resemblance to that of the Grandets' servant Nanon and, in some respects, to the fate of Eugénie Grandet herself.

But Amiens and its Cathedral also point in another literary direction. In that same year, 1880, John Ruskin was writing about the same town and the

---

[1] *The George Eliot Letters*, ed. by Gordon S. Haight, 9 vols (New Haven and London: Yale University Press, 1954-78), VII, 273. Further references to the *Letters* are given in the text.

same Cathedral, lecturing on them at Eton College in November and publishing *The Bible of Amiens* in December. And nearly twenty years later Marcel Proust was to break off writing a long work of fiction which he was never to complete — *Jean Santeuil*, a labour which sometimes made him wonder whether he was not coming to resemble Dorothea Brooke's husband in *Middlemarch* in simply heaping up ruins[2] — in order to write about Ruskin writing about Amiens. The articles he wrote were published in 1900 in the *Gazette des Beaux Arts* and the *Mercure de France* and were to reappear as the preface to his own translation of *The Bible of Amiens* which was to take him another five years to complete.

Thus at this moment in the last year of her life George Eliot looks back to Balzac and unwittingly points forward to Ruskin and Proust; and although this conjunction is simply a matter of chance, I wish to argue that it does have some bearing on developments in her own late fiction, that is in *Daniel Deronda*. If *Daniel Deronda* breaks new ground for the English novel, it does so in ways which invite comparison with the fiction of other European countries. Henry James suggested, quite rightly, that there was something German about it.[3] This chapter will contend that there are also some affinities with the French novel, with both Balzac and Proust. This is not to make any claim for influence: the Balzacian elements are not strong or precise enough to indicate a particular debt on George Eliot's part; and whilst there may be grounds for arguing Proust's indebtedness to *The Mill on the Floss* and its presentation of childhood and memory, there is no such strikingly Proustian material in *Daniel Deronda*, a novel which, in any case, he does not mention in his writing and may never have read. The claim is, rather, that any affinities with the work of the two French novelists are a measure of the bold new departure that *Deronda* represents.

Proust, of course, knew, and in different ways admired, the work of both Balzac and George Eliot. About Balzac he wrote at some length in *Contre Sainte-Beuve*, and about George Eliot briefly but warmly in a couple of pages of notes of uncertain date, and in a number of letters throughout his life. The notes concentrate on *Adam Bede* and *Silas Marner*, commenting on the poetic and sympathetic rendering of rural working life, on the sense of the mysteriousness of life and its changes, and on the nature of George Eliot's moral vision, which brings out the difference between the evil that we do to others and the evil that happens to us, and shows how the latter can be the

---

[2] Marcel Proust, *Correspondance*, ed. by Philip Kolb (Paris: Plon, 1970-93), II, 378.

[3] Henry James, '*Daniel Deronda*: A Conversation', in *Selected Literary Criticism* (Harmondsworth: Penguin Books, 1968), pp. 65, 76.

condition of a greater good that God wishes to bestow on us.[4] Proust notes, too, the conservative spirit of these works and the examples of a progressive capitulation of the will which they offer. As J. P. Couch has suggested in *George Eliot in France*, many of these observations 'could, with only minor changes, be applied to *A la recherche du temps perdu*';[5] and, together with the famous remark in a letter that two pages of *The Mill on the Floss* — the novel that he loved the most — could reduce him to tears,[6] they have furnished the material for comparisons between the two writers which, by now, have thoroughly covered the ground in focusing on rural life, childhood, time, memory, and moral vision.[7] I want to take a different approach in attempting to place George Eliot's last novel in the mainstream of European fiction that flows from Balzac's realism to Proust's modernist adaptations of realist practice, and this paper will concentrate on how *Daniel Deronda* both explores what might be termed Balzacian territory, the lives of the metropolitan rich, the 'beau monde', and at the same time anticipates Proust in some of its formal qualities rather than in relation to time, memory, childhood, and rural life.

About Balzac George Eliot had mixed feelings which are summed up in 1855 in 'The Morality of Wilhelm Meister', where she describes him as 'perhaps the most wonderful writer of fiction the world has ever seen', but one who 'drags us by magic force through scene after scene of unmitigated vice, till the effect of walking among this human carrion is a moral nausea'.[8] Her ambivalent attitude and the grounds of her criticism closely resemble those expressed by Lewes in both his 1842 article on Balzac in the *Monthly Magazine* and his 1844 article on Balzac and George Sand in the *Foreign*

---

[4] Marcel Proust, *Contre Sainte-Beuve*, ed. by Pierre Clarac (Paris: Gallimard, 1971), pp. 656-7; *By Way of Sainte-Beuve*, trans. by Sylvia Townsend Warner (London: Chatto & Windus, 1958), pp. 282-3.

[5] John Philip Couch, *George Eliot in France* (Chapel Hill: University of North Carolina Press, 1967), p. 151.

[6] *Correspondance*, X, 55.

[7] See, in addition to Couch, L. A. Bisson, 'Proust, Bergson, and George Eliot', *Modern Language Review*, 40 (1945), 104-14; Franklin Gary, 'In Search of George Eliot: An Approach through Marcel Proust', *Symposium*, 4 (1933), 182-206; P. McKenzie, 'George Eliot's Nightmare, Proust's Realism', *Modern Language Review*, 79 (1984), 810-16; Margaret Mein, *A Foretaste of Proust* (Farnborough: Saxon House, 1974).

[8] *Essays of George Eliot*, ed. by Thomas Pinney (London: Routledge and Kegan Paul, 1963), p. 146.

Quarterly Review.[9] In the latter, in particular, Lewes comes to blame and stays to praise. Initially claiming that Balzac is inferior to George Sand and deserves contempt as an immoral writer, he ends by maintaining that Balzac's 'strengths are great enough and rare enough to outweigh his faults' (293). George Eliot and Lewes are thus both exercized by Balzac's questionable morality. Writing to John Blackwood in 1858 she states that 'The Heart of Midlothian would probably have been thought highly objectionable if a skeleton of the story had been given by a writer whose reputation did not place him above question. And the same story told by a Balzacian French writer would probably have made a book that no young person could read without injury' (*Letters*, VIII, 201). There is an unmistakeable taint of Podsnappery here, which may be due in part to the susceptibilities of her correspondent that she is too ready to accommodate, but the remark is consistent with other judgements on Balzac passed by her at this time. A journal entry of 25 October 1859 runs as follows: 'We have just finished reading aloud Père Goriot — a hateful book. I have been reading lately and have nearly finished Comte's Catechism.'[10] The condemnation of *Le Père Goriot* — a novel which Lewes also found 'extremely disagreeable' (*FQR*, 287) — is her most specific, and best known, verdict on any of Balzac's novels, and it prompts the question of why 'hateful'? The conjunction of the two readings in this journal entry may suggest one answer. Whereas *Le Père Goriot* presents a story of filial ingratitude, of daughters who exploit and impoverish their generous, if stupid, father without scruple or remorse, the very structure of Comte's *Catechism* presents something like the opposite relationship. It consists of a dialogue between a woman who asks questions of, and receives instructions from, a man (the Positivist priest) whom she calls father and who calls her daughter. Here is a woman as dutiful daughter, intelligently taking lessons from a wise father. Patriarchal authority is affirmed by the structure of Comte's work, not challenged and overthrown by clamorous egoism as it is in Balzac's novel. Is it, then, the inversion of the proper and conventional relationship between father and daughter that George Eliot finds so disturbing and hateful? The death of Goriot on his squalid truckle bed, abandoned by his daughters, could scarcely be further from the death of Mr Tulliver with Maggie kneeling by his side, the scene towards which George Eliot was heading as she worked on the second volume of *The*

---

[9] *Monthly Magazine*, 95 (May, 1842), 463-72; *Foreign Quarterly Review*, 33 (July, 1844), 265-98. Further references to these articles will be given as *MM* and *FQR* in the text.

[10] *George Eliot's Life*, ed. by J. W. Cross (Edinburgh: William Blackwood and Sons, 1885), II, 139.

Mill on the Floss in the autumn of 1859. And in her following two novels exemplary father-daughter relationships were to play an important part: Silas Marner and the adopted Eppie; and Bardo and Romola. In her fiction of this period George Eliot implicitly defines in her own moral affirmations what must have been peculiarly 'hateful' in Balzac's novel.

The perversion of filial relationships may not be the only grounds for disapproval.[11] The spectacle of Parisian life which *Le Père Goriot* presents is one of heartless self-interest, monomaniacal obsessions, and insouciant adulterous liaisons, so that, from its famous opening in the sordid boarding house, it could be said to drag its readers 'through scene after scene of unmitigated vice'. In this respect it is typical of Balzac's Parisian novels, and it is clear that both Lewes and George Eliot tended to draw a critical distinction between his scenes of Parisian life and his scenes of provincial life. Lewes saw Balzac's failings, his 'affectation and moral blasphemy', his 'cleverness and coarseness', as those of the essential Parisian (*MM*, 463), and listed provincial novels as his finest work — *Eugénie Grandet, Le Médecin de campagne, Le Curé de Tours* (*MM*, 469; *FQR*, 273) — while in her days as a reviewer George Eliot praised Balzac along with Jane Austen for his high standard in the 'delineation of quiet provincial life'.[12] The critical assessment which they shared of Balzac, and of what she referred to in a later letter as 'the Balzacian view of Paris' (*Letters*, VI, 57), was matched on one occasion by their response to the capital itself. In a letter of 1872, written on their way home from Bad Homburg where *Middlemarch* had been completed and the first seeds of *Daniel Deronda* planted, Paris is tellingly associated with vices and contrasted with the quiet Germany they preferred:

> Our evil genius persuaded us to go to Paris and to make the journey by night — whence came headache and horrible disgust with the shops of the Rue de la Paix and the Boulevard. After going to Versailles in the rain, seeing the sad ruins of the Hôtel de Ville and buying gloves (missing the Theatre Français and getting 'Patrie' in exchange) we rushed away to this place where we are trying to recover the sense of benefit from our change, which forsook us on quitting old Germany. We have an affinity for what the world calls 'dull places' and always prosper best in them. George became quite rabid towards Paris, and only calmed down a few minutes when we found a comfortable knitted waistcoat with silk sleeves which is what we have been seeking for him these five years. The vices of great capitals are more tolerable when one gets just the thing one wants in them. (*Letters*, V, 318)

---

[11] Walter M. Kendrick, 'Balzac and British Realism: Mid-Victorian Theories of the Novel', *Victorian Studies*, 20 (1976), 5-24, argues that she saw in Balzac 'a demonstration of the dangers which lay in the attribution of an independent moral value to art itself' (15).

[12] *Westminster Review*, 66 (July, 1856), 262.

The contrasts here are instructive. The great city of vices may also be, despite the destruction wrought by the war with Prussia and the civil war of the Commune, the city of satisfied consumer desire; but George Eliot and Lewes are more repelled than excited, for their deeper affinity lies with the 'dull places' they have left behind them in Germany, a country still essentially provincial by comparison with Paris. The critical perspective from which *Eugénie Grandet* could be preferred to a lurid metropolitan fiction of rampant ambition and material desire like *Le Père Goriot* is implied in the expressed attachment to a particular type of location and mode of existence.

The George Eliot revealed in this letter seems to be little changed from the writer of the 1850s who criticized Balzac's questionable morality while praising his delineation of provincial life. But to judge from her occasional pronouncements on Balzac in the 1860s and from the evidence of her last novel, upon which she was soon to embark, her understanding of Balzac's work had in fact altered and deepened. She had come to value him as a fellow craftsman. When François D'Albert Durade was translating *The Mill on the Floss* into French in 1861 and having difficulty in rendering different shades of style determined by character and social position, she observed that she had 'discerned such shading very strikingly rendered in Balzac', who 'dares to be thoroughly colloquial in spite of French strait-lacing' (*Letters*, III, 374). When her poem *The Spanish Gypsy* received some critical reviews in 1868, she reminded her publisher of Balzac's remark: 'when I want the world to praise my novels, I write a drama; when I want them to praise my drama, I write a novel' (*Letters*, IV, 464). And when she reflected on how she was growing old and how the years in front of her were diminishing, she had recourse to Balzac's famous motif of the shrinking skin, 'the terrible *peau de chagrin* whose outline narrows and narrows with our ebbing life' (*Letters*, III, 475). There is evidence from the letters and from Lewes's journal that she and Lewes read or re-read Balzac extensively in the 1870s, and although there are insufficient grounds for claiming influence, it is clear that, in widening the scope of her fiction in *Daniel Deronda*, she produced a novel which, in its social setting and moments of melodrama at least, can recall the kind of novel she condemned in *Le Père Goriot*. Just as her view of Balzac seems to have become less censorious between the late 1850s and the 1870s in line with the general tendency of critical responses to him in Britain,[13] so her own fiction came to reveal other qualites than those praised by Proust, and to transcend

---

[13] Donald Adamson, '*Le Père Goriot* devant la critique anglaise', *L'Année Balzacienne*, N.S. 7 (1986), 261-79, points out that the vexed question of Balzac's morality was quickly forgotten after the 1840s (274-5).

the essentially conservative spirit he found in her early work. Radical and daring, *Daniel Deronda* could be said to be European not only in its scope and setting, but also in venturing beyond the conventional bounds of the English novel both in its subject and in its form.

At the beginning of *Daniel Deronda* an echo of Balzac and an anticipation of Proust are interestingly combined. The epigraph to the first chapter, which reflects on the 'make-believe of a beginning', draws attention in cosmic terms to the daunting vastness of the whole of which any fiction can only offer a fraction, and thus lightly touches on a problem faced by any novel that attempts an encompassing representation of social life. Balzac, of course, fired by a notoriously Napoleonic ambition to represent the totality of French society, found his own solution to the problem in the device of recurring characters who create the links between the different scenes of the *Comédie humaine*. George Eliot's insistence that in *Daniel Deronda* she 'meant everything in the book to be related to everything else there' (*Letters*, VI, 290) shows her to be performing a similar act of the encompassing imagination on a smaller scale; and in the opening chapter she initiates a pattern of relations in a manner that recalls Balzac in particular. At the beginning of a novel he frequently uses a single scene, exhaustively presented, to imply the nature of the social whole — the infamous boarding house in *Le Père Goriot*; the theatre in the second part of *Illusions perdues*; or the gambling salon in *La Peau de chagrin* — and it is this kind of narrative synecdoche that is at work in the opening scene around the gaming tables at Leubronn. Like Balzac in *La Peau de chagrin*, George Eliot makes gambling a central motif in *Daniel Deronda*. Just as the acquisition of the magic skin by Balzac's protagonist is a gambler's throw — a win that is only the prelude to ultimate loss; a gain in intensity of experience which finally destroys body and soul — so Gwendolen's marriage to Grandcourt is a self-defeating wager, bringing material security only at the price of suffering and despair. Behind both novels stands the figure of Faust, and any affinity between them is partly due to the Goethean inheritance which they have in common, and to which George Eliot alludes in the epigraph to the first chapter when she refers to a 'prologue [...] in heaven'.[14] The implications of gambling reach beyond Gwendolen's experience alone, however, to involve a whole class of the rich and powerful who are disposed to seek the 'gain [that] is another's loss'; and the moral emptiness of that acquisitive materialism is graphically rendered in

---

[14] *Daniel Deronda*, ed. by Barbara Hardy (Harmondsworth: Penguin Books, 1967), p. 35. Further page references to this edition are given in the text.

the faces of the gamblers around the tables at Leubronn, all 'marked by a certain negativeness of expression which had the effect of a mask' (37), an image which anticipates the 'long Satanic masquerade' (831) that is to be Gwendolen's life with Grandcourt. Thus in abandoning historical distance for the first time in a novel and attempting a comprehensive representation of the contemporary world, George Eliot recalls Balzac in the scope of her undertaking and the initial moves in its execution. At the same time the self-conscious meditation on the problem of a beginning contained in the epigraph suggests her readiness to go beyond the customary procedures of nineteenth-century realism, and this is confirmed by the opening lines of the narrative proper, with their daring stroke of plunging directly into the thoughts of an unidentified mind. The initial volley of questions — 'Was she beautiful or not beautiful' (35) — is, for the space of a paragraph, as disconcertingly unanchored in place, time, and named character as the famous opening of *A la recherche du temps perdu*; and it shows how George Eliot's last novel is intriguingly poised between the established practice of realism and the formal innovations associated with modernism, between Balzac and Proust.

Daniel Deronda's intermediate position can be seen in its use of melodrama on the one hand and its presentation of character on the other. The melodramatic mode, which nineteenth-century fiction so often exploits, may be deeply conservative in its moral simplifications and conventional resolutions, but it can be used, as Christopher Prendergast has shown in the case of Balzac,[15] in radical and subversive ways. In *Le Père Goriot*, for instance, the mystery of family relationships, of abandoned children and vanished fathers, that constitutes one of the patterns of melodrama, is inverted to expose the shameful secret underside of society. Rather than resolving the initial mystery in the solace of a reunited family, Balzac maintains the disturbing and scandalous nature of the relationship between father and daughters to the very end. G. H. Lewes found that relationship 'revolting' (*FQR*, 289), while George Eliot's vehement reaction to the novel is testimony to its power to scandalize and provoke. It is a measure of the conservative spirit which Proust found in her early work that in *Silas Marner* a drama of entangled father-daughter relationships is given the kind of consoling and morally appropriate resolution that Balzac avoids. *Daniel Deronda*, however, is very different, for here George Eliot uses melodramatic material in a way that is as radical and searching as Balzac's. The melodrama of mysterious

---

[15] Christopher Prendergast, *Balzac: Fiction and Melodrama* (London: Arnold, 1978), pp. 175-7.

family relationships involves both halves of the double plot, embracing Deronda's search for his own origins, the problems of Mirah's dispersed family, and Grandcourt's abandonment of his mistress and children to marry Gwendolen. But the relations of fathers and daughters, parents and children, are now beyond reconciliation. Mirah's father is a feckless sponger prepared to exploit his children until they expel him; the history of Daniel's mother, Alcharisi, is one of filial rebellion rather than filial piety, and his rediscovery of her is scarcely a reconciliation, but, rather, an uncomfortable encounter that leads only to a final parting. In this radically unsettling work the unity of the family, and by implication the unity of the larger national community, is never restored, and the pattern of absent or inadequate fathers is an important element in an uncompromising criticism of established society and its values. In place of the sharp and simplifying moral outlines of melodrama the novel presents a moral complexity which challenges even the simple opposition of contemporary English upper-class society and an idealized Jewish community. As the story of Alcharisi makes clear, the Jewish culture in which Deronda finds his origins and his vocation can be, for a woman, simply oppressive. If there is something Balzacian in *Daniel Deronda*'s sweeping indictment of Grandcourt and his world, there is also a subtler power to challenge, to complicate, and to raise questions that remain unanswered.

That power can be seen at work in the treatment of character, so that even where the action is at its most melodramatic as in Grandcourt's oppression of Gwendolen, behaviour cannot be understood in terms of melodrama's polarized moral extremes. Although he invites moral opprobrium, the reptilian and predatory Grandcourt is strangely indeterminate and enigmatically inert. Sartorially impeccable and exquisitely disdainful, he *looks* like a Balzacian figure, like an older version of one of those dandified young men — de Marsay, Rastignac — who represent social success in the *Comédie humaine* and act as a mocking chorus to its various chronicles of failure, most notably in *Illusions perdues*. But there is a significant difference. Lewes took particular exception to Balzac's *arrivistes* like Rastignac, maintaining that the way in which they succeed through cunning calculation represents a false view of life (*FQR*, 284), and his view is echoed by George Eliot in 'Brother Jacob', where the narrator refers disparagingly to 'the astute heroes of M. de Balzac, whose foresight is so remarkably at home in the future'.[16] It is just such an ability to predict and control events that the

---

[16] *Silas Marner, The Lifted Veil, Brother Jacob*, ed. by Peter Mudford (London: Dent, 1996), p. 236.

apparently self-controlled and imperious Grandcourt is denied, and whereas Balzac's young men on the make may appear transparent as embodiments of social success, Grandcourt is made not only inscrutable but also curiously opaque. The chapter in which he is introduced has the telling motto, 'the beginning of an acquaintance whether with persons or things is to get a definite outline for our ignorance' (145); and in a later chapter, headed by La Rochefoucauld's observation that it is easier to know man in general than one man in particular, he is shown to be 'a chancy personage, raising an uncertainty as to what he may do next' (364). In this novel, which is both psychologically acute in its understanding of how 'there is a good deal of unmapped country within us' (321) and highly self-conscious about its formal procedures, the presentation of Grandcourt serves to emphasize the problem of character and the limited power of the mind to fathom its workings. George Eliot's scrupulous reticence here seems to be far removed from Balzac's knowingness and zeal to explain, and yet a sensitive reader of Balzac like Proust was able to discern something similar on occasions beneath the busy surface of the *Comédie humaine*. There are, he observed, 'wonderful effects of silence' in Balzac, despite the fact that 'he hides nothing, he says everything'; and to illustrate that silence he singled out the figure of Rastignac as a character who eludes final understanding: 'You know Rastignac? Really?'.[17] What Proust's unusual sensitivity uncovers in Balzac, George Eliot deliberately underlines in the figure of Grandcourt, bringing to the surface the problem of character that is never more than latent in earlier realist fiction.

George Eliot's reticence with Grandcourt seems to occupy an intermediate position between Balzac's apparent knowingness and Proust's dramatically disorienting practice of putting his characters through surprising meta-morphoses, so that they become, like Odette does for Swann, increasingly 'chancy personages' about whom nothing can be known for certain beyond their capacity to escape final definition. However, *Daniel Deronda* is too radical a work to be so neatly positioned between conventional realism and modernist innovation. If its opening sentences can be seen to foreshadow those of *A la recherche*, its conclusion is more open and unsettling than Proust's; and if we juxtapose two moments which precede and prepare for those different conclusions, it is clear that George Eliot matches Proust in the way she relates precisely observed details of the external world to the subtle

---

[17] *By Way of Sainte-Beuve*, pp. 129-30; *Contre Sainte-Beuve*, ed. by Bernard de Fallois (Paris: Gallimard, 1954), p. 210.

workings of the inner life. The two well-known scenes are both moments of vision, made possible by a pause in a railway journey which is, at the same time, a pause in the progress of the narrative towards its destination, a moment of repose before the denouement.   The first occurs during Gwendolen's return to England after Grandcourt's death:

> Gwendolen had turned with a changed glance when her mother spoke of Offendene being empty. This conversation passed during one of the long unaccountable pauses often experienced in foreign trains at some country station. There was a dreamy sunny stillness over the hedgeless fields stretching to the boundary of poplars; and to Gwendolen the talk within the carriage seemed only to make the dreamland larger with an indistinct region of coal-pits and a purgatorial Gadsmere which she would never visit; till, at her mother's words, this mingled, dozing view seemed to dissolve and give way to a more wakeful vision of Offendene and Pennicote under their cooler lights. She saw the grey shoulder of the downs, the cattle-specked fields, the shadowy plantations with rutted lanes where the barked timber lay for a wayside seat, the neatly-clipped hedges on the road from the parsonage to Offendene, the avenue where she was gradually discerned from the windows, the hall-door opening, and her mother or one of the troublesome sisters coming out to meet her. All that brief experience of a quiet home which had once seemed a dulness to be fled from, now came back to her as a restful escape, a station where she found the breath of morning and the unreproaching voice of birds, after following a lure through a long Satanic masquerade, which she had entered on with an intoxicated belief in its disguises, and had seen the end of in shrieking fear lest she herself had become one of the evil spirits who were dropping their human mummery and hissing around her with serpent tongues. (831)

The comparable scene in the final volume of *A la recherche* occurs when the narrator is returning to Paris after several years in a sanatorium:

> The train had stopped, I remember, in open country. The sun shone, flooding one half of each of their trunks with light, upon a line of trees which followed the course of the railway. 'Trees', I thought, 'you no longer have anything to say to me. My heart has grown cold and no longer hears you. I am in the midst of nature. Well, it is with indifference, with boredom that my eyes register the line which separates the luminous from the shadowy side of your trunks. If ever I thought of myself as a poet, I know now that I am not one. Perhaps in the new, the dessicated part of my life which is about to begin, human beings may yet inspire in me what nature can no longer say. But the years in which I might have been able to sing *her* praise will never return.' But in thus consoling myself with the thought that the observation of humanity might possibly come to take the place of an unattainable inspiration, I knew that I was merely seeking to console myself, I knew that I knew myself to be worthless. If I really had the soul of an artist, surely I would be feeling pleasure at the sight of this curtain of trees lit by the setting sun [...].

> C'était, je me le rappelle, à un arrêt de train en pleine campagne. Le soleil éclairait jusqu'à la moitié de leur tronc une ligne d'arbres qui suivait la voie du chemin de fer. 'Arbres, pensai-je, vous n'avez plus rien à me dire, mon coeur refroidi ne vous entend

plus. Je suis pourtant ici en pleine nature, eh bien, c'est avec foideur, avec ennui que mes yeux constatent la ligne qui sépare votre front lumineux de votre tronc d'ombre. Si j'ai jamais pu me croire poète, je sais maintenant que je ne le suis pas. Peut-être dans la nouvelle partie de ma vie, si desséchée, qui s'ouvre, les hommes pourraient-ils m'inspirer ce que ne me dit plus la nature. Mais les années où j'aurais peut-être été capable de la chanter ne reviendront jamais.' Mais, en me donnant cette consolation d'une observation humaine possible venant prendre la place d'une inspiration impossible, je savais que je cherchais seulement à me donner une consolation, et que je savais moi-même sans valeur. Si j'avais vraiment une âme d'artiste, quel plaisir n'éprouverais-je pas devant ce rideau d'arbres éclairé par le soleil couchant [...]? [18]

This moment of disconsolate reflection, of seeing not feeling how beautiful things are, prepares the ground for the conclusion by the force and focus of its dejection. The narrator's lament at the absence of any poetic powers hints at the creative potential he is about to discover. His concern with the line which separates sunlight from shadow on the trunks of the trees reveals a mind dominated by division: not only is observation divorced from feeling, but the responsive past is divided from the indifferent present, the natural world from the human, the poetic life from the commonplace, the lost years from those still to come. Yet all these divisions point to the possibility of future connection. The voice which apostrophizes the trees, speaking simply and bluntly of desolation, is clearly to be distinguished from the one which carries the main body of the narrative: it seems to speak from, as well as of, a past condition that has been transcended. Recapitulating earlier moments of despondent self-assessment, this scene is the final expression of the narrator's sense of creative sterility, of time wasted and of a life emptily lived out. It is the dark ground on which the final, redeeming illumination is to be projected, when, at the Guermantes' reception, the experience of involuntary memory reveals that the past is still alive within him and that he has the power to retrieve it through the process of artistic creation.

Proust's scene is thus a strategic moment in the grand unfolding plan of a work which tells the story of its own conception and which turns back on itself in its closing pages to complete the circular pattern of a life transformed into self-contained art. The passage from *Daniel Deronda* seems to promise a similar closure through a redeeming return to origins. Instead of Proust's emphasis on division, however, there is a reverie which mingles past and present in a manner reminiscent of other moments in *A la recherche*. The pause in the journey creates a space for imagination and memory to work, and Gwendolen projects onto the Continental scene first a nightmare vision of

---

[18] *Time Regained*, trans. by Andreas Mayor (London: Chatto & Windus, 1970), pp. 207-8; *A la recherche du temps perdu*, Bibliothèque de la Pléiade (Paris: Gallimard, 1954), III, 855.

Grandcourt's estate at Gadsmere which he has bequeathed to her, and then the remembered landscape around Offendene, whose sheltering downs and pastoral peace offer a refuge from mental torment and a misdirected life. In remembering her recent family home she also imagines a homecoming in terms which define what she is escaping from: a homecoming in which she sees, and is seen by, her female relations alone. Offendene thus represents a refuge not only from society, but also from the demeaning scrutiny of men, who, with the exception of Deronda, have looked upon her as little more than an object of sexual and proprietorial desire. This dream return to an earlier life seems to reverse and redeem the misguided search for meaning in the world of fashionable society, rather as the rediscovery of his buried past is going to do for the narrator of *A la recherche*. But although Gwendolen's imagined return to Offendene does take place, it does not complete the circle of a life in Proust's redemptive fashion. In the first place it is not her childhood home, as has been emphasized earlier in the novel in the well-known passage celebrating the value of a life being 'well rooted in some spot of a native land' (50); but, more importantly, her rootlessness persists, to be reinforced by the loss of Deronda's support. When he announces his decision to marry Mirah and leave for the East, any shelter which the familiar horizons of home might have offered Gwendolen is obliterated and she succumbs to a frightening vision of the world getting larger around her, 'and she more solitary and helpless in the midst' (875). The expectations raised by the reverie in the train are, then, never entirely fulfilled, and, in its reticence about Gwendolen's future as well Deronda's journey to the unknown East, the novel remains disconcertingly open. In this respect it bears out Proust's observation that all the great works of the nineteenth-century have the defining characteristic of being always, although marvellously, incomplete.[19] He cites Balzac's *Comédie humaine* as an example, but he might also have cited with equal justification George Eliot's last novel.

In the light of the ending of the novel the pause on the return journey to England takes on a lightly ironic inflection. The foreign country station gives rise to a vision of a station in another sense, a fitting habitat among 'the unreproaching voice[s] of birds' on a country estate. The temporary halt raises expectations of a permanent and secure resting place. Contrasted with the Satanic masquerade and hissing serpents, the well-tended English countryside looks like an Eden to which Gwendolen is to be granted a miraculous return. But, in retrospect, that second station may be as

---

[19] *A la recherche*, III, 160.

impermanent as the first, another temporary stopping place on a journey whose course and end remain unknown. In her final interview with Deronda there is repeated emphasis on movement, on 'the great movements of the world' (875) which now erupt into her life, and on 'the pressure of a vast mysterious movement' which disturbs her narrowly settled horizons, giving her 'a sense that her horizon was but a dipping onward of an existence with which her own was revolving' (876). Her secure retreat is that no longer; here is a life being set in bewildering motion again. George Eliot shakes up the patterns she has established and, with her variations on the word 'station', exploits the mobility of language itself in her resistance to conventional closure.

In his review of Cross's *Life* Henry James seized upon George Eliot's condemnation of *Le Père Goriot* as a 'hateful book' to argue that this moralizing reaction indicated her principal weakness as a novelist, 'the absence of free aesthetic life' which followed from her view of the novel not as 'primarily a picture of life' but rather as a 'moralized fable'.[20] If there were not already sufficient grounds in her earlier novels for rejecting such a criticism, *Daniel Deronda* would provide evidence for a conclusive rebuttal. What is suggested in the passage under discussion, but then subtly undermined, is precisely the kind of neat patterning that might be associated with a 'moralized fable'. Rather as there is a counter-current of movement in Proust's work to qualify the certainties of the concluding revelation,[21] so George Eliot here qualifies the clear contours of a moral pilgrimage by the 'free aesthetic life' of an imagination with no restrictively moralizing purpose but, rather, a readiness to leave her characters still unfinished and in motion.[22] With its unresolved questions and mutually qualifying or conflicting elements, *Daniel Deronda* has a continuing power to disturb any attempt to discern in its complexity a simple moral scheme. Its ironic openness and imaginative boldness seem to be far removed from the conservative spirit that Proust found in George Eliot's earlier work, and these qualities bring it closer

---

[20] *George Eliot: The Critical Heritage*, ed. by David Carroll (London: Routledge & Kegan Paul, 1971), p. 497.

[21] As Gérard Genette has argued in 'Proust palimpseste', *Figures* (Paris: Editions du Seuil, 1966), pp. 39-67.

[22] The opposite case has been made by Timothy Pace, 'Who killed Gwendolen Harleth? *Daniel Deronda* and Keats's "Lamia"', *Journal of English and Germanic Philology*, 87 (1988), 35-48, who argues that Gwendolen's final note to Deronda fixes her in 'a static pose of good' (46). But this touching epistolary gesture does not, in my view, overcome the sense of new and disturbing movement initiated by her last meeting with Deronda.

to the French tradition of fiction which Henry James admired and against which he unfairly measured her in interpreting her reaction to *Le Père Goriot*. In beginning *Daniel Deronda* with an arresting volley of questions and ending it with journeys into the unknown, George Eliot takes the English novel into new territory where both Balzac and Proust are fellow explorers.

Chapter Sixteen

Playing with Shawls: George Eliot's Use of *Corinne* in *The Mill on the Floss*

Gill Frith

'Take back your *Corinne*,' said Maggie, drawing a book from under her shawl. 'You were right in telling me she would do me no good. But you were wrong in thinking I should wish to be like her.'[1]

This chapter deals with the serious business of dressing-up, with the games girls play together as part of the process of moving towards adulthood: trying out new roles, taking up different positions and discarding them, putting clothes on and taking them off. It is also an essay about cultural hybridity: I want to identify a cross-national literary tradition in which the influence of Madame de Staël's *Corinne* (1807)[2] is paramount.

My sub-title for this chapter is 'George Eliot's use of *Corinne* in *The Mill on the Floss*', but it might more accurately be sub-titled George Eliot's *mis*-use of *Corinne* in *The Mill on the Floss*. My concern is not to identify precise allusions and explicit borrowings: Eliot's direct allegiance to *Corinne* has been fully and effectively discussed by Ellen Moers in *Literary Women*.[3] Rather, I want to consider Eliot's novel as one version of a story which

---

[1] George Eliot, *The Mill on the Floss* (1880), ed. by A. S. Byatt (Harmondsworth: Penguin Books, 1985), p. 432. Further page references to this edition are given in the text.

[2] Germaine de Staël, *Corinne, or Italy* (1807), trans. by Avriel H. Goldberger (New Brunswick and London: Rutgers University Press, 1987). Page references in the text are to this edition. My discussion of *Corinne* in this chapter draws in abbreviated form on Gill Frith, 'Embodying the nation: gender and performance in women's fiction', *New Formations*, 27 (Winter 1995-6), 98-113. See this essay also for a fuller discussion of the 'half-sisters' novels of the 1840s.

[3] Ellen Moers, *Literary Women* (New York: Anchor, 1977), Ch. 9.

225

nineteenth-century women told themselves, a story about the relationship between gender and national identity which has its origins in *Corinne*.

Nationalism, says Benedict Anderson, is 'an imagined political community', a community whose members 'will never know most of their fellow-members, meet them, or even hear of them, yet in the minds of each lives the image of their communion'.[4] The importance of *Corinne*, for my purposes at least, is that it provided a means of placing women in the 'imagined political community', and, also, of working towards envisaging a community *beyond* the everyday, beyond the constraints of the existent imaginings.

Now, *Corinne* is, famously, the novel which Maggie Tulliver failed to finish, and I know that Maggie is not alone here, so, on the assumption that not every reader will be entirely familiar with de Staël's novel, I think some summary is necessary. *Corinne* is ostensibly an affirmation of national diversity — or, rather, of the 'natural' diversity of 'imagined political communities':

> The art of civilization tends to make all men seem alike and almost be alike in reality. But our mind and imagination enjoy characteristic differences among nations: men are the same only in their insincerity and selfishness, diversity is the sign of everything natural. (12)

Diversity is located in Corinne and her English lover, Oswald Nelvil. Nelvil represents the 'best of Britishness': courage, honour, duty, moral principle, wit, restraint. Corinne is the embodiment of Italy: warmth, passion, beauty, spontaneity, grace, culture. But the narrative is propelled by the need to bring the two together: by the desire for, and the impossibility of, union between the qualities — the collective imaginations — of the two nations.

Nelvil first encounters Corinne on the day of her greatest triumph: she is to be 'crowned' at the Capitol. All of Rome has gathered to celebrate her achievements: she is poet, singer, dancer, musician, fluent in many languages, an inspired and eloquent *improvisatrice*, and the loveliest woman in Rome. But her real accomplishment is to embody, to make material, the Italy 'that must be understood through imagination' (17). Corinne not only pulls together the 'imagined community', but tells her audience *how* to imagine it, as the prince who pays public tribute at her 'crowning' makes clear:

> Corinne is the common bond shared by her friends; she is the impulse, the interest of our life; we depend on her goodness; we are proud of her genius. To foreigners we say:

---

[4] Benedict Anderson, *Imagined Communities: Reflections on the Origin and Spread of Nationalism*, rev. ed. (London and New York: Verso, 1991), p. 6.

'Gaze on her, for she is the image of our beautiful Italy; she is what we would be except for the ignorance, envy, discord and indolence to which our fate has condemned us'. (25)

The subject of Corinne's improvisation on the day of her coronation is 'The Glory and Bliss of Italy': her spectacular performance is observed through Nelvil's mesmerised eyes. What the narrative stresses at this point is her amplitude: 'Her arms were ravishingly beautiful; her tall full figure, reminiscent of Greek statuary, vigorously conveyed youth and happiness' (21). She is dressed like Domenichino's Sibyl: and she wears, on her head, an Indian shawl wrapped into a turban. Note the Indian shawl: I shall be returning to it later. Corinne is, like the sibyl, obscure: her origins and history are unknown. She has no patronymic, and even the name 'Corinne' is one she has chosen for herself. She is, then, the perfect embodiment of the autonomous super-heroine, but de Staël goes to great pains to stress Corinne's womanliness, her naturalness. As Christine Battersby has emphasized, the narrative goes through considerable contortions in its attempt to negotiate a balance between Corinne's femininity and her genius.[5]

Corinne and Nelvil fall passionately in love. Corinne embarks on Nelvil's 'sentimental education' and takes him on an extended guided tour of Rome and Naples. She implants the paintings, buildings, music, theatre, ruins, literature and landscape of Italy into Nelvil's sensibility. But this meeting and merging of nations and genders is destabilized when Corinne's origins are revealed: she proves to be only half-Italian, the daughter of an English aristocrat. She has an English half-sister, Lucille, who is positioned as Corinne's opposite, the exemplar of English bourgeois femininity: blonde, reserved, silent, insipid, child-like, domesticated. Nelvil returns to England and marries Lucille. From the moment of his return, Corinne's amplitude is progressively undermined. She loses control over her body, and over language. Her physique shrinks: she becomes pale, thin and dishevelled, prone to fainting and tears. The depletion of Corinne's body is parallelled in the narrative by the gradual effacement of Italy, and the possibilities which Italy represents, from Nelvil's imagination.

Germaine de Staël is perhaps best known now as the woman who made Napoleon very cross, but for my purposes in this chapter, what is significant is that she had no particular personal allegiance to Italy.[6] She was Swiss-

---

[5] Christine Battersby, *Gender and Genius: Towards a Feminist Aesthetics* (London: The Women's Press, 1989), pp. 98-100.

[6] For de Staël's life, see J. Christopher Herold, *Mistress to an Age: The Life of Madame de Staël* (London: Hamish Hamilton and the Book Society, 1959).

Protestant by birth, and resident in France for most of her life. Her celebration of Italy in *Corinne* may be attributed to her disaffection with Napoleonic France, or to her recent visit to Rome with her lover, but her Italy has a primarily symbolic function: it is a country of the mind which, the novel fantasises, might be realized in the body. For Corinne, England is both the object of desire and the source of death: her girlhood years in Northumberland are presented as a kind of living death, in which her creative talents were stifled. She cannot breathe in England.

De Staël's novel had a profound influence on Victorian women writers. In the next part of this chapter, I want to look at the impact of *Corinne* on a long-standing literary tradition. Many nineteenth and twentieth-century novels by British women writers depict a relationship between a woman who is English and a woman who is wholly, or partly, foreign. From the 1840s to the 1930s, the scenario is almost invariably the same. The foreign friend is enigmatic and alluring; she is a little older, more cultured, more sophisticated, more knowing than her impressionable English friend. She has a more secure footing in the world of adult femininity. The English heroine is on the cusp between girlhood and adulthood, and, again almost invariably, she has certain unarticulated yearnings, passions, ambitions which are not shared by the women of her community but which she finds mirrored in her foreign friend.

Many Victorian novels contain a ritualised scene in which the young English heroine — often on the occasion of her first ball, often in front of a mirror — is dressed up by her foreign friend, who arranges her simple white dress, crowns her with flowers, arranges jewellery around her neck. It is an initiation ceremony, a rite of passage which signals the heroine's entry into adult female subjectivity. This dressing-up ritual seems clearly to evoke the much discussed concept of the masquerade, and there is certainly some kind of masquerade going on here. But I do not think it conforms to Joan Riviere's configuration of the masquerade, in which women who wish for masculinity put on an exaggerated mask of womanliness to avert the retribution feared from men.[7] Nor does it quite fit with Luce Irigaray's account of the masquerade as a parodic imitation in which women participate in men's desire at the cost of relinquishing their own.[8] I would argue that the dressing-up rituals in Victorian fiction comprise a fantasy of agency, which, like most fantasies, procludes — magics away — certain rather significant questions

---

[7] Joan Riviere, 'Womanliness as a Masquerade', in *Formations of Fantasy*, ed. by Victor Burgin, James Donald and Cora Kaplan (London and New York: Methuen, 1986), pp. 35-44.

[8] Luce Irigaray, *This Sex Which Is Not One*, trans. by Catherine Porter (Ithaca, NY: Cornell University Press, 1985), p. 76.

about power, and who holds it. Entry into adult femininity is transformed into a game played by women together, a game which women control, and the significance of the foreign friend is that she simultaneously inculcates the younger women into the mysteries of adult femininity, and ratifies the ways in which the heroine does not conform to the prevalent womanly ideal.

In these scenes, there is often a sensuality somewhere in the air, but it is never precisely located. It is not quite clear whether there is a sensual current floating between the women, or whether the younger woman is absorbing, by osmosis so to speak, the sexual knowledge which her more sophisticated friend possesses. But what is clear, throughout nineteenth and early twentieth-century fiction, is that access to sexuality is being represented as something which is achieved through the model of another woman. The male gaze and male control over female sexuality, are, apparently at least, erased.

The influence of *Corinne* is most apparent in a cluster of novels published in the 1840s, each of which depicts a relationship between a young English woman and a woman who is part-Italian: Geraldine Jewsbury's *The Half Sisters* (1848), Georgiana Fullerton's *Grantley Manor* (1847), Elizabeth Sewell's *Margaret Percival* (1847) and Grace Aguilar's *Woman's Friendship* (1850).[9] The 1840s was also the decade in which Victorian bourgeois domestic ideology was consolidated, notably through the proliferation of conduct manuals which set out the terms of the middle-class Englishwoman's mission. Underpinning the nature of this mission, as it is presented in the manuals, is an appeal to origins: to the fixity and naturalness of both gendered and national identity. I want to suggest that the double identity, the hybrid origins, of the half-Italian heroine provided a means by which the woman writer could attempt to negotiate a position beyond that fixity. Once origins are placed in question, so is nature.

All of the 1840s novels listed above interweave questions of nation and gender to question some of the constraints upon the middle-class Englishwoman, but the two novels which most closely follow the model of *Corinne* are Jewsbury's *The Half-Sisters* and Fullerton's *Grantley Manor*.

In all three novels, the two women are half-sisters. The half-Italian sister is illegitimate, either literally, or because she has been rejected by her biological father. She is also a performing heroine: she sings, acts, improvises, plays the

---

[9] Geraldine Jewsbury, *The Half-Sisters* [1848] (New York and Oxford: Oxford University Press, 1994); Lady Georgiana Fullerton, *Grantley Manor*, 3 vols (London: Edward Moxon, 1847); Elizabeth M. Sewell, *Margaret Percival*, 2 vols (London: Longman, Brown, Green and Longmans, 1847); Grace Aguilar, *Woman's Friendship: A Story of Domestic Life* (London: Groombridge and Sons, 1850).

piano publicly, on stage. She has a hybrid personality: innocent and passionate, creative and domestic, autonomous and dependent. During the course of the novel she discovers and encounters her English half-sister, who conforms to the English domestic ideal. The two women fall in love with the same man, an Englishman.

Foreignness might simply be seen here as providing a licence for transgression: the non-British heroine can act out desires, adopt positions, realize talents which are illegitimate for women within the terms of the English community. But — like Corinne — she performs, nevertheless, *for* the community: her performance mediates the aspirations and profoundest feelings of that community: she pulls together its scattered members, articulates desires it did not know it had, and gives a shape to its imaginings. Her position, then, is on the face of it a thoroughly contradictory one: that of the foreign woman who gives cohesiveness to the community but remains outside its boundaries.

Or, we might say — drawing on Homi Bhabha — not contradictory, but 'in-between'. In *The Location of Culture*, Bhabha urges us to 'locate the question of culture in the realm of the *beyond*'; to look beyond singular positions and unitary identies, and *at* the 'in-between' and the 'unhomely'. These 'in-between' spaces, he suggests, provide the terrain for elaborating new strategies of selfhood and contestation.

> It is in the emergence of the interstices — the overlap and displacement of domains of difference — that the intersubjective and collective experiences of *nationness*, community interest, or cultural value are negotiated.[10]

Bhabha is describing a contemporary phenomenon which he relates to 'the new internationalism' but his words describe precisely what is happening in the Victorian half-sisters novels: origin is displaced, and the 'in-between' serves to negotiate new signs of identity. It is, however, a *fantasy* of shifting the boundaries of the legitimate, which can only be realized in fiction, and even the fantasy is circumscribed. The heroine's illegitimacy places her outside normal kinship structures. Her foreignness, her religion, her illegitimacy place her too far outside the boundaries of what the community can imagine. She can perform *for* the community, but the performance cannot be sustained *into* the community. It is beyond the limits of its collective imagination. The moment when the heroine reaches her creative peak comes relatively early in the novel. She is feted and adored by a (primarily male)

---

[10] Homi K. Bhabha, *The Location of Culture* (London and New York: Routledge, 1994), p. 2.

audience which is putty in her hands. But this integration is followed by her gradual disintegration; she falls sick, becomes pale and emaciated, and loses her powers. At the end of the novel, she marries an English aristocrat, and is absorbed into the English domestic community.

In the half-sisters novels of the 1840s, then, the *Corinne* plot is adopted and modified. What we are finding here is an attempt to interrogate de Staël's attack on English domestic ideology while negotiating a place for Italy within that ideology. And at this point I want to turn to another 'mother-text' for these novels, a novel which could not be more different from *Corinne*, but which was also a profoundly influential text for Victorian women writers. I am referring to Harriet Martineau's *Deerbrook*, first published in 1839,[11] a panoramic realist fiction of provincial life which is the precursor of *Middlemarch* and many other Victorian novels. Charlotte Brontë, in the guise of 'Currer Bell', wrote to Martineau to say that *Deerbrook* ranked with 'the writings that have really done him good, added to his stock of ideas, and rectified his views of life'.[12] Anna Jameson continually urged her friend Ottilie von Goethe to read it, emphasizing its Englishness and adding on one occasion 'you must read it, tho it may tire you'.[13] Her caution was warranted: *Deerbrook* is a compelling, exhausting and profoundly didactic novel. Yet its appeal for Victorian women is easily understood. For its female readers, *Deerbrook* touched a chord because it turned the bourgeois Englishwoman's mission into high drama, representing her continual personal struggle between strength and weakness as a matter of urgent *social* importance, vital to the stability and harmony of the community in which she lives. The novel focuses on two sisters, Hester and Margaret. Hester is beautiful and courageous, but hopelessly self-absorbed, possessive, jealous and unstable. The novel's heroine is her sister Margaret, who exemplifies the self-renunciatory strength and quiet calm of the woman who has struggled against the desires of the self, and won. (*Deerbrook*'s influence is most clearly evident in the proliferation of Victorian heroines with the name of Margaret.) Both sisters are in love with Edward Hope, a dissenting surgeon of radical views who represents hope for the future. Hester gets him: Margaret does not.

---

[11] Harriet Martineau, *Deerbrook* (1839), with an introduction by Gaby Weiner (London: Virago, 1983).

[12] Letter written in November 1849, quoted in Harriet Martineau, *Harriet Martineau's Autobiography*, with memorials by Maria Weston Chapman, 3 vols (London: Smith, Elder and Co., 1877).

[13] *Letters of Anna Jameson to Ottilie von Goethe*, ed. by G. H. Needler (London: Oxford University Press, 1989), Letter 74, June 1839, p. 112.

What I am suggesting is that the 1840s half-sisters novels not only have hybrid heroines, but are also hybrid texts. They attempt, with visible difficulty, to mesh the Englishness of *Deerbrook* with the foreignness of *Corinne*; to negotiate a fusion between *Deerbrook*'s sober affirmation of the bourgeois Englishwoman's mission in her community, and *Corinne*'s flamboyant celebration of the passionate, creative woman. Something strange, exotic, energizing, dangerous is injected into the current social frame, only to have its danger assimilated and defused. Transgression — creativity, sensuality, entry into the public domain — are located onto the foreign woman: no Englishwoman would behave *like that*. Ultimately, however, foreign subversiveness is muted and modified by the heroine's integration into the provincial community.

In the Victorian novels I have discussed so far, there is a clear polarization between the English and the foreign, but some transgressive foreign attributes are given qualified affirmation. Here it is worth noting that *Corinne*'s fictional English daughters of the 1840s are pre-revolutionary texts: all were completed before 1848, but written when revolution was in the air, I want to move on now to look at three post-revolutionary novels, published in the less turbulent, more complacent climate of the 1850s. In these novels, foreignness itself is suspect: but the influence of *Corinne* may be seen at work in the ways in which elements identified as foreign are assimilated into the bourgeois English community.

The heritage of *Corinne* is evident in Dinah Mulock Craik's *Olive* (1850),[14] which makes use of the half-sisters plot, but Craik's novel, which had a long run of popularity, also draws freely upon *Jane Eyre*. Olive and her half-sister Christal are (loosely, never explicitly) the fictive daughters of Mr Rochester by Jane Eyre and Bertha Mason. Christal is the illegitimate daughter of a ferocious and passionate Quadroon; Olive, the heroine and legitimate daughter, is a quiet, reserved young woman whose concealed depth of feeling and extraordinary visionary gift find expression in her paintings. Unlike Jane Eyre, Olive takes her talent into the public sphere, achieving fame and fortune as an artist. She is also a hunchback.

Victorian women writers persistently truncate the physiques of their creative women: it is a way of marking out the woman artist as different, rationalising her entry into the public domain by making her something less than a full woman, but it also acts as a way of reducing and containing her

---

[14] Dinah Mulock Craik, *Olive* [1850] (London: W. Nicholson & Sons, n.d). Page references to this edition are given in the text.

'phallic' threat to received notions of gendered identity. Olive's handicap is, however, flexible: initially represented as a crippling deformity which repulses even the heroine's mother, it later becomes more or less noticeable according to the demands of the plot, and, by the time Olive moves towards marriage, domesticity and the renunciation of her career, it has been modified to a barely visible defect in posture.

The contortions involved here illustrate the anxiety of women writers over the question of female creativity. It is not so much that creative production itself was the problem; by the mid-nineteenth century women's writing had a long history, and the literary scene contained a number of highly competent professional women who, like Craik herself, handled their business affairs with confidence and were sometimes, like Harriet Martineau and Geraldine Jewsbury, in positions of considerable influence.[15] The anxiety focuses on the implications of this for gendered identity: on the question of whether such a position somehow involved being less of a woman and more of a man. The reputation of George Sand stood as an admonitory example of the way in which transgressive femininity, whether it was in the form of female genius or irregular sexuality, was most easily accommodated as a manifestation of bisexuality. Sand's novels were extremely widely read and discussed in the 1840s and 1850s, but discussion of her work was often overshadowed by the relentless fascination with Sand's 'hermaphroditism', her cross-dressing, her cigars, the scandal of her extra-marital affairs, which, while largely heterosexual, somehow fed into the received framework of Sand's 'masculinity'.[16]

For English women writers, the most important of Sand's novels was *Consuelo*, first published in 1842; Mary Taylor commented that it was worth taking the trouble of learning French simply to read it.[17] Like Corinne, Consuelo combines genius with unblemished femininity. Reared on the streets of Florence, the waif with a golden voice grows up to be a celebrated

---

[15] See Shirley Foster, *Victorian Women's Fiction: Marriage, Freedom and the Individual* (London: Croom Helm, 1985), Chs 1 and 2.

[16] For a full account of the reception and influence of George Sand in Victorian England, see Patricia Thomson, *George Sand and the Victorians* (London and Basingstoke: Macmillan, 1977). See also Isabelle de Courtivron, 'Weak Men and Fatal Women: The Sand Image', in *Homosexualities and French Literature*, ed. by Elaine Marks and George Stambolian (Ithaca and London: Cornell University Press, 1979), pp. 210-27.

[17] Letter to Ellen Nussey written in 1843; quoted in *Mary Taylor, Friend of Charlotte Brontë: Letters from New Zealand and Elsewhere*, ed. by Joan Stevens (Auckland, New Zealand: Auckland University Press, 1972), p. 49. The first of many English translations of *Consuelo* appeared in 1846.

prima donna while retaining her perfect simplicity and purity. Consuelo's distinguishing attributes — gleaming black hair, gypsy-like appearance, simple black dress — appear again and again in the heroines of Victorian women writers. But in *Olive*, Consuelo is split in half: the gypsy-like waif is the artist heroine's wicked half-sister.

Christal appears first as a ragged child with fierce black eyes, 'the very image of a half-tamed gypsy' (149). When she re-enters the narrative after a spell in a French boarding-school, it is as a 'Frenchified' (170) adult whose haughty elegance and artificial grace barely mask her real nature. Olive's rise towards selfless fame and virtuous domesticity is parallelled and disrupted by Christal's fall from repressed rebellious venom to demonic violence and uncontrolled sexuality: Christal tries to kill Olive, becomes a fallen woman, goes mad, and ends up, bitter and humiliated, confined to the convent she had chosen as her 'spirit's grave' (373).

The locking-up of the monstrous female clearly draws on *Jane Eyre* and, like Bertha, Christal may be seen as expressing the resistance and rage that the text represses.[18] Nor is this entirely a covert process: Craik points the finger at patriarchy and imperialism in the story of Christal's mother, who appears briefly in the novel as a ravaged tigress, once an artist's model with the exotic beauty of an 'Eastern queen' (147), who has been seduced and abandoned by Olive's father. She comes, as she tells Olive, from a country where there are thousands like herself, delicately nurtured young girls 'whose mixed blood is too pure for slavery, too tainted for freedom. Lovely, accomplished, brought up delicately, they yet have no higher future than to be the white man's passing toy — cherished, wearied of, and spurned' (150). Christal's wrecked life is similarly the offshoot of this casual seduction, but whereas *Jane Eyre* suggests an identification between Bertha and Jane, paralleling their entrapment, the narrative of *Olive* works to effect a clear separation between the heroine and her 'other', detaching Olive from the foreign, the exotic, the strange, and confirming her as, despite her transgressive talent, truly English and thus, truly feminine.

---

[18] For the most influential analysis of *Jane Eyre* along these lines, see Sandra M. Gilbert and Susan Gubar, *The Madwoman in the Attic: The Woman Writer and the Nineteenth-Century Literary Imagination* (New Haven and London: Yale University Press, 1979), Ch. 10.

I want to turn now to two other novels written in the 1850s, Elizabeth Gaskell's *North and South*[19] and George Eliot's *The Mill on the Floss*, which set out to re-imagine the English community from within. Both novels draw on codes and motifs taken from *Corinne*, but reinflect them to extricate them from their association with foreignness and to locate them within English kinship structures. Both novels depict a relationship between two cousins, and what happens during the course of the narrative is that the reigning 'princess' abdicates in favour of a new 'queen'. The little, kitten-like princess — Edith in *North and South*, Lucy in *The Mill on the Floss* — is the pattern of conventional femininity: soft, sweet, submissive, cossetted, at one with her own image, perfectly at home in a drawing-room. Her taller, gypsy-like cousin — Gaskell's Margaret Hale, Eliot's Maggie Tulliver — is more restless, at odds with the constrictions of feminine discourse, out of place in the female indoor space. The motifs which signal the heroine's claim to the 'throne' are taken from *Corinne* and *Consuelo* — the Indian shawl, the gypsy, the heavy 'coronet' of black hair.

In the first chapter of *North and South*, Edith is on the brink of marriage. She chatters on about wedding dresses, marriage ceremonies and tuning pianos, and falls asleep in a kittenish ball of muslin and ribbon and silken curls. As she sleeps, Margaret stands in for her to display the exotic Indian shawls lavished on Edith by her doting mother.

> No one thought about it; but Margaret's tall, finely made figure, in the black silk dress which she was wearing [...] set off the long beautiful folds of the gorgeous shawls that would have half-smothered Edith. Margaret stood right under the chandelier, quite silent and passive, while her aunt adjusted the draperies. Occasionally, as she was turned around, she caught a glimpse of herself in the mirror over the chimney-piece, and smiled at her own appearance there — the familiar features in the unusual garb of a princess. (39)

That Margaret is the true 'queen' and the proper recipient of the Indian shawls is emphasized at several points in the narrative. When she meets Thornton, her future husband, she has over her plain dark gown 'a large Indian shawl' which she wears 'as an empress wears her drapery' (99). What has happened to Edith's shawl, by contrast, is revealed in one of Edith's characteristically chatty letters:

---

[19] Elizabeth Gaskell, *North and South* (1855), ed. by Dorothy Collin with an introduction by Martin Dodsworth (Harmondsworth: Penguin Books, 1970). Page references to this edition are given in the text.

> I tried to wear my great beauty Indian shawl at a picnic [...] but it was of no use. I was like mamma s little dog Tiny with an elephant's trappings on; smothered, hidden, killed with my finery; so I made it into a capital carpet for us all to sit down upon. (299)

But 'playing with shawls is very different work to drawing up settlements' (41), Henry Lennox warns Margaret early in the novel. The Indian shawl licenses Margaret as a strong-minded heroine, who goes out of the drawing-room into the streets, but if Margaret is something more than a lady, she is, equally, never not a lady, and by the end of the novel she is fairly thoroughly settled. In *The Mill on the Floss*, Eliot gives us a heroine in much more flagrant breach of the communal codes, a heroine who wears pink, runs away with her best friend's lover, and longs for knowledge and freedom for its own sake. Stretching the boundaries of the imagined community to negotiate a place for Maggie is a delicate business. As Eliot famously acknowledges, the cultural arbiters of that community are female. 'Public opinion, in these cases, is always of the feminine gender' (619). It is women who preside over what, according to Benedict Anderson, sustains the community's homogeneity and its boundaries: shared ceremonies and commodities, replications which reassure each member 'that the imagined world is visibly rooted in everyday life'.[20] Food, china, linen and clothes are the ceremonies and commodities which are so lovingly and lavishly evoked in *The Mill on the the Floss*, and it is on the last of these — clothes — that I want to concentrate. I shall argue that *The Mill on the Floss* presents us with a double narrative in which Maggie's subversive qualities — her passionate and hybrid nature, her unhomeliness — are simultaneously rejected and nurtured, constrained and validated, by the female members of the community.

As Ellen Moers points out,[21] the moment when Eliot's narrative draws most closely on *Corinne* comes when Maggie's naked arms are exposed:

> Who has not felt the beauty of a woman's arm? — the unspeakable suggestions of tenderness that lie in the dimpled elbow and all the varied gently lessening curves down to the delicate wrist with its tiniest, almost imperceptible nicks in the firm softness. A woman's arm touched the soul of a great sculptor two thousand years ago, so that he wrought an image of it for the Parthenon which moves us still as it clasps lovingly the time-worn marble of a headless trunk. Maggie's was such an arm as that — and it had the warm tints of life. (561)

This description closely evokes the moment of Corinne's triumph at the Capitol, but it must be said that Maggie is hardly a performing heroine. She does not create: the sum of her achievements, it might be said, is exquisite

---

[20] *Imagined Communities*, pp. 35-6.

[21] *Literary Women*, p. 274.

plain sewing and death by drowning. Rather, Maggie responds to, and stimulates, the creativity of men: Stephen's singing and Philip's painting. Her naked arms are represented to us through Stephen's sensual and fetishising gaze: the limbs are separated from the head. But it is, precisely, in Maggie's unfulfilled potential — her unsatisfied intelligence, her passionate longings and conflicting desires, her lack of a sense of home — that Maggie can be said to extend the boundaries of the imagined community, to mediate aspirations it did not know it had. And it is on the body of Maggie that these desires are located in the narrative; the novel is propelled by a sequence of moves in which the censoring of Maggie's body is parallelled by its unveiling, a complicated process of clothing and unclothing, robing and disrobing, in which the women of the community are complicitous.

The elaborate unshrouding of Aunt Pullet's bonnet is the moment which most clearly replicates the community's boundaries: its allegiance to custom, tradition, respectability, show, the claims of kin. The funereal solemnity with which the bonnet is temporarily released from its shrine of rose-leaves and silver paper is, to Maggie, a 'painful mystery' (152) from which she is excluded. Now, our first glimpse of Maggie is of a small figure in a beaver bonnet, a figure at the centre of a pastoral English landscape, perceived through the nostalgic retrospective lens of the unspecified adult narrator. Thereafter, however, Maggie is repeatedly disbonneted: she casts her bonnets aside, fretfully refuses to wear them, is divested of her bonnet by the gypsies, and stomps on Aunt Glegg's handed-down bonnet 'so as to give it a general resemblance to a sage cheese garnished with withered lettuces' (115). What lies beneath the bonnet is, of course, Maggie's abundant hair: hair which is initially recalcitrant, failing to curl, failing to please, falling into her eyes, until Maggie herself chops it off. In the hands of her mother, the potential of Maggie's hair is gradually realized: Mrs Tulliver patiently brushes, braids and coils until the hair is turned into a coronet, a massy jet-black crown. But although Maggie now has a 'queenly head' (388) above her old frocks, she still persists in her refusal to confront her own image in the mirror. It is only in the final chapters of the novel that Maggie is unified with herself, and this process is again facilitated by women.

It is Aunt Pullet who insists that Maggie should wear pink, and who provides the dresses that Maggie wears at the scenes of her social triumph. But it is, above all, Lucy who sets out to turn Maggie 'from a drudge into a princess' (526), Lucy who insists that Maggie's arms should be exposed to the world, Lucy who propels Maggie into the arms of her own lover, Lucy who brings Maggie into harmony with her own image, when she takes Maggie before the cheval-glass and insists that she recognize 'the full length of her

tall beauty, crowned by the night of her massy hair' (555). Lucy dresses
Maggie, but she also undresses her: in the intimate confidential scene in
Maggie's bedroom, Lucy coaxes Maggie into taking off her clothes,
encourages her into her pink gown, watches her with a spaniel's affection as
she unplaits her long black hair.

But as Lucy propels Maggie towards a unified self, she becomes
disconnected from her own: as she effaces herself to fashion Maggie into a
queen, she becomes noticeably submerged by her own clothes, subordinated
to her drapery of silk and crape, smothered by her ample white dressing-
gown.   All this might be seen simply as dramatic irony: Lucy's self-
obliteration is part of the process by which she innocently impels her own
downfall. But Lucy's collusion in Maggie's transgression is part of a larger
pattern in the narrative, which draws closely on the model of *Corinne*.

Ellen Moers perceives *The Mill on the Floss* as a revenge fantasy which
interrogates *Corinne*'s plot by validating the unruly brunette over the
conventional blonde.[22]   But I think that Moers is colluding here with
Maggie's misreading of *Corinne*: George Eliot, unlike Maggie, had read to
the end of de Staël's novel, and she would have seen that the 'blond-haired
woman' does not actually carry away all the happiness, as Maggie suggests.
The conclusion of *Corinne* is a beautifully-staged melodrama, in which
Corinne orchestrates the manner of her own death, and is reunited with
Oswald Nelvil. But it is Lucille who orchestrates Nelvil's return to Italy and
Corinne. And Corinne, in turn, delivers Nelvil back to Lucille, telling her
'May he live with you in happiness' (418). Eve Kosofsky Sedgwick has
identified a longstanding and extensive literary tradition in which homosocial
bonding is mediated by a ritualised 'traffic' of women: women act as the
conduit of a relationship in which the final object is the affirmation of male
collectivity and power.[23] *Corinne* is an influential text in an alternative
tradition in which 'gynosocial' bonding is affirmed through the exchange of a
man.

In *The Mill on the Floss*, as in *Corinne*, Maggie delivers Stephen back to
Lucy. The primary structural difference between the two texts is that
Maggie's amplitude is not diminished during the course of the narrative: she
remains robust, brown and healthy until taken by the flood. I think the
difference might be attributed to the fact that Maggie's transgressiveness is

---

[22] *Literary Women*, pp. 266-7.

[23] Eve Kosofsky Sedgwick, *Between Men: English Literature and Male Homosocial
Desire* (New York: Columbia University Press, 1985).

rooted within the English landscape which has nurtured her and, also, to the imagined, potential elasticity of her community. That elasticity is identified in the novel, with some irony, as peculiarly English:

> [...] is not the striving after something better and better in our surroundings, the grand characteristic that distinguishes man from the brute — or, to satisfy a scrupulous accuracy of definition, that distinguishes the British man from the foreign brute? (222)

What Eliot is implanting here, in the minds of her English readers, is a re-imagining of what elsewhere in the narrative she calls 'the mother tongue of our imagination'(94): the sensibility produced by English habits and the English landscape. As Maggie tells Tom, words can have several meanings. Eliot inflects the mother-tongue of her imagined community with the potential for a new meaning: one which will allow its mute inglorious Corinnes, its disbonneted Maggies, a sense of home. The shawl which Maggie wears in the novel is not an exotic and colourful Indian shawl, but 'an hereditary black silk shawl of some wide-meshed net-like material' (393). It is a garment which signals both Maggie's roots, and the wider possibilities which she represents, and it is surely significant that it is under this shawl that Maggie covers up her copy of *Corinne*.

www.ingramcontent.com/pod-product-compliance
Ingram Content Group UK Ltd.
Pitfield, Milton Keynes, MK11 3LW, UK
UKHW020355010325
455677UK00021B/479